PAIN KILLER

Pain Killer

A MEMOIR OF
BIG LEAGUE ADDICTION

BRANTT MYHRES

VIKING

VIKING

an imprint of Penguin Canada, a division of Penguin Random House Canada Limited

Canada • USA • UK • Ireland • Australia • New Zealand • India • South Africa • China

First published 2021
Copyright © 2021 by Brantt Myhres | Foreword © 2021 by Michael Landsberg

www.penguinrandomhouse.ca

All photographs are from the personal collection of the author unless otherwise specified.

LIBRARY AND ARCHIVES CANADA CATALOGUING IN PUBLICATION
Title: Pain killer / Brantt Myhres.
Names: Myhres, Brantt, 1974 - author.
Identifiers: Canadiana (print) 20200239104 | Canadiana (ebook) 20200239112 |
    ISBN 9780735239418 (hardcover) | ISBN 9780735239425 (EPUB)
Subjects: LCSH: Myhres, Brantt, 1974 - | LCSH: Myhres, Brantt, 1974 -—Drug use.
    | LCSH: Myhres, Brantt, 1974 -—Alcohol use. | LCSH: Hockey players—Canada
    —Biography. | LCSH: Recovering addicts—Canada—Biography. | LCGFT:
    Autobiographies.
Classification: LCC GV848.5.M94 A3 2021 | DDC 796.962092—dc23

Book and cover design by Lisa Jager
Cover images: skull © Golden Shrimp / Shutterstock.com; hockey stick, puck, bird, and flowers by Lisa Jager

Printed and bound in Canada

10 9 8 7 6 5 4 3 2 1

Penguin
Random House
VIKING CANADA

*I dedicate this book to those who kept me on a path
that enabled me to write this—my daughter Chloe,
my grandma Jo, and my grandpa Bob.
Thank you for being my reason to keep swinging.*

"New beginnings are often disguised as painful endings."

—LAO TZU

CONTENTS

FOREWORD BY MICHAEL LANDSBERG

I hate sports books. I really do.

Most sports books are about success. For me, that's the turnoff right there. For me, reading about success in pro sport is dull, predictable, and, for most of us, also unattainable. I want to read about struggle. Struggle is what teaches us about the world around us and the world inside us. So, why did I read this book? Pure struggle. Let's face it: Brantt Myhres had eight points in 154 NHL games, so you know his book isn't about tickling the twine so much as riding the pine. But there is plenty of struggle.

One thing you will learn quickly in *Pain Killer* is that Brantt Myhres liked strippers. Brantt liked to party with strippers. Brantt liked to drink and do coke with strippers. In the end, his stripper friends taught him well. As you hold his book in your hands, consider it your entry into the champagne room of Brantt's life. Brantt's gonna show you everything, and it will engage you in a way that might shock you. It shocked me. It wasn't so much the wild life he led that shocked me. What shocked me was that there is so much about mental health and addiction that I found out I didn't know. I know more now. So will you.

I should tell you about my mental health, or rather my mental illness. Not because you need to know anything about me—this is Brantt's book. But it helps explain why he invited me to read his book, and why we became bonded in such an unusual and deep way.

I grew up being scared of too many things to list. Here's just a sampling: I was scared of sleepovers, I was scared of camp, I was scared of girls, I was scared of liquor and weed and anything else that would cause me to lose some control. Oh yeah—add to the list every illness imaginable. And that's it, except for elevators and middle seats at movie theaters. Basically, I was scared of most of the things other teenagers lived for. Most of all though, I was scared of throwing up. Petrified of puking, vomiting, heaving, ralphing. Under any name it was the enemy, and more than that, the fear of being around someone who even hinted they might vomit was overpowering and all-consuming. It ran my life.

I was constantly afraid that people would find out about my ridiculous fears, so I became adept at making excuses for not doing things. The overriding feeling for me was one of shame. I felt like I was somehow responsible for my fears. I was sure I was the only person on the planet who had these fears, so it was a great day for me when I read about phobias and discovered there was something called *emetophobia*. Emetophobia is in the medical books as the fear of throwing up or being around someone who throws up.

I was thrilled to learn that I wasn't the only one and that my affliction actually had a name—and that it wasn't *loser*. That, my new friends, is vindication. I wanted to race around waving it in people's faces: "See, I wasn't making it up. I am not immature or weak or lazy." I wanted to stand up in class and yell it. Then I realized I was too scared to stand up in class and yell. Not with all those girls there.

So, there was that.

And then there was depression. Like most of the world, I had no clue what it was until I felt it. I figured depression was like another Disney World Kingdom. Tomorrowland, Fantasyland, Frontierland, and Excuseland. In Excuseland the most popular attraction is a bunch of beds in the dark that people lie in and whine about how they don't have the will to get up. Of course, the ghosts don't just say boo, but boo-fucking-hoo.

It wasn't until I felt severe depression that I realized it was nothing like I'd imagined. I remind myself of my own former ignorance when I hear people today expressing the same stigmatizing things that I used to think. Fact: If you haven't felt depression, do not think you understand depression. Don't tell people like Brantt and me, "We all go through it." We don't all go through it. You aren't stronger than me or Brantt or your wife or your kid or anyone else with depression. You haven't had it, not because of your strength, but because of your luck.

One of the things that hit me hardest in this book was Brantt's "less than ideal" upbringing. When I think of what I was given, compared to what he was given, it's not surprising that his struggles to find his way were a million times tougher than mine. It was like I was born with a flashlight in my hand. I would have preferred a silver spoon in my mouth, but the flashlight was the love I received from so many who loved me unconditionally—and that allowed me to find my way out of the darkness. Brantt didn't have that. You will learn that, and you will sympathize with him like I did. But you will not detect a hint of *self*-sympathy. He makes no excuses for his behaviour. He reports it as an observer of his own life, not as a participant. It's like he's telling the story in the third person. I love that.

Oh yeah, the lesson Brantt learnt from the strippers I was referring to was pretty simple—the more you expose, the more effective you are.

Pain Killer is that strip bar that allows anything. Hide nothing, show it, shake it, write it.

Dignity is a weird thing. There's no dignity in getting on stage and talking about the one time you were so hammered you got in your car naked (a Brantt story). There is enormous dignity in getting on stage and talking about a *lifetime* of getting hammered and getting naked in your car.

The more undignified stories you tell, the more dignified you become. Self-awareness and humility are precious and the key to sobriety. This is 300 pages of dignity by volume. Brantt will show you the worst of what he is capable of, and in the end you will see the very best.

For however long it takes you to read this book, you will be in the company of a real man. I don't mean someone who fights for a living.

I define manhood as the willingness to share your pain for someone else's benefit. That's what real men do. Real women do it too.

I met Brantt in late 2011. We booked him to be a guest on the show I hosted, *Off the Record (OTR)*. We wanted to do a show with and about NHL enforcers. Three men who did that job had died earlier in 2011. That included a guy I loved—Wade Belak.

People were, for the first time, realizing that being a fighter in the NHL was not a victimless crime. Almost everyone that has ever done the job has paid a terrible price. "No one gets hurt in a hockey fight" was always a stupid comment made by those who wanted to preserve the tradition. The truth is, everyone gets hurt, not always *by* the fight, or *in* the fight, but *because of* the fight. You will never see hockey fighting the same way after reading this book.

I greeted Brantt in the green room. I was shocked by what I saw. Try to imagine for a moment what the face of long-term addiction might look like. Well, this wasn't it. I don't know what I expected. I knew he'd been sober for a few years, but damn, I thought, he is a good-looking man. Handsome, well dressed, fit, with a demeanor that didn't match the look. I found him to be humble, poised, and perhaps a bit fearful. He had a good reason to be afraid. Not of me—I told him I had his back and that it was my job to make him look good and all he had to do was answer questions about his own life. How tough could that be? *Pain Killer* will show you how tough, and why he was worried.

I knew a lot about what was in Brantt's head. First off, I understood his mental illness.

As I told you I've been crippled at times with anxiety and depression and I understand the desperation for relief.

Before reading this book, I also understood self-medicating. My brother started drinking and taking prescription drugs in his teens and it wasn't until years later I realized he was medicating for the pain caused by the same illness I had. I also understand the rationale behind self-medicating and it's surprisingly simple. When you're desperate for relief from pain, tomorrow becomes irrelevant. Long term damage to your body and your life is irrelevant. All that counts is right now. Offer someone like Brantt or my brother instant relief, even if the cost is enormous and they will almost always take it. Almost. So why not me? Answer: I was too afraid of puking. For real. I've never been drunk.

I also understood how tough his job in the NHL must have been. As I've mentioned, I was buddies with Wade Belak who, like Brantt, was an NHL enforcer. I knew from Wade how tough the job could be and the toll that it could take. I knew from Wade that there was a pressure that came with the job that isolated him in a room filled with his teammates. I also knew from Wade that if a person is described as big, strong, tough, rugged, and fierce, they could also be described as lovely. Wade had a sweetness about him that was so profound, ran so deep that when he died by suicide, he crippled everyone who knew him. Two weeks before his death Wade had sat at my kitchen table. We ate pancakes together and spoke about one of the things we had in common: depression.

So when Brantt and I spoke before the show, we talked about Wade. The two of them had never fought. I wish they had. I wish Wade had softly said, "You wanna go?" as they lined up for a faceoff. Why would I want that? The answer is something Brantt writes in this book. It's one of the most illuminating things I have ever read or heard when it comes to a hockey fight. It explains so well how you don't have to dislike a guy to fight him. It's one word: *intimacy*. Read the book to find out how that word applies.

Because of my job, Brantt is just one of dozens of tough guys that I've spoken to. In the world of hockey, the unwritten rule (I unwrote it right now) for players in an interview is to "talk a lot but say nothing."

Sure, there are many exceptions, but if you ever get the chance to hang out with three hockey players, and Myhres, Domi, and Laraque are looking for a table, as are three Hall of Famers, go with the tough guys. I have never met an NHL enforcer that I didn't like (Sean Avery wasn't an enforcer).

I have a theory. Einstein had his theory of relativity, I have the Landsberg theory of creativity. The amount of creativity a guy has (or is willing to show) to make a decent conversation is inversely proportional to the number of goals he's scored. Also the more PIMs (penalties in minutes) a guy accumulates, the greater his ability to make those around him feel special.

The greatest enforcer ever was Bob Probert (he could also score). Everyone feared Bob. Brantt talks about his love for Bob. I knew Bob. He was one of the kindest, sweetest, most gracious people I've met. Oh yeah, and gentle. That's right, gentle. Years ago, my daughter interviewed him for a school project. I will never forget how kind and gentle he was. He knew she was nervous. He knew how just saying his name intimidated people. His treatment of Casey was wonderful, but not unusual. Most of the guys I know go from being enforcers on the ice to Lady Byng candidates in real life. Bob died in 2010.

I'm glad Brantt didn't die. I say that because he writes about his near misses multiple times in the book. The fact that no coroner had to fill in the "cause of death" line on a Brantt Myhres death certificate is a near miracle. Brantt could have filled out his own forms in advance. He would have needed three. Cause of death: Cocaine overdose. Cause of death: Injuries caused by driving drunk in his car. Cause of death: Injuries caused by driving drunk on his motorcycle. Ironically, even doing one of the most dangerous jobs in sports, he was far safer on the ice than off.

After Brantt's appearance on *OTR*, I did something I only did a handful of times over 18 years—I asked him over to my house for dinner with my family. I had gone out with guests the night of the show plenty of times—one day ask me about Vin Diesel at the Brass Rail (strip club). I don't even remember why I asked Brantt. I guess it was as simple as me just liking him and feeling an unusually deep bond with him.

That was 2011. We talked from time to time over the next nine years. When the pandemic hit, we really reconnected. The charity my daughter and I started, #SickNotWeak, chose to start a daily show. We called it *Isolation Nation*. Brantt was a guest a few times and helped us get others like him. By that, I mean other former NHL players who were in recovery. I was struck by how much influence he's had and still has on their lives. They look at Brantt as an example of what is possible when you want it badly enough. Now, even great players like Sheldon Souray look at Brantt, with his eight career points, as a superstar. Now, he is measured not by goals and assists, but by length of sobriety.

You know the Gordie Howe hat trick, right? A goal, an assist, and a fight. Well, after reading this book I am making the smoke, the coke, and the Jack the Brantt Myhres hat trick. Imagine if you had told him as he was putting one of those on the board that one day he would be an inspiration and model for so many. He would have thought you were crazy.

So, get ready for a book filled with stuff that will shock you. Brantt's journey from addiction to sobriety had all kinds of false starts, and failures. It would be quite the understatement to say Brantt and AA didn't exactly hit it off.

I imagine, if he was honest, his first AA appearance would have sounded like this:

"Hi, my name is Brantt and I am NOT an alcoholic. You know how I know? Because alcoholics are losers and I'm not a loser. You losers joined because you can't quit drinking. Well, I can quit anytime I want, but I don't want to because a smoke, a pull of Jack, and a line of coke is heaven. Why would I give it up?"

If that thinking makes sense to you, you need to read this book.

If that thinking would make sense to someone you care about, you need to read this book and get them to read this book.

As you can guess, the truth about this book is that it's filled with lies. The lies helped teach me that the first casualty of addiction is truth, but they also taught me that the first rule of sobriety is that the truth shall set you free. As it did Brantt. As it can you.

PAIN KILLER

PROLOGUE

I used to work out in Los Angeles with Bob Probert. I thought that was pretty cool. More than cool. For one thing, Bob was my idol. He was a lot of people's idol, but my respect for the man probably ran a little deeper than most, since he and I did the same job for a living. We were both tough guys, and tough guys respect each other. Still, Bob was the coolest tough guy ever to put on skates, so I figure I probably respected him a little more than he respected me. But that was fine.

The San Jose Sharks were paying for my trainer at Gold's Gym in Venice Beach. They were also paying me millions of dollars to play hockey, so they'd hired the trainer to take care of their investment. I thought that was pretty cool too. On my first day at the gym, the trainer told me to go warm up on the bike and meet my training partner for the summer: Bob Probert, legendary Chicago Blackhawks enforcer.

So I was pretty close to having it all. The job I'd wanted since I was a little kid. Hitting the weights with a legend, at the gym where Arnold Schwarzenegger got huge. Gold's has an outdoor workout area. On one side of the chain-link fence are a bunch of huge guys pumping iron under the California sun, and on the other is the ocean, the boardwalk, and a parade of beauties a young guy from Swan Hills, Alberta, could have hardly imagined.

Not many people get to live out their dreams down to that kind of detail, but there I was. I had it pretty good.

One day Probie said, Hey Myze, you like Harleys?

Yeah, I love bikes, why?

Well, me, Jeremy, and Chris are going to hit the canyons tomorrow for a ride. Want to join?

That would be his Blackhawks teammates Jeremy Roenick, who went to the All-Star Game pretty much every year, and Chris Simon, one of the toughest guys in the league. So, pretty cool guys to hang out with.

Sure Probie, I said. But I don't have a motorbike licence.

Don't worry about the licence, buddy, I'll rent the bike for you. I'll put the deposit on my Visa and we'll be good to go.

So there I was on the back of Probie's bike, riding down the highway to the dealership. It must have been quite the sight. Two six-foot-four, 225-pound guys doubling on a Harley.

When it was time to go our separate ways, he said, Okay, we're going to meet at Malibu Chicken around nine a.m. See you then.

I was renting this house that was about ten minutes from the beach, a nice little spot. I took the bike home and sat down to watch some TV. But that evening I was getting a little restless. I started thinking, Brantt, are you really going to just sit here and watch TV? How fucking boring is that? You're only twenty-five years old. You've got some cash in the bank. If you head down to the beach on this Harley, you never know—you might meet a nice girl to take for a ride and enjoy the sunset.

You might even go for a beer.

In fact, anyone would be crazy not to. Unless they'd already been through two stints in rehab.

Which I had.

I'd been kicked out of the league twice. I'd been drafted, because someone thought I would make his team better. And I'd been kicked out, twice, because the league thought I was making it worse.

Now I was back. I was with my third team. I was doing better than ever. Making more money than ever. Enjoying the breeze off the ocean in Venice Beach. All I had to do to hold on to all this was stay sober.

But I told myself that one beer isn't really a relapse. That I'd just head down to the bar by the beach. That I'd have just one.

I jump on the Harley and off I go. As I'm driving I'm not concentrating on how beautiful the palm trees are or how the ocean is looking as the sun goes down. I'm wrestling. I'm saying the words *Don't do it, Brantt. Turn the bike around. You're going to fucking blow this again.* Couples are walking down the narrow streets in flip-flops and loose-fitting clothes. Everyone is tanned and relaxed. No one has any idea what I'm going through. They probably think I'm just like them. Just enjoying the evening, like a normal person.

I'm not. The funny thing is, I'm not enjoying this at all.

The bars are all lit up and everyone inside looks happy. I feel left out, like everything is happening without me. It's one bar after another. It's as though all anyone does here is drink. I park the bike, put my helmet on the handlebars, and walk into this Mexican place for my one beer.

I sit down at the bar. It's sickeningly familiar. The taps of draft, the specials on the chalkboard. The bottles lined up shoulder to shoulder across from me, where I see myself in the mirror. Catching myself in the act. The beer doesn't even taste that good. Not really. When you haven't had a drink in a while, the buzz hits right away. You're not convinced you even like it. A minute before, I was sharp. Now I'm not so sure.

Not for that first sip anyway. That first, guilty sip.

By the time I finish that beer, though, it's not hard to remember what I loved so much about booze. And let's be honest.

I've *never* stopped at one.

Soon it's two. Then three. Now the guilt is draining away. The rush is a relief, bordering on giddy joy. The world transformed in a few short minutes into a better place. Why would I stop now? Now when the bar is a sea of smiling faces? When the lights are swirling around me, and the music is irresistible?

I had money. I felt the warm glow of security knowing I could drink as much as I wanted.

I went outside for a smoke and noticed my helmet had disappeared. I just laughed.

By two thirty I've finished a bottle of tequila.

I said to this Mexican guy sitting next to me, Hey pal, know of anywhere I can get some blow? Of course he does. Not far away. Perfect, I tell him. Let's roll.

When we get outside I'm surprised the street is empty. The tanned, good-looking couples have all gone home. The storefronts and restaurants have gone dark. I'm having a hard time standing.

How are we getting there? the guy asks.

I point at the Harley.

We're going on that thing?

Hell yes.

Where's our helmets?

Don't worry, bro, I've been riding bikes since I was five. We don't need helmets. Jump on.

There we were, driving down Washington Avenue, only now the night is cool and the hum of traffic is gone. All I can hear is the thunder of the Harley echoing down the empty street.

We were cruising along when I looked back at the guy and said, Yo bro, where are we going? Are we close? I was shouting over the roar of the wind. The wind can be deafening when you're not wearing a helmet.

He said, Oh shit, it's right here, turn right! I turn the handlebars and the next thing I see are these two little snakeskin cowboy boots fly by. The bike is in full flip mode, and I'm bouncing on the road. When I open my eyes I notice that I'm in a real bad neighbourhood.

My bike is about fifty feet from me and it looks mangled. I look at my arms and legs. I'm mangled too. I get up and run over, lift it up, jump on, and hit the start button. I'm relieved when it starts. I looked around for the Mexican but all I see are his cowboy boots sticking out of the ditch. I have no clue what condition he's in but I'm not sticking around to find out. I put the Harley in gear and take off down the highway. It's now three thirty in the morning. I'm not having fun anymore.

All of a sudden I hear the cop sirens going, telling me to pull over.

I've been pulled over before. I'm not intimidated by cops. But this time I'm really fucked. It's funny how a siren can clear your head. Jail for sure. One hundred percent, my career is finished. I pull over and shut the bike off, sitting there with no helmet on and blood all over my clothes. The cop walks up to me and says, Licence and registration please. I'm so hammered I can't even get my hand into my pocket to grab my ID.

Whoa, whoa, you've been drinking a lot tonight, mister.

Yes, officer, I have been drinking tonight. I know I should not be driving in this state.

Then I had to grovel.

Officer, you got to understand. The reason I was drinking was I just signed a five-year contract in the NHL. I was celebrating.

I actually started to cry. If you bust me my contract and my career are over. Please give me a chance.

He said, Well, I don't usually do this, but how far away do you live?

Five minutes from here.

Okay. Lock that bike up and walk your ass home. If I see you within two feet of that bike I'm arresting you and you're going downtown.

Needless to say, I thanked him from the bottom of my heart and promised I'd never drink and ride again.

I may have even meant it.

I lock the bike and start walking down the road. Then I turn the corner and pull myself under this truck, wait for the cop to drive by, and then get up and walk back to the bike. Then I unlock it, fire it up, and away I go again down the road.

I made it home somehow, but when I pulled into my driveway I forgot to hit the brake and ran the bike right into the side of the house.

I wake up naked on my floor to the sound of my cell phone going off. It's Probie: Myze, it's nine o'clock, where are you?

Shit: Probie! I slept in, is all I can say. And that much is true. I grab the bottle of Advil and pop three of them. I take stock of the road rash and the dried blood, but I'm still pretty drunk so I'm not really feeling much. I'm just focused on meeting the boys.

As I'm driving there, all I'm thinking is, I'm so fucked, Probie is going to kill me, maybe I should start thinking of an excuse! I'm having a hard time keeping the bike between the lines, mostly because the handlebars are bent, so I have to steer to the left to make the bike go straight. The front fender is broken half off and I'm still drunk. The gas tank has a big dent in it. All I can think about is, What the hell am I going to say to Bob?

I pull up and see the boys waiting outside, and as I get closer I see Bob's eyes open wider.

Myze, holy shit! What happened to the Harley?

Well, Probie, did you see the construction going on? The gravel was loose and I put 'er down.

Come on, Myze, that's not what happened. Let's chat about it later, but Jesus, were you hammered?

Just a tad, I said.

I'd like to be able to say I learned a lesson that night. But I was pretty much immune to lessons back then. I had been for a while. Some people respond to a mistake by doing things differently next time. Wiser people than me say, *Never waste a mistake*. That's supposed to mean you can figure out what to do by keeping track of the things you've done that you shouldn't.

But I wasted a lot more than mistakes. I wasted just about everything that came my way. Millions of dollars. The love of two wonderful women. More second chances from people I admired than I can count. I'm sure there were some I didn't even notice. I wonder which is worse, losing that first million dollars or squandering that first second chance. The missed opportunities cost me more. They cost more than a million dollars, and they also cost me the respect of the people who offered them.

By the time I finally put my mistakes to good use, it was nearly too late. I could hardly have cut it any closer. I'd been a professional athlete once, now I was a bloated, bleary-eyed husk who could barely walk outside to light a cigarette without getting winded. I used to turn away autograph-seekers, now I was invisible. I'd made a living intimidating the toughest of the tough, now I was pathetic. Others looked down on me. I made them sick. I made myself sick. I was about as close to the bottom as you can get.

But something straightened me out. I'm not saying I pulled myself up by my bootstraps, because I don't get to take the credit. And I'm not saying I deserved it, because if life were truly about balancing out rights and wrongs, I probably still have some misdeeds to pay for. But I did put in some hard work, and I did get lucky, and the two things happened at the same time.

It's funny. I'd had more than my share of good luck, and no one makes it to the NHL without hard work. Neither had saved me before. But on February 27, 2008, something fell into place that gave me a chance to finally make use of all those mistakes. This book is about mistakes, then, lots of them, and my belated efforts to make the most of them.

PART I

WANNA GO?

1

It must have been minus thirty outside, but all I wanted was to get out the door. My mother had cooked up some homemade pizza while my sister Cher and I watched *Puff the Magic Dragon*. I was five, eating pizza in front of the TV. I remember saying to my mom that I was done my dinner and that I wanted to go to the rink. She said, Get those boots on then. You can walk. We had to when we were young.

So I put my hockey bag over my shoulder, grabbed my stick, then walked in snow up to my knees to get to the rink. I don't remember how long the walk was, but my feet were still frozen when I put my skates on. You don't forget what it feels like to stuff cold feet into cold skates.

We lived in a trailer park on the edge of a town called Swan Hills, pretty much right in the geographical centre of Alberta. Around us lived the loggers and oil rig workers who populated our trailer park.

I remember getting on the ice and skating along the boards to help me stand up. Outdoor ice doesn't feel like indoor ice, or the soft ice of an NHL rink. It's rock-hard and rutted, and a little kid's skates chatter over the rough patches. Not that I was much of a skater at that age. When I went too fast I'd just run into the boards to make myself stop. But there was nowhere I'd rather be. It still amazes me that I was able to get to that rink and put a smile on considering what was going on back home.

The night before I could tell that my stepfather, Brad, was not in the best of moods because his eyes were this fiery red, which meant he was hammered drunk again and looking for someone to pick on. There was a five-year-old boy, a six-year-old girl, and a twenty-three-year-old mother to choose from. It was only a matter of time. Then my mom said something to him, and the next thing I knew, Brad jumped up and grabbed her by the hair, threw her to the floor in the kitchen, and started to stomp on her head with his foot. There was blood coming from her nose and her mouth. My mother's scream has stayed with me to this day.

She was begging me and Cher to get help, and I ran for the door. As I reached for the doorknob Brad grabbed me by my neck and said, Shut that fucking door, you little prick. If you dare leave this house or tell anyone, I'll kill you and everyone in it.

I had enough sense to surrender and promise to keep my mouth shut.

What was just as scary as the beating he gave my mom that night was the fact that no one in the world cared, that I could see. The police did show up, and by that time my mom's eye had already swelled completely shut. When the cops left fifteen minutes later, Brad was still sitting on the couch. I remember praying to God to please take him to jail and never let him come back. But no one was going to take care of Brad for us. That's what I learned that night.

I was better off on the outdoor rink, even in the brutal cold. Me and Cher were just terrified of what could happen anytime, any day, back home. When Brad had that look in his eye we'd run to our bunk beds and pull the blankets over our heads and pray he wouldn't come storming through the door. I remember calling my grandma Jo one of those nights and telling her what was happening. I begged her to call my dad, who lived somewhere in Edmonton. I always believed that once my dad heard that Brad was physically abusing me and Cher, he would come rescue us. That time never came.

One night I heard my mom getting beat up again, and the next thing I knew she was whispering in our ears to be quiet and get into the car, that we were going to Grandma and Grandpa's. As soon as I heard that, I felt this overwhelming feeling of joy rush through my body. That meant we were going to be safe. It was my favourite place on earth.

So we packed up our old car. My mom called it the "Green Machine." Off we went. I never saw that trailer park again.

My grandparents owned a hardware store called McCloud's in a small town of five thousand, about five hours away, just south of Cold Lake. They were hard workers and respected in the community.

There's this town called Bonnyville about thirty minutes before we got to my grandparents, and about fifteen minutes before Bonnyville, there were these two little flashing lights at the top of a huge pole or antenna. Whatever it was, whenever I saw those lights flashing I knew I was safe. We were almost there. That night I didn't sleep the whole way.

We stayed with my grandparents for about a year. Compared to Swan Hills, life was good there. I was always playing outside with my friends, mostly road hockey for hours. If I needed to get to hockey practice my grandpa would come pick me up and drive me. I don't ever remember my mom being at a game, but I'm sure she was.

Eventually, though, Brad came back into our lives. It took me years to make sense of that. At the time it was like a horrifying dream, watching something awful unfolding, knowing that an unpredictable menace was coming for you but being powerless to stop it.

It started with visits to Swan Hills, when I was around nine. On one trip back there I went out with some friends to a secret spot down by the river in the forest. Just being kids, one of my friends pulled out a cigarette and asked if I wanted to try a puff. I said sure. I grabbed the smoke, took a drag, then stood up and threw the cigarette into the bush next to the river. Then we turned to walk home. Only about a minute later, one of my friends said, Jesus Christ, look at the forest!

It was lit up like a torch. We could already hear it as the fire took on a life of its own. As we started to run home we were seeing the fire trucks flying by with their sirens on. I just remember keeping it to myself, because I knew what would happen if Brad heard about it. But the next day when I went to see my buddy, it was obvious that his father had heard about it. Each of his fingertips was burnt. His dad explained that ten burns might convince him to stop playing with fire.

By this time my mom had her own place on top of the hill called Brady Heights. Back then our neighbourhood was called Grand Centre, before it merged into Cold Lake in 1996. Eventually Brad moved in with us, and it wasn't long before things went back to what my mom had run away from.

One night when my mom was at a friend's house, I was lying in bed trying to fall asleep, anxious because I could hear my sister outside playing with her friend. More than anxious. Brad was yelling from his room to shut the fuck up. I kept thinking, Oh, Cher, you better be quiet, please Cher be quiet—when all of a sudden my door swung open and Brad ran over, picked me up by my hair, punched me in the face, and smashed my head against the TV.

I kept screaming, Please stop, I didn't do anything!! It seemed like forever that he was laying that beating on me, and once the last punch came, I remember thinking, Wait till I tell Mom what just happened, she's going to kill you.

I picked up the phone and called her at her friend's house. Mom!! Brad just beat me up real bad—he punched me in the face and choked me!

All she said was, Cry me another river, Brantt. It couldn't have been that bad.

The next day was brutally cold, as it often is in northern Alberta. That afternoon I asked my mom if I could go skating on the outdoor rink and play some hockey. It was a weird day because when we got to the rink no one was there, just me. So, just before my mom left I asked her if she could pick me up in an hour. Knowing that it was absolutely freezing outside, she said, Yes, I'll be back soon to grab you.

I went out and started to skate around, shooting some pucks. Later I noticed that it was getting really dark out, that it had been much longer than an hour. I must have stayed out there for three hours, until something inside of me said I'd better start walking downtown to Grandma's or I'd die out there. I didn't have my boots, so I walked in my skates about half a mile on the paved road to the store.

When I walked in, my grandma saw that my face was completely red from the frost and that I had a black eye. She said, Oh my god, Brantt, what happened to you! I blurted out that Brad had beat me up the night before and that Mom had forgotten to pick me up at the rink. She looked at me and said, This will be the last time you ever spend another night at your mother's house. You're living with me and your grandpa from now on.

I was finally saved.

From that point on I was loved and taken care of, and most importantly, I felt safe. My grandpa worked his ass off and so did my grandma, so when they got home they would unwind with a bottle of rum. I always waited till they were on their second rum and Coke before I asked permission to do something—that way there was a 75 percent chance they'd say yes.

My grandparents were very strict, very old school I guess you could say. My grandpa didn't fuck around when it came to asserting discipline when needed. One night when I was fourteen I waited till he fell asleep on the couch, snoring away from the rum. Then I went into his pants and grabbed his truck keys, snuck outside, put the truck in neutral and rolled it off the driveway, and went to go pick up my buddy Blake for a little joy ride. Later I snuck back in and went to bed—only to be woken up by a knuckle sandwich! You didn't want to piss off my grandpa. But they also showed love, more on my grandma's side, but again, I felt safe and that was all that mattered.

My grandpa never knew much about hockey. I don't think he'd ever even put on a pair of skates, but he'd always take time off work to drive me to the rink. Neither of us ever missed a practice or a game. And since he owned a hardware store that sold hockey equipment, I'd always have the best to choose from.

I knew from an early age that hockey was the love of my life—I'd watch *Hockey Night in Canada* and marvel at what I was seeing. My dream was just to play one shift in the NHL. And I was going to do whatever it took to play that one shift.

When I was eleven, one day my grandfather said, Hey, son, what do you think about getting a big brother?

Big brother, Gramps?

Yeah, you know that Big Brother and Big Sister program?

Yeah, I've heard of it.

Well, since I'm always working, it would be nice for you to have a big brother to spend time with.

I was like, Sure Grandpa, that actually sounds fun.

About a week later my grandpa says, So there was a guy who fits the bill, his name is Charlie, and he lives on the air force base, about ten minutes away.

Charlie shows up on our doorstep a few days later. He's an older man, tall, with light hair and blue eyes. Hey Brantt, so nice to meet you— what kind of food do you like?

I love Boston Pizza!

Okay, little guy, let's go for some pizza then.

We went out for pizza a few times. We'd be sitting there eating, just talking about small stuff. One day he said, Want to check out where I work on the base?

Sure, that sounds fun!

We went to this warehouse where he drove a forklift. After that first visit he'd let me drive that machine around. It was a blast—I loved anything that had wheels and a gas pedal.

One day he said, Hey Brantt, do you think your grandparents would let you stay over for the night?

I'm not sure, Charlie, but I'll ask.

Brantt: Hey Grandpa, Charlie wanted me to ask you if it was okay to spend the night at his place. He says we can get pizza and watch movies.

Grandpa: That's fine with me, son, but listen carefully. If that guy tries anything funny with you, you tell me right away. I'll grab my shotgun out of my case in the bedroom and shoot that fucker dead.

I didn't really understand what he was talking about. I mean, I was only eleven, and Charlie seemed like a good guy.

We get to Charlie's barracks on the base, and he tells me to go have a shower, to clean up. I started to get nervous, but I took my clothes off anyway and jumped into the shower. As I was showering he was just standing there. Watching me. Then he said, When you're done, just come into the living room. Charlie only had one room.

As I walk into the living room I see Charlie on the bed naked; he's got a *Playboy* in front of him with a ruler. I start to shake as I walk over and say, Hey, what are you doing?

Oh, not much, just playing around. Brantt, can you do me a huge favour?

What's that?

I'm going to get a hard-on right now, and I'd like you to measure my penis.

The only thought going through my head was that he was going to kill me if I didn't do as he asked.

I grab the ruler, my hands shaking. He puts his hand on my ass and says, Why don't you just go down and give it a kiss?

At that point I throw the ruler on the bed, run across the room, and curl up in a ball on the floor. Then I start crying. Please, Charlie, don't hurt me, please just take me back to my grandparents!

He runs over to me, saying, I'm sorry little guy, I was trying to have some fun, *please* don't tell your grandparents or anyone else. If you promise not to ever tell anyone I'll drive you home right now.

Yes, I promise! Just please take me home.

As I walked into the house, all I could think about was my grandpa telling me that if Charlie touched me in any way, he'd shoot him dead.

Now, I was old enough to know that people who killed people went to jail for a really long time, and there was no way I was letting my grandpa go to jail. Funny thing is, I knew my grandpa would have pulled that trigger.

I never told a soul.

And Charlie never came back to pick me up. Grandpa never asked why.

A couple of weeks passed. One day we were on the air force base playing in a hockey tournament. Someone had the radio on in the dressing room, blasting tunes to get us pumped up. Then the news came on.

What I heard made me feel sick to my stomach. The police had arrested a guy for six counts of sexual assault on young boys. It was Charlie. My heart sank. I was thinking about those young boys who weren't so lucky, those young boys who didn't know what to do when he handed them a ruler.

Trusting men after that day became a little harder.

Still, my life was pretty good. I was able to ride my little dirt bike after school as long as I'd finished my homework. I was doing average in school, but was turning into one of the better players in my area. Then, when I was twelve, my grandpa told me we were going to go pick some berries. It seemed like just another normal day. But he had news. When we got to the farm he told me that my dad had called and that he wanted me to live with him in the city.

My first reaction was extreme joy and happiness. I'd known only a little of my father, Bob Myhres, when I was young. What I knew made him seem like a hero to me. He coached a men's senior hockey team and knew a lot about the game. It wasn't until later that I'd get to see firsthand just how much he knew. He'd send Christmas cards and birthday cards with money in them. He'd come and take me out for dinner, and I'd stay a night or two at his place in Edmonton. Hockey was pretty much all we talked about. So I didn't know much about my dad, but hockey was something that brought us together. My dad to me back then was a god. He was really muscular, in great shape, and seemed to just be bigger than life. He used to make me his homemade clam chowder every time he saw me—I was crazy about it, and still make it to this day. He had a new car, and seemed to always have money.

But after that first reaction, I got scared. What if he did to me what Brad had done? My grandpa reassured me that I'd be safe, and that he wouldn't let anything happen to me.

So I moved to the city with my dad. He picked me up in a brand-new silver van and we drove to a little community in Edmonton called Mill Woods, where he'd rented us a really nice townhouse. He took me to the furniture store and bought me a water bed; back then you could heat those things up big-time in the winter. I went to this Catholic school about ten minutes from home.

It seemed to be going awesome—I was so happy to have my father back in my life and really looked up to him. I remember I was eating like three packs of ramen noodles a day, ten cents each, or soup and sandwiches. I don't think my dad was making much money at his job selling carpets. But he did come and pick me up, and he loved hockey as much as I did; that's all we talked about. And not only that: he was the coach.

One day, when I was sitting outside on the deck suntanning while he was cooking dinner, I said, Hey Dad, do you think I could ever make it to the NHL?

He said, Not a chance.

I was a bit taken aback. What do you mean by that, Dad?

Son, you haven't the first clue about what it takes to make the NHL . . . but if you listen to every word I have to say, then you'll have everything in the world you ever wanted—money, girls, the best parties—it will all be there waiting for you.

So from that moment on I made the decision to listen to him and do what he said when it came to hockey, no matter what. It's crazy that my father saw something in me at that moment that needed structure and discipline at such a young age. He saw the talent, but he knew I had lazy written all over my body language. He understood that talent would only get me so far—but that if I listened to him, he'd know the way to get there.

That year, 1986, I made the best AAA peewee team in Edmonton. Grand Centre didn't have a AAA team since the population was so small, so this was the first really good team I made. And my dad was the coach.

I remember that year as being close to perfect. My dad and I seemed to have it all: we did everything together. I played hockey every day, and I now had a coach to guide me. That season was when the Edmonton Oilers were becoming one of the best teams in the history of the NHL. They had a player by the name of Wayne Gretzky who was smashing the league's record books and just looked plain cool with his jersey tucked in, the number 99 on the back.

I went to a game that season where I'd somehow lucked out and got a seat right next to the bench. At one point Gretzky came off the ice, took his tape off his stick, and threw it on the ground. I looked at the stick boy and said, Please could I have that tape he just threw away?

You want his *tape*?

Please, I said again, he's my hero!

So I went home that evening with a piece of Wayne Gretzky's tape. I set it right next to my bed, and every night after that I'd grab it and dream of the day when I'd play that one shift in the NHL.

There was also a player named Marty McSorley, the team's tough guy. I had the chance to ask for his autograph, and as he was signing it I was in awe of just how huge this guy was—he seriously looked like the Hulk to me at that age. Afterwards he gave me a wink and said, Take care, kid . . . Little did I know that in eleven years I'd be fighting him in front of nineteen thousand people. Back then, I was so young that all I remember is seeing his big smile and long blond locks. He was very nice to me.

During that season I was scoring quite a few goals and really enjoying the time I had with my dad, since now we were together every day. We'd been living in Edmonton for almost a full year by then, and I couldn't be happier: everything just seemed to be coming together. Then I went home to visit my grandparents for the weekend. My grandpa asked if we could go for a walk. I had no clue what was about to happen. As we walked, he told me that my dad had lost everything. They were coming to take his car and all the furniture. That meant I had to come and live with them again—my dad couldn't afford to take care of me. I was devastated.

As a twelve-year-old boy who finally had his father in his life, it truly crushed me. I moved back to live with my grandparents and my dad moved back to Grand Centre. I was back to playing hockey, so my dad had rented an apartment to be close.

My mom was actually in the same town, since she worked at my grandparents' hardware store for years. So that was sort of weird: I was living with my grandparents but seeing my mom all the time at the store, although the two of us would get together only now and then. My sister Cher lived with her, so she was in and out of my life. Meanwhile, my uncle Marvin and auntie Carolyn (my grandma and grandpa's daughter) were my favourite people. They had this cabin at Marie Lake about twenty minutes from Grand Centre, and it was my happy place in the summer. I'd go quadding, boating, fishing with my uncle Marvin, who was almost like a real big brother to me.

But it was my little 60-cc dirt bike, a 1981 Yamaha YZ60, that was my favourite thing in the world. I'd ride from after school till dinner, and knew all the trails all over town—I loved that bike. When I was thirteen my grandpa bought me a bigger bike, a 1986 XR100. I loved that thing too. Grand Centre was the best town to grow up in, small, but with lots of great memories.

I often wondered why it was only me that my grandparents took into their home. It made me sad later on in life because my sister was going down a really bad path. She got pregnant when she was fourteen.

I remember the call clear as day. I answered the phone and she said, Hey Brantt, I have something to tell you: I'm pregnant . . . I hung up the phone and didn't talk to her for quite some time. I also had two younger brothers, Devon and Derek, who were Brad's sons. I wasn't close with them at all, not the way brothers should be, anyway.

For the next few years all I did was practise and play games. Whether it was playing road hockey or playing on the ice, I lived and breathed it. One day in grade six our teacher asked us to write a paper on something, but when she walked by my desk all I had was a page full of my signature. Brantt Myhres, over and over. She said, What is all over your page and why are you not doing what I asked you to do? I said I needed to practise because one day I would play in the NHL and didn't want my autograph to look bad because people would want it. She looked at me and said, Brantt, stop it. You'll never play there—do you know how many kids in Canada have the same dream you have? Give it up.

That moment, when she just dropped that bomb on a young kid and his dream, never really fazed me, though. I had this inner giggle that was like, I can't wait for the day when I sign my first autograph. I'll be picturing your face.

There seemed to be a lot of drinking going on with my grandparents. They'd come home after work and pour themselves a rum and Coke, have four or five of them, then go to bed. That happened every night. I remember smelling their drinks one night and almost puking. I could not imagine how anyone could like the smell of that shit. By the time I was seventeen it was my favourite cocktail.

2

When I was fifteen I met the most beautiful girl I'd ever laid eyes on. I'll call her Brooke. We spent every minute together; she'd come to all my games and cheer me on. Meeting someone like that changes you. One day you think things will just keep rolling along the way they always have, and the next day you have a new most important thing in your life.

Brooke and I first met at a friend's house. I was with my friend Blake; we'd been cruising around on quads. I remember leaving that house and saying to Blake, God, I need to see this Brooke again.

One night I was driving around in my buddy Ryan's car when I spotted Brooke and her friend hanging around Grand Centre's main street. I yelled out, Ryan, dude, there she is! Let's go over and ask if they need a ride home.

They did. Little did I know she lived out on this acreage about thirty minutes from Grand Centre. It was a night I'll never forget. We were in the back seat of Ryan's car, a long boat of a car, just bouncing down the gravel road to her house. We had Bon Jovi playing—that was my favourite band. I had my arm around Brooke and could smell her shampoo, but she still seemed somehow far away. I said, Hey, how much longer to your house?

Umm, about five minutes?

My heart started racing. I wanted to kiss her, so I knew I had to be quick. I leaned over and we pretty much kissed the whole five minutes. That feeling of first love is something I never want to forget. The rest of the world just felt empty without her, and somehow shabbier. Just by existing, she made it better.

What could I offer her? I always wanted Brooke to know that I could protect her. One day I was sitting next to her on the school bus, heading to her house on the acreage. There were these two brothers on the bus who used to pick on me from time to time, and it turned out they lived next to her. They started in on me. Calling me a pussy. Asking Brooke why she'd be dating a fag like Myhres. If you've ever ridden a high school bus, you'll know it's like being in a cage with a bunch of teenagers. The only authority is the driver, but no one really respects him and he's got his back to you anyway. The only justice you're going to see on a school bus is the kind you arrange yourself.

Not that I was a tough guy. Most kids back then could handle themselves if they had to. A lot of things got settled with fights. But it wasn't like I swaggered around looking for trouble. I just wanted to sit with my girlfriend. The fact is, I was scared. It's normal to be scared when someone wants to fight you. It's even more normal when two guys want to. Who knows what I would have done if I'd been by myself? Maybe I would have done the stupid thing and tried to talk my way out of it.

But I was with Brooke, and I'd rather get punched in the face than show her I was scared. So I just thought to myself, Fuck this. I looked at one of the brothers and said, You wanna get knocked out? The brothers' names were Wade and Ronnie Myers.

We stood up and squared off. There we were, barrelling down a gravel road with the northern Alberta scrub rushing by outside, all the teenagers now electrified by what was about to happen. No one ever looks away when a fight is about to start.

I dropped Wade with one punch.

Then his brother Ronnie jumps on my back, we're rolling around on the seats and then on the floor, and I can feel all the blood rushing to my face. Then I can feel the school bus swerving and the driver yelling, *Stop it!* That gave me the chance to land one clean—and it was enough to bloody up the other brother's face. Then the bus stopped and the driver had us by our shirts, shouting that the principal was going to get a call. Let's just say the brothers never bothered me again. Actually me and the brothers became great friends after that.

When I was fifteen my dad thought it was a good idea to try out for the Junior B team in Bonnyville, called the Bonnyville Pontiacs. We'd been debating whether to try out for the Midget AA team or the Junior B team, but my father thought that playing against bigger and stronger guys would help my development. So I went with the Pontiacs.

These guys were men, full moustaches and beards. When I walked into the dressing room for the first time I was terrified. One guy had 666 written on his neck and EAT CUNT on his back. Another guy was dressed up like the Ultimate Warrior: painted face, long hair, with a band around his arm and KILL KILL KILL on his workout shirt. Everyone was chewing tobacco and spitting it on the floor. I wasn't expected to make the Pontiacs; players my age usually don't. But I was scoring goals and making plays, so they felt I could help the team. So I made the team.

Now came the time to be initiated.

The first part of the process is to strip naked and lie on a table. Then out comes the razor. They shave your head, then your armpits, then your balls. For a fifteen-year-old boy, just coming into puberty, nothing could be more horrifying.

But that's only step one.

Then they called the first rookie to get back on the table and lie on his back. They tied his hands and feet to the table. Above the table was a pipe that ran across the room. They tied one end of a string to the handle of a bucket and then looped it over the pipe.

The other end they tied to his penis.

Each veteran on the team was holding a puck. The rookie had to tell a joke. If a single one of the veterans didn't laugh, he got to throw a puck in the bucket. With each joke that didn't provoke a laugh, the weight would increase.

There I was, naked and hairless, my hands literally shaking from terror. I see two or three pucks being thrown into the bucket and now the kid was crying, almost screaming for them to stop. Eventually they did, but there was a problem with removing the string from his penis. The weight of the pucks had tightened the string, and the players couldn't untie it. I pretend to go use the washroom, but what I really do is hide in a hallway behind a door for an hour so they couldn't find me. I was fucking losing my mind. I found out later that the kid had to go to the hospital to get the string removed.

But even that wasn't enough to end my Junior B hockey career. The final straw came after the ten-game mark with the team. We had this kid with a mental disability who worked for the team filling the water bottles, picking up tape, carrying the sticks—just basically helping out around the rink. One day before practice some of the older players took him out on the ice, put a hockey sock over his head, and taped him to the goal post. Then they stood on the blue line and fired pucks to see how close they could come to hitting him. My dad walked into the rink and saw what was going on, and that was the last time I ever played for the Pontiacs.

At fifteen I was beginning to grow quite a bit. I was tall but pretty skinny. I was playing midget hockey and had a great year: I believe I had around 140 points. But I'm not going to lie—I didn't have everything figured out when I was fifteen. I wasn't a great student. I was probably scared half the time and scaring others the other half of the time. But on the ice, everything seemed right. Everything made sense. In class, or in the cafeteria, the rules never seemed clear to me. But once the puck was dropped, not only did I know instinctively what to do, I could just do it. And there weren't many people who could stop me. I loved the game, and I loved the way the game made me feel. I loved the person I was when I was on the ice. Hockey was fun at that age. Little did I know it would be one of my last years playing real hockey.

I'd been listed by a Western Hockey League team in Oregon called the Portland Winterhawks the year before. My father told me that a man named Bob Tory, the head scout for the Winterhawks, was coming to watch my game, so I needed to put it all on the line. I don't remember exactly what I did, but I do remember having a great game, and getting a rare word of approval from my father afterwards. Whatever I did, Bob Tory liked it. Getting listed meant I was the property of the Winterhawks. No one else could sign me.

For those who don't know about the WHL, it's one of the best junior leagues in the world. Me and my father, as well as my grandparents, were through the roof with happiness. The next step was to actually make the team, and from there, the next stop was the NHL. For me, though, the WHL *was* the NHL. And most NHL players came from major junior hockey in Canada. That was me. It was at that point where I thought to myself, Wow, Brantt, you may just be on your way. When I turned sixteen, I would be eligible.

Right after my sixteenth birthday I got my first car, a 1981 red Camaro Z28. My grandpa and my dad had both said that if I saved half the money they'd pay the other half. The car cost $2600, and I'd saved around $1300 from cutting the grass around town and chores around the house. The only problem was that it didn't have a stereo—and there's no point having a red Camaro if you can't crank tunes. So I decided to get a job at a stereo store. Within a week of working there I went downstairs, loaded up on a bunch of Alpine stereo equipment, put it in my bag, and went home. Then I left it on my dresser.

When I got back from school my grandma said, Hey Brantt, there's some stereo equipment in your room with the new wrapping still on it.

Yeah, some guy at school got it for his birthday and had no car, so he gave it to me.

Well, it sure looks like it's brand new, and it may be stolen. Maybe I should call around to see if someone stole it?

My guts were turning at that point, but I said, Yeah, make your calls.

Sure enough, she called the right store and they pressed charges. I had to go to court. While I was on the stand the judge, Mr. Fraser, who I'll never forget, said to me, Well, son, I see that you're quite the hockey player, and that you're listed by Portland. You know that I can, as of now, make it so you can't cross the border, and your so-called hockey career will be over.

I promised him that I'd never steal again and asked for one more chance.

All he gave me was thirty hours of community service. I never did steal anything again.

At the time, though, I was pissed at my grandma. She had strong morals and would never let me get away with stealing—she knew I had to address the situation and not get away with it. It was weird: as me and my grandma were walking to the courthouse, even though I was pissed, there was a feeling of, She really loves me and only wants the best for me. And that was exactly what she said after we left the courthouse. She said, Dear, I love you very much. I didn't do this to hurt you, I did this so you can learn a hard life lesson here—you'll thank me down the road.

Brooke found out nothing about any of it.

When I was fifteen I got invited to the Winterhawks' main camp in Edmonton: my chance to make the big step to the WHL. And I planned on going there and turning heads. I scored a couple goals during the game and was playing really well, but every time I skated by the other team's bench their backup goalie would yell at me: Myhres, you fucking hot dog, you pussy, you suck, nice white gloves, you homo. So when the game ended I skated by their bench and said, Go fuck yourself, dickhead. That was probably exactly what he wanted. His response was a phrase I would hear hundreds of times over the next eighteen years.

Wanna go?

I didn't even have to decide. This wasn't like being on the bus, defending my reputation in front of my girlfriend. That time, I was like a cornered animal. Fight or flight, with nowhere to fly. Maybe it was because this guy had been yapping at me for an hour already, and I'd just had enough. Maybe the guy was just good at pissing people off. Whatever it was, that was the first time I experienced tunnel vision. I backed up to centre ice and tossed my gloves and stick to the side while the guy scrambled out off the bench, shedding his glove and blocker as he went. My dad was in the stands along with all the head brass for the team. My heart was racing, but the arena seemed silent. My focus was on one thing only—my target.

I'm like, Okay, what now, Brantt? As he's skating towards me, I turn sideways with my left hand cocked back. I reach out with my right to grab his jersey and start throwing my left hand as fast and as hard as I can, staring only at his face so I don't miss.

The fight was over real quick. He was hunched over, with blood all over his face.

If you've never been in a hockey fight, I can tell you what I learned that day. It feels pretty great to win. But it feels even better not to lose. I was pumped, but the real elation, I realized later, was *relief*. When you agree to tangle in front of a bunch of people, the thing you really fear is getting embarrassed. Half the time you don't even feel the fists on your face. But getting embarrassed hurts in a way that takes a long time to recover from. Not that I knew that part then. I was 1 and 0. I was undefeated.

There was a guy standing at the door as I was leaving the ice. I just thought he was a fan and that he was going to congratulate me on a good fight. Wrong. He punched me right in the face and then landed on top of me. My dad and the team's brass came running down and pulled him off. Turns out it was the goalie's brother.

My swagger of thirty seconds earlier was gone. I thought to myself, Holy shit, if this is what the WHL is all about, I'm in big trouble. What I didn't realize was that the head brass loved it. The owner came into the dressing room and gave me a pat on the back, saying, Way to not take any shit, Brantt, good job. My dad looked like a kid on Christmas morning, just this huge smile: Atta boy, son, boy did you kick the shit out him. I'm proud of you for taking a stand.

No one had to tell me twice what I needed to do to make the team.

I didn't make the team that year—pretty much no one does when they're 15. But when I came back the following year, I hadn't forgotten what I'd learned. There was another sixteen-year-old guy in camp, named Josh Erdman. He was a highly touted player in the province and looked like he might make the team. In our first shift on the ice together we met in the corner and he punched me in the side of the head, saying, Come on, let's go! I guess he knew I'd scored some points by dropping the gloves and wanted a chance to prove himself too. We were both close to making the team—and maybe the last roster spot would go to the guy who wanted it more.

He didn't have to ask me twice. My gloves were off and we were swinging for the fences—teenagers don't worry about defence. I cut him over the eye real bad. He had to go off and get stitches over his right eye.

But when he came back from the trainer's room, stitches sticking out of his eyebrow, he was looking for redemption. So as soon as we hit the ice the gloves were off again—and again I got the better of him. I remember sitting in the penalty box saying to myself, Oh my god, what have I got myself into? I could see that this guy was going to keep challenging me until he won.

Just as I'd thought, the next time we got out on the ice he came after me for a third round. We dropped our gloves, circled each other like a couple of snarling dogs, then reached in to get a grip and started throwing. But by this time I guess the team's owner had seen enough. He came flying down the stands and leaned over the glass to bark at us, You fucking guys are going to be teammates, so lay off, no more!

That's how I found out I'd made the team. The two of us were standing in the middle of the ice, our fists cocked and with a handful of each other's sweater, our teammates clustered around us to see how the fight would end. But the news took all the anger out of the fight. We just smiled and looked at each other.

Josh and I would become best friends on the team that year. It's strange, but nothing brings you closer to someone than trading punches.

Moving to Portland was one of the most exciting days of my life. I was really sad to leave Brooke and my family, but I could smell the NHL now. I packed up my Camaro and drove the seventeen hours to Oregon. I was by myself but was following our goalie, who lived in Edmonton. I had a huge smile on my face the whole way.

When I got there I was introduced to my billets, the family I'd live with while I played. They were nice people and made the transition pretty easy for me. They also had a real nice house and a Mercedes and would buy Kraft Dinner by the case, as I'd eat at least one box a day. I was totally addicted to Kraft Dinner (or Kraft Macaroni & Cheese, as it's known in the U.S.).

Everything seemed so new to me. I had to get a visa, which the team helped me get. I had to go to a new school in a new country, make new friends, and live with a new family, plus I was away from Brooke, which was really hard. I think my phone bill back then was like eight hundred bucks a month, just talking to her and to my family. As usual, I wasn't really focused on my classes. The work seemed difficult, but the bottom line was that I really only went to please the coaches. I never actually completed any courses.

I know a lot of people hated high school, and I can't say that I loved it. But there are worse ways to go through those years than as a six-foot-four major junior hockey player. No one fucked with me. It's not like prison—I didn't have to go pick a fight with the toughest guy in school. Maybe everyone just assumed that I *was* the toughest guy in the school. And since there were other guys from the team to hang around with, I never really made any friends in Portland. Girls were a different story. They were always asking to come to our team parties, asking for tickets to the game, so it was sort of like shooting fish in a barrel, if you know what I mean.

Back then we got paid only sixty dollars every two weeks, so I was pretty much broke. After practice we'd all go to Taco Bell and eat like pigs for six bucks. We couldn't afford anything else. My billets were nice people, but to me, living with someone other than my grandparents always felt off. I missed them very much.

Me and my dad talked pretty much every day. He was my rock when it came to the pressures of the game and would give me great advice on how to handle myself. My mother was never really in the picture. I guess there were just too many bad memories with her for a sixteen-year-old to work on.

I went from playing in front of a hundred people to playing in front of ten thousand. Everyone had facial hair and looked real old. I may have been tall, and I probably looked pretty intimidating. I mean, I wanted to look intimidating, so I hope it worked. But I was just a scared kid. Anyone who's not scared of fighting is probably insane. You *should* be afraid. I don't care how tough you are or how skilled you are, you're going to get punched in the face. You're going to lose some. And you lose a lot more when you don't know what you're doing. I can't imagine what it would be like not to worry about that.

And remember, just a few months before, I'd been playing minor hockey with kids my own age. I'd put up over a hundred points skating on the first line. Now I was on the fourth line and barely playing. I certainly wasn't scoring. But again, I was six four. So I decided to do what I seemed to be pretty good at, which was to fight.

Actually, I didn't decide that. My father told me to "play tough." He said, Son, play like a prick out there. There's going to be NHL scouts in the stands now, and they're all looking for players that are six four and can skate.

I ended up that year leading the league as a sixteen-year-old with twenty-three fights.

I loved the game of hockey. I never dreamed about being a fighter; I wanted to be the player I'd been in midget, making a difference on the scoreboard, not in bloody knuckles. But after my first few fights that year, it started to sort of just roll. I was adopting that gladiator mentality, and nothing was going to stop me. Don't get me wrong. I was overwhelmed at times. That first year, I was overwhelmed a lot. I was fighting big, mean guys who knew how to handle themselves. Part of that is technical, and part of it is just controlling your emotions. But whatever it is, experience is a huge advantage in a fight. I didn't have it, but I was accumulating it quickly.

One thing I didn't know at the time is that anxiety and excitement are the same thing, at least from a neurochemical point of view. Your body experiences the same reactions. The difference lies in how you respond to that rush of chemicals. If you fight a lot in front of cheering fans and with the momentum of a hockey game in the balance, with your coaches and father watching, with scouts in the stands and your dream of a career in the NHL on the line, it's hard to know where the anxiety ends and the excitement begins.

Hockey fans know the excitement. Let's say the game has been chippy. Let's say someone from the other team takes a run at one of your guys. The coach sends the fourth line over the boards. Everyone in the building knows what happens next. Everyone can feel the pressure mounting. Everyone wants justice. There has to be a fight, and there's no one among the ten thousand fans who doesn't want the fight to happen.

Including the guys who are going to fight. They have the same sense of honour. And they know they can lift their teams. In a few moments they can take their buddies on their shoulders and change the game. They're also young men, with more than their fair share of testosterone, probably. It's generally not all that hard to get a young man to fight.

And if you've ever won a hockey fight, you know it's one of the best feelings in the world. It's addictive.

On the other hand, those two guys may have been up all night worrying about this fight. They may be scared of getting hurt, but probably not. One of the secrets of experienced fighters is that the punches don't really hurt, at least not at the time. Sometimes you barely feel them. But if you challenge a guy in front of thousands of people and you lose; if you tell your team, Don't worry, I've got this, and you lose; if you drop your gloves at centre ice with an NHL scout in the stands and you lose; you know there are few things in life more crushing.

There aren't many ways to shake off that awful feeling. But one is to fight again.

Anxiety or excitement, winning or losing, exhilaration or humiliation. It all leads back to the same thing. Another fight. It's not long before you feel like you're on a runaway train.

Not that my first year in Portland was some kind of hell of homesickness and fear. Major junior hockey is exactly what teenage guys think they want. You get to play hockey all the time and make a little money. You're treated like a hero pretty much wherever you go. People actually want your autograph. Girls want more than your autograph. In many ways you're treated like a professional athlete, and you get to party like one.

At this point I never drank that much, from time to time a beer or so. I'd be at a team party and would dump out the drink just to make it seem like I was keeping up. It's funny to look back and wonder how many guys were dumping out their beers. We weren't old enough to get into the bars in Portland, so there were always house parties to go to. As I was sober at all these parties, I'd see our older players drink a ton. And if they didn't see you drinking they'd think you weren't mature enough to play in that league, hence I'd always have an empty beer can in my hand.

There wasn't much going on as far as wild goes. We had this other sixteen-year-old on the team, a high pick in the bantam draft, who everyone thought was going to become the star of the franchise. The owner of the team had even rented him a new Mustang; it was in his contract. Well, he was a crazy fucker. One day we were on our way to the rink for practice and saw his Mustang in the ditch. He'd let some fifteen-year-old girl take his car home, and she'd crashed it. He got suspended from the team for a couple weeks.

The NHL entry draft is the way every eighteen-year-old hockey player in the world hopes to make it to the big league. That's when every hockey player's dream is put to the test. If you're not drafted, chances are the dream is over. There are exceptions, but not many. If no one wants you when you're eighteen, who's going to look at you when you're nineteen and every GM in the league has already passed on you?

That means your seventeen-year-old year is the most important of your life. I'll never forget that summer my dad pulled me aside and said, Son, how bad do you want to get drafted to the NHL?

More than anything, Dad.

Okay, he said. Well, you're going to have to lead the whole Canadian Hockey League in fighting majors.

I was like, What?!

He said, You need to get noticed every time you hit that ice. Make those NHL scouts write your name down when you're out there.

Things in Portland were coming to an end. I wasn't getting much ice time. My dad had moved down there to give me support, knowing that this was my most important season. He was crucial for me that year, never missed a game or practice—if I was dogging it out there, I'd get an earful.

One game, the team was sitting in the dressing room during the second intermission. I'd played so little I was hardly even sweating. Like everyone else I was leaning with my forearms on my thighs when my dad walks right through the dressing room and into the coach's office. We all looked at each other to make sure we'd actually seen a parent in the dressing room. Parents hadn't been allowed in the dressing room since we were nine years old.

Then the yelling started in the office. My dad was tearing into the coach. And although I finished the third period, I had a feeling it would be my last with the Winterhawks.

My father convinced me to walk off the team and request a trade. It took two weeks, but they traded me to the Lethbridge Hurricanes. I was headed back to Alberta, a couple hours' drive south of Calgary. I didn't really know much about Lethbridge other than that they had a good team that year. A couple friends of mine said, Well, at least you'll be able to hit the bars now (the drinking age was eighteen, lower than in the States, although I was still only seventeen). Plus, Brooke and I were thrilled to be close together again.

I drove from Portland to Kamloops to meet my new team for my first game. I wanted to make an impression. So during a time out, when the other team's goalie Cory Hirsh was skating by our bench to go to his own bench, I punched him right in the face. Next thing I knew it was a full line brawl. All of a sudden I felt right at home. I always remembered my father telling me to make sure the scouts in the stands write your name down—to do something to make them notice you.

I don't think that's why I did it, though. Not that I would have put it this way at the time, but there was only one thing in my life I could control. I couldn't control my ice time, or what city I lived in. I couldn't control my career. I couldn't be with the people I cared about. I sucked at school. I wasn't even scoring anymore.

But when the gloves came off, I was back in charge.

At some point during that season I stopped pouring out my beers. I began to love booze too much for that. And it is no exaggeration to use the word "love." I loved booze more than I loved anyone I knew. I loved it more than hockey.

I know that sounds crazy. But it was like falling in love with Brooke: one day there was the life I was accustomed to, and the next there was life with booze. Alcohol gave me an inner feeling as if the world was a beautiful, fun place, whereas hockey gave me that feeling of, Well, time to turn the switch on that crazy animal for three hours. Hockey wrung me out, and when I discovered that booze could release me from that roller-coaster of anxiety and excitement, I was in love.

The truth was, there was nothing I could do that would make me feel half as good as booze did. I could laugh unselfconsciously. I could dance. I could talk to girls without feeling embarrassed. I didn't feel lonely when I was drinking. Alcohol made the world seem better.

Like most teenagers, we thought we were adults. And we loved thinking of ourselves as pro athletes. But we were also just a bunch of kids living far from home, without much supervision, and under a lot of pressure. Every athlete faces the pressure to win, but major junior players face the anxiety that any mistake, any bad decision, any bad bounce, is going to be seen by the NHL scouts. Was my shift too long? Too short? Or should I have gone harder? Should I show more grit? More coolheadedness? And don't forget, we're also playing against our teammates for ice time. Because more ice means more exposure, and more points. And more of those things means better chances of getting drafted higher. Or getting drafted at all. It's hard enough trying to win a hockey game. It's even harder when you're trying to win the next few years every time you step on the ice.

And as a tough guy, I had a different kind of pressure. If you've ever been in a fight, you know that your heart races, your adrenalin spikes. You're carried along by a rush of fear and excitement and aggression that makes whatever you were doing five minutes ago seem tedious and boring. You have tunnel vision—the world fades away, you can't hear a thing, it's just quiet, and all that matters is winning. All that matters is the next few seconds. You can't think about anything else.

Then it's over, and the world comes charging back in. You have to account for what you've just done. You've still probably got a few lumps, and very sore hands. You've got the buzz of victory to take a lot of the pain away, but that fades. And part of you wonders whether you're proud of the part of you that just tried to physically hurt someone in front of a few thousand people. You're proud, but pride may not be the only emotion. There are other emotions that come with the territory, and they're not all good.

And that's if you win. If you lose—and everyone loses sometimes—then you feel a different kind of shame. A shame that no one wants to feel. You stepped up to protect your teammates, and you failed. You just lost some of the respect you've built up, fight by fight.

Fighting is hard. Fighting night after night as a teenager is much harder. Bare-knuckle fighting. But fighting like that, when the stakes include your future employment and the respect of your peers? That's pressure.

Put a bunch of teenagers under pressure, take away the kind of control that most kids' parents are there to provide, and stand back. Those kids are probably going to blow off dangerous amounts of steam. That's what happened in Lethbridge anyway.

One evening we were in a strip club watching the dancers, a few of my friends sitting in the front row while I was sitting in the back, when suddenly I saw a guy stand up, grab his chair, and smash it right over a teammate's head. I ran over, grabbed the guy by his neck, and choked him till he collapsed. I saw more guys coming towards me, so I thought the best way to tackle the situation was to jump on the stage with the stripper and pick them off one by one. After the fights were over we left, all bloodied, and decided to head down to the country bar to chat about what had just gone down. Naturally we all thought it was hilarious.

The next day, when I got brought into the GM's office to explain what happened, I said it was all out of self-defence. (That became a common theme during my career.) We were banned from the strip club after that. Actually it got so bad that by the end of the year we were banned from all the bars except one. My running mates were Todd MacIsaac, Slade Stephenson, and Maurice Meagher. I would say that there'd probably been eight to ten guys at the club that night. All the guys I ran with went just as hard as I did. We weren't boy scouts.

Funny how drinking and fighting go together. The more I fought, the more I drank. And the more I drank, well, as the year went on I was fighting almost every night. I ended the season setting a record for the most penalty minutes ever by a seventeen-year-old: 381 minutes in fifty-three games. That's forty-five fights, maybe more if you include exhibition games. I was rated as the toughest junior player in North America. Not many seventeen-year-olds get in forty-five bare-knuckle fights in a year.

3

The NHL's Central Scouting rated me as going late in the second round of the draft. By that time I had an agent, Carlos Sosa, who'd approached me and my dad when I was seventeen. He was a real awesome guy, treating me like I was already playing in the NHL, and that I'll never forget. Carlos even agreed to fly my family to Montreal, where the draft was being held, so my sister Cher, my grandma and grandpa, and my dad were all there supporting me. My grandma was so cute—she was walking across the hotel lobby when young kids came up and asked me for an autograph, and I could hear her say to my grandpa, Bob, look! I can't believe my little boy is signing autographs! That has always stuck in my mind.

I'd never been so nervous. That was 1992. Everyone was talking about all the Europeans and where they would go in the draft, which made things even more competitive. Still, I'd done everything my dad had told me to do. I led the whole league in fighting majors. I had four goals and eleven assists. In my mind I'd done absolutely everything I could do to hear my name being called. So that morning I woke up, opened the blinds, and just had this big smile on my face. Time to shower and put your suit on, Brantt, and make sure your tie is nice and straight—this will be the biggest day of your life!

We get to the old Montreal Forum, and all you see are the draft tables with all the teams' logos on them. Then you look up to the rafters and see all the Stanley Cup banners, with all the Hall of Famers. I was blown away. This was the mecca of the hockey world.

We sit down in our seats in the stands, which are packed with suits, all these young men who've worked so hard and given up so much to be moments away from belonging to an NHL team. Meanwhile, all the GMs in the league are down on the trade floor. Basically, everything I'd done for the past few years was to impress these guys, and now there they are, all in one place, drinking coffee out of Styrofoam cups, talking on the phone, making notes. With my fate in their hands.

When the first round was finished, I was confident my name was about to be called. But then the second round went by. Then the third. Then the fourth, and I still did not go. By now the crowd was thinning out. The reporters were heading back to the office. The GMs were loosening their ties. The big names were long gone. I was looking at my dad and agent, saying, Holy shit, I may not get picked. Carlos leaned over and said, Brantt, I have a feeling you're going to go real soon.

Then Tampa Bay Lightning went up to the podium with their first pick in the fifth round. Their GM, Phil Esposito, leaned over to the mic and said, With the fifth pick in the 1992 NHL Entry Draft we take Brantt Myhres from the Lethbridge Hurricanes of the WHL.

I could not believe my ears. I hugged all my family and with a big smile went down to the table to meet the personnel from the team. My first thought was, Oh my god, I get to meet Brent Gretzky, the little brother of my idol Wayne Gretzky—Tampa had picked Brent in the third round. Then, as I was shaking the hands of the Tampa staff, all I could think was, Where's that jersey, I want to put it on! Finally they handed me the jersey and a hat—I slid both of them on and took some pictures with the media. I was so happy, not only for myself, but for my grandparents, my father, and my sister. I knew the love and sacrifice that had gone into this day, and it was as much theirs as it was mine. Every hockey player says that. Because it's true.

That night Tampa had a party for all the draft picks, and there I got to meet Brent Gretzky and everyone else. I was standing there with my family when Phil Esposito came up to me and put his hand on my shoulder. Man, he said, I can't believe how big you are! All the fans in Tampa are going to fall in love with your style of play, so get ready.

Now, I knew I wasn't going to make the team that year, but just hearing that with my family standing there was pretty inspiring.

So, as usual, my first thought was, Where was I going to get loaded? With about two hundred dollars to my name, I decided to head down to Saint Catherine Street.

Around three a.m. I was stumbling around when this girl on the street said, Hey cutie, wanna have some fun? I had no clue what she meant. My buddy Jeff said, Myze, she's a hooker. All I said was, How much and where do we go? That was my first experience with not respecting sex or women.

When we landed back in Edmonton, I was in the car with my dad and we were still talking about hockey. His view was that the draft was just a minor step in the process—that now the work really begins, but if I took the summer to work on my skills and put some weight on, I could have a shot at making the team.

And so I did: I took that whole summer to practise and hit the weights from time to time. Back then, though, I had *no* clue about how to work out. I thought playing shinny was enough to get me into shape.

I went into camp for Tampa that year at 228 pounds. Nobody was going to fuck with me, and I was going to make a statement. I was playing pretty good in camp, playing inter-squad games.

At one point I went to get a puck and this guy named Larry Melnyk, a veteran in the NHL and probably thirty-three or thirty-five years old, hit me and said, Hey you big fucking monkey, wanna go? I said, Sure, and with one left bomb, I knocked him to his knees.

———

For their first pick in the NHL draft that year Tampa went for Roman Hamrlik, their golden child—the favourite not only of the Tampa Bay Lightning but of the NHL. Real good-looking guy, six-foot-two, 210 pounds. He had this long hockey hair, drove a brand-new Lexus, and had this girlfriend who looked like someone off of *Baywatch*. I was definitely envious of this kid, and I can't say that about many other players. We were in our second day of training camp, playing another inter-squad game. I was covering the point when the puck gets rimmed around the boards on my side. When I go to get it I feel this hard fucking whack on the back of my leg, and when I look back it's Hamrlik. I'm like, You cocksucker, you ever touch me again and it's bedtime for you.

Well, the next time we get out there together, the puck gets rimmed again around the boards, I go to get it, and what do ya know, this fucking guy slashes me again hard on the back of the leg. I turn around and start chasing him. I know he has a visor on, so I have to be careful, but he actually drops his gloves first, so I grab on, give him two hard uppercuts to his face, and he goes down to the ice.

As I stand up, I see Phil Esposito running down the stairs with his suit on yelling at me to get the fuck over there. I'm like, Oh shit, this is not going to go very well.

Espo: What the FUCK do you think you're doing? You're going after our number-one draft pick?! Settle the fuck down, and I want to see you in my office after this game. LEAVE HIM ALONE!

The game ends and I'm dreading this meeting. I walk into Espo's office.

Espo: Grab a seat, Brantt. I just have one question for you.

Brantt: What's that, Mr. Esposito?

Espo: If the puck gets rimmed again around the boards, and Roman slashes you again, what are you going to do?

Brantt: I'm going to give it to him again.

Espo: That's exactly the answer I was looking for.

Even though I had a good camp, I was still only eighteen years old and I got sent back to junior for another season.

That year in Lethbridge it seemed like now I had a target on my back because of my reputation. Everyone wanted to fight me. That's the way it works at every level. As soon as you start winning, everyone wants a shot at you.

One night we were in Saskatoon where the Blades had a killer named Rhett Trombley, who looked like he was about forty years old, beard and all. They started me in the opening lineup, and guess who else was in the starting lineup? Yes sir, Rhett. When we lined up before the puck was dropped, I said, Hey Rhett, what's shaking tonight?

Not much, Myze. Wanna go?

You bet, I said. Let's just wait for the puck to drop. That way we could take our helmets off and get at it properly.

So we came together. I hit him with about ten lefts to the side of his face, and he went down to his knees.

When we were in the penalty box I could see that his cheekbone was purple and really swollen. He had an ice bag on it.

He looked over at me and said, Hey Myze, can you give me another shot?

Are you sure, Rhett? Your face is pretty messed up.

I have to, man. Just one more.

Sure, pal.

We got out on the ice together again and squared off . . . and this time I wanted to make sure he wouldn't want to fight me again. I was going to aim right for the fucked-up side of his face. Fifteen punches later, the fight was over and Rhett had to hit the dressing room to put on a full protective cage.

At the start of the year I told Carlos that I was tired of putting two dollars in my gas tank to get me to the rink. I mean, we got paid only eighty dollars every two weeks, so I was always broke. I said, Let's get a contract done with Tampa so that I can get a signing bonus.

Carlos got a deal done in the next couple of weeks: I got $75,000 in a signing bonus, and if I made the big club I'd make $200K. So I went out and bought a brand-new Jeep and new clothes. And when we went out to the bars, the drinks were on me. By this point, me and Brooke were on the rocks because I was screwing everything in that city.

I was in a country bar one night with the team when I bought a hundred rum and Cokes for last call. So I was absolutely hammered when I wheeled this hot chick out of the bar and into my convertible. I put the top down, started doing doughnuts right in the parking lot, and when I came to a stop, there was a cop in his car staring right at me, smiling. I looked at the girl and said, Well, I'm off to jail, nice knowin' ya. The cop walked over and said, What's with the stunting?

I just got a new car, I said, and wanted to impress this beautiful lady.

He asked for my licence. Then he said, Oh, hey Brantt, you guys are having a great season so far. I'm a big fan. Have you been drinking?

Not a drop, officer.

Well, he said, be safe and good luck the rest of the year!

I put the Jeep into first gear and took off. Then I lit a joint and cranked Bon Jovi on the way back to my house.

Brooke's dad, Bob, came down to visit and watch a game that was going to be on TSN. He said that if we won the game he'd buy drinks for everyone. We did end up winning, so off we went to the bar. By the time we left the bar, about twelve of us were wasted, and we had been joined by some girls. We ended up getting a room at a hotel called the Magic Mushroom. I was with Bob, of course, so I was planning on being pretty tame. Now, I don't want to go into too much detail about what goes on between teenaged hockey players and teenaged girls. If you know much about the game, you probably know that what passed for normal back then would not be tolerated today, and I'm sure a lot of guys are not too proud of the way they behaved. Maybe the girls aren't either. I'm not proud anyway.

Things got pretty wild that night. Bob and I were just standing there, laughing and having a smoke. He was puffing on a big cigar. But then he headed out to his truck to grab more beer, and my behaviour went downhill from there. Before the night was over, Bob had stubbed out his cigar on my penis.

Somehow this story of the Magic Mushroom Hotel got back to the GM and the coach. They called me into the office the next day and said they were suspending me—my drinking was getting out of hand and I was becoming a bad influence on the other guys.

I was like, Give me a fucking break, these guys are big enough to make their own decisions. That argument didn't work. They recommended I take a one-week leave of absence and go stay with my agent in Seattle: maybe that would smarten me up a bit. I ended up sleeping with his seventeen-year-old daughter.

That summer I was nineteen years old and heading to Tampa's training camp to make the team. I got in my first exhibition game against the St. Louis Blues. When I went to the faceoff the guy lining up next to me had the eyes of someone who's not afraid of anything. His neck was the size of a fire hydrant.

Hey kid, wanna go?

Sure.

When we square off, all goes quiet again. I can see just how big this guy's hands are, and how he's got this old helmet that was a knuckle breaker. I go in to grab him, and he just turns sideways and starts throwing bombs! The fight ended up being pretty even.

I didn't know who he was, but after the fight was over and I skated back to the bench, the guys all had this look on their face like, What the fuck were you thinking?

It was Tony Twist. Twist was one of the top killers in the NHL. Probably one of the reasons why I did so good in the fight was that I didn't know who he was! The guy threw sledgehammers. He hit me so hard that I couldn't open my jaw for two weeks.

I was the last cut on the team that year, so back to Lethbridge for one more season.

That year, 1993, I played hockey again. I didn't have to fight, because no one would fight me. I was playing on the first line, and ended up with twenty goals and forty-three assists for sixty-three points in sixty-one games. People wonder why there's still bare-knuckle fighting in a modern sport like hockey. Well, that's why. When a big guy who can handle himself goes to the net or heads into the corner to retrieve a puck, he has considerably more time and space than other guys. You need confidence to play hockey at a high level—so a good tough guy can make his teammates better by spreading around some of that confidence. He can also make the other team worse. They're all a little less aggressive when a bona fide tough guy is cruising around the ice. And hockey is a game of aggression.

For the past couple seasons I'd been telling myself that I was drinking because I was sick of fighting. But that year I was playing the game the way I wanted to play it. And I was still drinking.

Actually, my drinking was getting the best of me.

I was staying with an awesome family: Linda, who was a nurse, and her husband, a cop. I came home drunk one night and stumbled into the spare room. Linda had a friend in from out of town, and she was sleeping.

I sat on the end of the bed. Hey, wake up, hey wake up.

She woke up and said, What the hell are you doing in my room?

I said, I want to have a little fun—what do you think?

She got right up and ran into the living room. I was chasing her around the coffee table saying, Hey, relax, just settle down, don't wake up Linda or I'm fucked.

Linda and her husband woke up, and then kicked me out of their house. I had to go stay with another family until the waters cooled down. Then I begged them to give me one last chance. They said they would as long as I stopped drinking. I made a promise to them that I would stop.

Four days later I was wasted.

4

All I did that summer was drink, smoke pot, and chase girls. When I showed up at Tampa's camp I was in the worst shape of my life.

Also in camp that year was the league's first female goalie: Manon Rhéaume. When I realized that she'd be on my team for training camp, I was like, Wow, this girl is really attractive. Manon and the French guys hung out together; her English was not too good.

By that time I was hanging out with Roman Hamrlik. It's funny, sometimes you become best friends with a guy you've fought, and that was the case with me and Hammer. We ended up always hanging together—we liked the same heavy metal music and the same food. I was always amazed, though, by how he'd never drink, and when I say never, I mean never. We'd go out to the bar after a game on the road and he'd just order his cranberry juice. It blew my fucking mind how a guy could just sit at a bar and drink juice.

One night I went out for dinner with Manon and Roman. I was like, Hammer, how the hell can I hit on this girl if she can't understand a word I'm saying?

He said, Myze, I'd leave this one alone. Focus on making the team.

Before each scrimmage we'd all sit in the middle of the dressing room to stretch, and Manon would be sitting there with her long underwear on, stretching away, all the guys with these little-kid smirks on their faces. And when she'd be in net for practice, I truly believe guys were trying to take her head off with bombs. Petr Klíma would come down in warm-ups and just blast one at her head. We'd all be saying, Welcome to the show, sweetheart! I must say, though, that I was really impressed with just how good she was. I was expecting this girl to come into the net looking like a "shooter tutor" with a hundred holes. And that was not the case. She held her own, and good for her.

After we did our fitness testing, GM Phil Esposito called me into his office.

Brantt, how do you think you did?

Not bad, I guess . . .

You know Manon? Well, she beat you in the VO2 bike test.

I felt pretty embarrassed about that. It was becoming clear that all the dreams I'd ever had of playing that first shift in the NHL were getting trumped by my partying. I never really gave much thought to it, other than I may like to go just a bit harder off the ice than some of my teammates. It's not like I was the only guy who liked to drink. Just about every guy I knew would get wasted if we had the next day off. And I figured that as long as I kicked the shit out of someone, I'd be safe and keep my job.

That's not how it ended up this time, though. I got sent to Atlanta, Tampa's farm team in the International Hockey League (IHL). They were called the Knights. I was going down to the minors with something to prove, knowing that the NHL was just down Highway I-75.

Atlanta was one of my favourite cities ever to play in. I was only twenty years old in this massive city that loved their hockey team. And the Knights were filled with older guys who had NHL experience, so now I was so fricken close to my first shift in the big leagues.

If you like to party, you'll love Atlanta. I did. They had this district called Buckhead that had blocks of bars, and the strippers were the best I've ever seen. For a guy who loved to booze, it was heaven. I got a fake ID since the drinking age was twenty-one. It was just so cool now to be playing with guys who'd played in the NHL, and they were awesome with me; they didn't treat me like a rookie at all, it was just one big happy family.

Somehow, whatever wake-up call Esposito had tried to give me was forgotten whenever I got near Buckhead.

My first roommate in pro hockey was a Mormon, a great guy. Aaron Gavey was a pretty straight arrow; I don't think he knew what he was getting himself into living with me. We actually got along really well, most of the time anyway. We'd always be eating out or cooking simple meals. The thing is, he would freak out when his girlfriend came to visit.

Myze, he pleaded one night, please, please do not bring any girls back while my GF is here. She's only here for three days, I'm sure you can handle that, right?

I was like, Oh yeah, Gaves, no problem, bud.

That night I got sideways drunk and ended up bringing back two strippers to play strip poker. As the girls and I were nearing the end of the game, all of a sudden Aaron's door opens, and his GF pokes her head out and screams. Naturally, all of us were pretty much naked at that point, and I really didn't care about anything other than keeping the party going. So I asked her to put some clothes on and come out for a cocktail! Aaron didn't talk to me for quite some time, but it blew over.

Pretty much everything blew over in those days. I did pretty much whatever I wanted, and there wasn't much anyone could do about it.

I had a girlfriend, Nicole, for a while that year. She was a stunner, a dentist. After dating for about two weeks or so, we all went out for drinks at the bar—myself, Nicole, and a couple players and their girl-friends. There was a guy there who was always hanging around practice, one of those guys who was a real ass kisser. At one point I had to go to the washroom and told Nicole I'd be right back. By the time I returned she was crying her eyes out. I asked what was wrong.

She said, You see that big guy over there, the one you were doing a shooter with about ten minutes ago?

Yeah, why?

Well, when you went to the washroom, he told me that when you guys went on the road you were a pig and you were fucking chicks all the time.

Nicole, now are you sure that's the guy who said that? I pointed to him, and she confirmed.

I walked up to him as he was talking to someone, so his back was facing me. I tapped him on the shoulder, and when he turned around I punched him so hard in the face that one blow was all it took to put him on the ground. Then I grabbed him by his hair, saying, You're gonna get it even worse when I get outside, you fucking weasel!

The bouncers broke it up and me and Nicole went home. At six a.m. the police called and said I needed to come down to the station because the guy was charging me. So I got dressed, drove over, and when I walked in, there was the guy I'd just smacked in the face. Let's just say his face didn't look so good. I was told it was up to him and his lawyer to decide whether they'd press charges.

His lawyer called the next day and said, Brantt, he can't see out of his eye so he's going to miss at least a week, maybe two, of work. Why don't you pay three grand now and let's put this to bed. I told him to go fuck himself.

The next year I had to pay sixty thousand.

Every day in the minors is a bit like playing the lottery. You're busting your ass, but to some degree, your fate is out of your hands. You have to just hope each morning that today is your day. It can't be everybody's day, and not everybody's day comes. Some guys wait their whole careers thinking that every time they drive to the rink today is going to be different. Hope can wear you out.

I didn't have to wait long. One unremarkable day, March 4, 1995, as I was just skating around, my coach said, Hey Myze, come over here for a second.

I skated over. What's up, coach?

He tapped me on the back of the pants and said, Kid, you're going up to the show. You're on a flight tonight to Hartford, playing the Whalers tomorrow, so be ready.

At that moment, the five-year-old kid carrying his hockey bag over his shoulder in snow up to his knees, the kid in grade six practising his autograph with his teacher telling him he'd never make the NHL—that kid came to life.

I was about to get that first shift in the show. When I went back to my apartment to pack, I called my dad. He could not believe that all those countless hours on the rink working with his son, all the hours and days of travelling to hockey practice, had finally paid off.

Hey Dad, any advice before I play the game tomorrow?

Yes, son . . . Keep throwing.

I knew at that point I was going to fight in my first game no matter what. The next day I woke up and could not eat a thing. My guts were churning, I was so nervous. I knew I had to have a good game.

I got on a plane and flew to Hartford. When I got to the arena I walked into the dressing room, and there was a Tampa jersey with the number 27 on it and the name: Myhres. I almost started crying, but held it in of course. As I sat there I looked around at all the players I'd been watching on TV for years. Petr Klíma, Denis Savard, Darren Pupa. It seemed surreal. I didn't say a word to anyone that day—even though I was in awe of my surroundings, I was getting into gladiator mode. I knew that all those years of practice, all those years of fighting, were going to come down to one moment in about two hours. And that if I lost, I'd probably be sent right back to the minors. Talk about pressure.

After I got dressed I looked at the lineup for that night. The tough guy suiting up for Hartford was a player named Mark Janssens. Six-foot-four, 220 pounds. So there was my target. I put the jersey over my head, went to the bathroom and smeared Vaseline on my face like a prizefighter to help punches slide off, then went out for warm-up with no helmet on. Back then you didn't have to wear a helmet in the NHL, so that alone really made you feel like you made it.

I was trying to stay loose, looping around our end of the ice, toying absentmindedly with the pucks. But really I was soaking it all in. The lights were brighter. The ads on the boards were for international brands, not local real estate brokers and car dealerships. The guys shuffling into their seats with beers were wearing suits, not baseball caps.

And there was Mark Janssens at the other end, smiling and cracking jokes with his teammates, not a care in the world. You don't have to worry about the angry, red-faced guys. It's the calm, smiling ones who can hurt you.

Warm-up ended and the national anthem began. By now I was just bouncing on the bench, nervous as hell.

The game started and about three minutes later my coach Terry Crisp tapped me on the shoulder and said, Myhres, you're up next.

I jumped out on the ice and launched myself into the play. Just the way I'd practised it a thousand times. It was familiar and strange at the same time. I went into my end along the boards, looking for a breakout pass. When the puck came to me, so did a guy named Mark Janssens. I was no longer even thinking about the puck. He came crashing into me, and the words were all but scripted.

Wanna go?

Our gloves were off. We were throwing hard punches, back and forth. He connected hard and I went down on one knee. The only thing going through my mind was my dad's voice: *Keep throwing.* I got up and threw a hard left hand that caught him on the chin.

We were tangled up. Because I'd been holding on to him for balance—and he had a fistful of my sweater for the same reason—we were close enough that I could see his eyes roll back in his head.

I landed on top of him. Then I leapt to my feet, this crazy emotion coming over me as I skated to the penalty box. The rink was crackling with adrenalin and testosterone. And I felt invincible. Nothing could touch me. I said to myself, Holy shit, I just knocked out a guy in the

NHL! My dad told me later that he was watching the game back home in Cold Lake at a bar called Thumpers with a big cigar in his mouth and a huge smile on his face.

Much as I wanted to enjoy what had just happened, I was getting sick to my stomach knowing that in two days we'd be in Tampa playing the big bad Flyers. I called my father on the pay phone the next day and was like, Dad, fuck, it looks like I'll have to fight Brown, hey?

Son, he said, there's really no way out of it—if you want to prove yourself against the best, well, he's the best.

They had guys on that team I'd idolized as a kid growing up: Eric Lindros, Paul Coffey, John LeClair, and Ron Hextall, just to name a few. They also had a tough guy by the name of Dave Brown, and for those who don't know that name, he was a monster and rated the top heavyweight in the league. One guy I was not too excited about fighting, that's for sure. When they wrote the opening lineup for the game and his name wasn't there, I almost laughed for joy. Now I'd be able to just go play and not worry about fighting.

I was playing quite a bit during that game, running around trying to hit everything and trying not to stare too much at all the stars. Coaches always say that if you do the little things right, the puck will follow you around out there. One shift, the puck came to me along the boards. I did what every player knows to do when you're out of options—I put it back deep in the corner. Another basic rule that every player knows: go to the net. That's what I did, and the puck came right onto my stick. I stuffed a backhand right between Hextall's pads.

I threw my hands up in the air. Then I tore screaming down the ice while twenty thousand people stood up and cheered. It was easily the most invigorating feeling I've ever had. In my first two games I'd knocked a guy out and scored a goal. Not a bad start, I would say.

It was almost as though hard work and playing by the rules were the key to success.

I scored a goal three games later against the Quebec Nordiques and seemed to be rolling along just fine. I moved into Chris Gratton's house, which looked like a mansion to me. It was still hard to believe that I was living my dream of playing in the NHL, but as the days went on, I felt like I belonged there.

On the schedule I saw that we were going to fly into Edmonton soon and play the Oilers, the same team I'd grown up watching, looking at those guys as gods. That to me was the most important game. All my family and friends would be there. Hockey is not just a game, not just a job. Going back to play in the Northlands Coliseum was a way for me to prove to everyone what Brantt Myhres was capable of.

The day we flew in was March 18, my birthday. As we were walking through the airport I noticed two police officers standing on the other side of customs. After I'd cleared customs they walked up to me and said, Are you Brantt Myhres?

I said yes.

They said, You're under arrest. Then they handcuffed me.

My coach, Terry Crisp, was standing there next to me. I looked at him and said, Crispy, is this some kind of birthday joke?

He said, Nope, I have no idea what's going on.

It didn't take me long to figure out what was happening. During the summer before, I was at a downtown bar in Edmonton with some friends, hammered out of my mind, when I decided to get into my convertible Mustang with my buddies. I drove out and started doing doughnuts in the middle of the street with the tunes cranked. When I stopped at a red light I saw two cops running down the middle of road, heading for me. One cop jumped on the back of my car, pounding his fist on my trunk, yelling *Pull over!* Instead I put my car in first gear and floored it. I knew that if I pulled over I was done.

Sure enough, when I asked why I was under arrest at the airport, they said it was an unpaid stunting ticket from last summer. Off I went in the cop car to the station while my teammates got on the bus to go to the hotel. All my family was at the hotel waiting for me to get off the bus. When they asked where I was, my teammates said I was at the police station. Talk about an embarrassing moment. The next day the headline in the Edmonton sports pages was "Bad Boy Myhres Gets Arrested."

I figured I'd made myself part of the team by the end of that season, but I'd figured wrong. In the fall of 1996 I was back in Atlanta. I was a little pissed that I hadn't made the team, but looking back, I was so out of shape they must have had no choice but to send me back down.

I started out good, playing lots, when during one game I was on a breakaway and the other guy tripped me. I slid into the net and my foot hit the post. As I was lying there I couldn't feel anything, but their goalie said, Holy fuck! I looked up and said, What? Then, within half a second, I looked down at my foot. It was pointing the wrong way.

I started to scream. The medical staff came out on the ice and took me into the dressing room. Then the doctor came in, looked at my face, and told me to hold on tight. He grabbed my foot and forced it back into place . . . and I almost passed out from the pain.

If you want to know how good cool water can taste, try it when you're dying of thirst. If you want to know how important sleep is, try collapsing into a soft bed when you're bone-tired. And if you want to understand how people get addicted to painkillers, try a Percocet when you're in physical agony. There is really no pleasure quite like pain fading away like a cube of sugar dissolving in a cup of coffee.

I was out for the rest of the season. During that time I ate painkillers by the fistful. I'd be playing video games and just puke up a pool of half-digested Percocets. I pretty much put on twenty pounds of fat and just lay around the house, not able to really walk for two months. They'd put in ten screws and a plate in my bone to keep it stable, but after six months I decided to let the doctors know I wanted the hardware out. I felt that if I could feel the screws in my ankle rub against the boot of my skate, the metal had to go.

After that I'd travel down to Tampa once in a while to check in with their team doctor and see how the foot was coming along. On my way back to Atlanta one night I was driving my convertible Mustang, doing about 120 mph, when I noticed that two semi trucks ahead of me had slowed down to about 10 mph. That sure seemed strange—until I saw the cop lights going off behind me. I pulled over. The cop had his door open with his gun pulled out, yelling, Put your hands up and get your ass out of the car now! Thank god I was sober that night.

I had my crutches with me in the car, so I stuck one outside the window, saying I had a broken leg and wasn't going anywhere. He rushed over to the car, grabbed me by my hair, and dragged me to the cop car. Then he handcuffed me, threw me in the back, and said he'd be right back—he was going to search my car for drugs.

Luckily I had an old hockey card in the car. Even luckier, he recognized me as the guy in the picture. When he came back he said he was sorry for being a bit stern, but he'd thought I was a drug dealer or something going that fast. As I was sitting there, counting my blessings that I had nothing incriminating in the car, he said, Well, do you have eight hundred dollars?

I was like, Nope, not on me.

Well Brantt, unless you come up with eight hundred dollars, I'm going to have to take you to jail.

So that's where I spent the night. With my one phone call I dialed a stripper friend in Tampa and said, Hey darling, can I get eight hundred wired into my account, as in asap? She said she would, but there was still the fact that it was the middle of the night. So I took the roll of toilet paper as a pillow and tried to catch some sleep till I got bailed out.

I got through that season somehow and went back to Edmonton for the summer. I had money in the bank and could flash my NHL hockey card around, and that meant I could live every day pretty much the same way—exactly the way I wanted it. Get up around one or two p.m., have a shower, make some Kraft Dinner, call a few girls, hit the bank machine, hit a pub at five p.m. Spend about $500 at the bar, call the coke dealer around ten p.m., spend $300 on an eight ball, finish the eight ball around four a.m., spend another $300 on another one: total cost for a Friday night: $1100. And that's when I was making only $200,000 a year.

And life back in Florida was even more entertaining. Playing in Tampa was incredible—the weather, the taxes, the fans, not to mention the strippers. Tampa strippers were the top of the charts in my opinion. I spent a lot of time with strippers back then. More than most guys do, I admit. But it's not hard to explain why. They always wanted to have as much fun as I was having, and those were the kind of people I wanted to be with. And when girls like that find out you play for the Lightning, the party picks up a couple of notches at least. Of course, they don't mind cash or coke either, and I had a steady supply of both.

Many nights I could be found at a place called Thee Dollhouse. One evening I met these two dancers. We partied until last call, and then decided to keep the fun going back at their place. These were two girls I became close with: whenever I'd walk in they'd come sit at my table all night. They didn't want me to buy any dances, just maybe give them a couple tickets to our game.

One time, as I was sitting there not long before the night ended, they told me to open my mouth, and when I did they put an ecstasy pill on my tongue.

When we left I got in my car, put the top down on a beautiful Florida night, and started driving on the highway back to their house. By this time the ecstasy was kicking in; I was really stoned. All of a sudden one of the girls said, Fuck, Brantt, you better speed up.

What the heck are you talking about, darling?

Take a look at the speedometer.

I looked down and saw I was doing ten mph.

When we got to their place in one piece, they said, Come on up, we want to do something to you.

I went to the fridge, grabbed a beer, and they pulled a chair to the middle of the living room. Then they said, Get naked, sit in the chair, and don't move. You're not allowed to touch us until we say.

They started performing sexual acts on each other for what felt like an eternity, then said, Okay, your turn.

I realized I had no condoms on me, so I said I'd be right back. I ran out to my Mustang, jumped in, put it in reverse, hit the gas, and smashed right into a light post. The next thing I saw were the two girls yelling, Brantt, oh my god, you're naked! Get your ass back in this house now— turn your car off and give us the keys!

I put a dent in my car, but in the end that was probably a good thing. Better than showing up naked at the 7-Eleven, anyway.

At this point in my life, at twenty-three years old, I figured I may drink hard and party really hard, but I never believed I had a problem, even though my agent would tell me he was getting calls from the head brass in Tampa concerned about my off-ice habits. I lived my life on and off the ice to extremes, and so far it was all working. I remember joking with a close friend, saying that people would always ask me, Brantt, why the hell do you live in the fast lane with no pressure on the brake? And I'd always say, If you were me, you'd do it too.

But I wonder if I believed that even then. I wonder whether that guy was who I really was. The reason I'm not sure is that when I look back, it's not the strippers and the blow that I remember fondly. The thing that meant the most to me was my first game against Wayne Gretzky.

We were playing the L.A. Kings at home, and it was going to be a full, packed house because the Great One was coming to town. During that day I was in a fog, having a hard time knowing I was really going to be playing on the same ice as 99. I mean, I'd had posters of this guy covering my bedroom walls when I was a kid. I'd slept with his hockey tape next to my bed. Now I'll be skating next to him?

When we went out to take warm-up, I couldn't keep my eyes off the other end of the ice, watching the guy who had his jersey tucked in on the right side. I made one lap, then on my second he's skating right at me along the red line. His hair breezing back. The shiny trademark aluminum stick. The turtleneck. No one looked like Wayne. I had frozen eyes, staring at him adoringly in a way he was probably used to. I gave him a little smile as we passed each other. Maybe he thought I was threatening him. That was my job after all. The Kings' tough guys were probably keeping an eye on me. But if there was one guy Wayne didn't need to worry about, it was me.

I stared at him for the whole game. I paid zero attention to the play. I was all about taking in the fact that I was playing against the Great Gretzky. I suppose it's a bit like finding an old love letter, or seeing the annual lines on the doorjamb in the house where you grew up and getting a glimpse of the way things were when you were that small. The world had changed, and in many ways I guess I'd changed too since the days when I was the goal scorer on my peewee team and would lie in bed each night imagining I was skating with the Great One. But I hadn't changed *that* much. I still would have taken a bullet for that guy, even though he was playing on the other team.

I ended that season in Tampa pretty excited about the year I'd had, having scored a few goals and gained a reputation for being one of the tougher guys in the league. I was blowing through my money pretty good that year, and my contract was up in the summer, so I was counting on my agent to get me a good deal.

Even though I played for almost a full year in the NHL (I got called up early November), I still had this vision or dream that once I was driving a real nice sports car, had an expensive watch on, and owned a house on the lake with a ski boat, *that* would be the day I'd actually made the NHL. And then it would all be complete. Meanwhile I needed more money, so I had to make sure my path would lead to more contracts.

I went back to Edmonton for the summer, rented a nice house on the west side, bought a dog named Levi, and noticed that I was doing more and more cocaine every time I drank—it seemed like once I had two or three cocktails I'd get this urge to do a line of blow. But being young and cocky, I never paid too much attention to it. One morning I was sitting with my dog on the couch watching TV when my phone rang: it was my agent, Ritch Winter.

Are you sitting down?

Why yes I am, why?

I have some good news: I talked to the Oilers and they're very interested in you; they want to make a trade for you. But first the GM, Glen Sather, wants you to commit to a drug test once every couple of weeks, just as an insurance protocol.

I had mixed feelings about getting traded. I loved Tampa. But I also loved the Oilers, my team since I was five years old. And yet they wanted me to take a drug test! When I'd asked a few friends how long it took cocaine to leave your system, they'd said three days, no big deal. So I said, Let's get the trade done, and yes I'll agree to a urine test. But Ritch, Will he sign me to a one-way contract? I'm not signing a two-way deal!

A one-way contract means they have to pay you your big-league salary no matter where you play; it's guaranteed money. Whereas in a two-way deal they could send you to the minors and pay you peanuts.

Ritch said he'd work on it; just leave it to him. Then he said, Oh yes, they're also going to pay for a trainer for you during the summer—they heard conditioning was an issue and they don't want that to be an issue there.

The trade happened shortly afterwards—and you can imagine how excited I was about the chance to put on an Oiler uniform.

But early one morning in July a guy called asking me to confirm my name. Once I had, he said he'd be at my house the next day around noon for a urine test. My heart started beating a bit faster—I'd smoked a joint the night before and knew that weed stayed in your system for at least two to three weeks. Why I'd smoked up knowing I'd be tested, I can't say. All I knew was that I needed to use someone else's urine.

So I called up a buddy who was a hairdresser—he drank quite hard but stayed clear of drugs.

Hey pal, hope all is well. Can I borrow some piss?

Really? You want my piss?

Yes I do. I'm getting tested tomorrow and I'll fail it if I use mine.

Off I went downtown to grab the goods, still not having a clue what doing a urine test involved. All I had was an empty plastic Pepsi bottle. So there I am, in the back alley behind the hair salon, watching my buddy piss into this thing. As I'm driving home I see the bottle on my seat, and all I can think is, Jesus, I sure hope this works or no one-way contract, my chance of playing for my childhood team gone.

The next day right at noon (those guys were never late), my doorbell rang. Hello, come on in. The guy made me fill out a form and sign it at the bottom. Then he gave me a cup and told me to go fill it up.

That sounded perfect. Not a problem. I stepped into the bathroom, poured in a splash of my friend's urine, walked out, and said, Here ya go, take care, see you down the road.

It seemed to be a pretty easy transaction, so I thought I'd really pulled the wool over his eyes and Sather's. Still, it was getting close to training camp and I was in horrendous shape. My nights of having a few friends over for a so-called couple beers would wind up with me chopping up lines of blow at seven a.m. and missing workouts. I ended up going to camp in just awful shape.

I look at pictures of myself from that time and can't believe I didn't see then what I see now. I looked like the Michelin Man. My body fat was 23 percent, where it should have been at least under 10. I really had no clue about how to train, eat, or act as a professional athlete. I mean, I *did* have a clue. I was pretty sure that a steady diet of booze and drugs wasn't the way to go about it. But I figured I'd do what I always did: go to camp to get into shape.

Our first exhibition game in 1997 was against the Vancouver Canucks. My whole family was going to be there. Well, except my mom. I'd invited her, but for some reason she decided to stay in the hotel right across the street and watch the game on TV. I never really figured that one out.

That morning we were supposed to have practice at ten a.m. for the seven o'clock game, which meant I had to be at the rink no later than nine. So I woke up at eight fifteen, figuring I'd give myself ten minutes to get out the door.

Naturally there was a girl in my bed. Hey hon, she said, don't games on Sunday start at six, not seven?

FUCK! I jump out of bed, jump into my truck, and run every red light in my path. I get to the arena at eight fifty-five. I could hear my teammates on the ice warming up. That is the worst feeling ever. Ask any hockey player. I know that when most people have anxiety dreams, they imagine themselves late for an exam they haven't studied for. For a hockey player, it's trying to get your gear on in an empty dressing room when everyone else is on the ice. It's an awful feeling. And it wasn't a dream.

I hit the ice at five after nine. I remember Ryan Smyth saying, Holy shit, Myze, what the hell happened to you? You look like you're still sleeping. I was late and I felt like shit.

After practice, Glen Sather calls me into the office and says, Listen Brantt, I don't give two shits why you were late. I like you and that's why I traded for you. But the coach Ron Low doesn't want to play you tonight. I went to bat for you, so you're in. Don't disappoint me or you. Have a great game.

As if I needed someone to tell me that. I mean, this was the Northlands Coliseum. I'd actually be sitting on the same bench where Gretzky sat for all those years. That's where he tossed a ball of tape that a twelve-year-old Brantt Myhres begged for. I wasn't a little kid anymore. But part of me was.

Still, at some point I was going to have to kick the shit out of someone. As the national anthem starts, I look behind the net where I'd gotten my family some tickets. There's my grandma, grandpa, dad, sister, and some cousins. When the game starts, it's chippy. Those divisional games always were. That's why the Oilers traded for a guy like me. The Canucks were running around, pushing us around in our own rink. Especially their biggest guy. As he skates by our bench I stand up and bark, Hey Brash, next shift I'm going to knock your fucking head off.

He just smiles and says, Don't worry, Myhres, I'll come find you.

I jump the boards for my first shift and then I hear this deep voice say, Hey Myhres, wanna go?

Now, for those of you who don't know the name Donald Brashear, he was huge: six three and 245 pounds of sculpted muscle. A neck that started at his ears, and the cold eyes of a killer.

You bet, I said. Let's do this, big boy.

We shake our gloves off. All I can think about is my family sitting in the stands. *Don't lose this one, Brantt.*

We square off, and I start throwing left hands. The next thing I remember is I'm holding the ref's ankles. Brash had caught me on the nose, then the chin, then my knees gave out. I stood up and headed to the penalty box. Then I looked up in the stands and saw my grandma crying.

It was the first time in my hockey career that I'd been demolished in a fight, and as I was skating to the box, I was so embarrassed. I'd just got my ass kicked in front of nineteen thousand people, in front of all my family members, in front of all my new teammates, not to mention in front of a general manager I was trying to ask for a one-way contract. Then, as I was sitting in the penalty box, my eye felt numb and was starting to really swell up. Plus my nose was broken and I could hardly breathe out of it. Needless to say, this was not a good way to start out with my new team.

The game ends and I have to shower, put my suit on, and go meet my family. They're waiting for me outside the dressing room. My eye now is black and blue, my nose is pointing the wrong way, and I see the look on my dad's face. What I see is not pride. It's worry. My grandparents looked stunned, as though they're embarrassed for me. I didn't really know what to say to them other than, Well, win some lose some, hey guys?

The next game was against Ottawa. Before the game Sather told me that I better put on a good show. *Make a difference in the game, Brantt, time's running out.* That night when I played I didn't do a thing. I stayed away from their tough guy, Dennis Vial. The truth is I was really scared of losing again, going through all those embarrassing emotions I'd just gone through a couple days before. The next day in the paper, one of the headlines was "Myhres, Quiet as a Mouse."

I called my agent. Ritch, I said, call Glen and try to get this deal done. I'm not going to continue sticking around this team without a contract.

Ritch called me the next day and said Glen wasn't budging. The contract on the table was two-way.

So I went into the dressing room before practice and packed my bag. On my way out the boys were saying, Myze, what the hell are you doing?

I'm heading to Cold Lake till they trade me, I said. See ya . . .

I was trying to sound like I didn't care, but I could hardly believe the words myself as I heard them coming out of my mouth. Maybe I was talking tough because that was the only language I knew. But I felt like a complete bag of shit as I walked out of Gretzky's barn with my bag over my shoulder—and not because I'd been cut but because I was quitting, because I froze when my moment came. I'd just blown my one and only chance of playing for my favourite team, and this was all on my shoulders, no one to blame here other than myself. It was a gross pill to swallow.

But blaming yourself and taking responsibility are two different things, in case you're wondering. As I jumped in my truck to head back to Cold Lake, I called Ritch and told him where I was going. He just said, Are you out of your mind? What is that going to accomplish? Then I called a friend and asked him to get me a couple grams of cocaine. Fuck it.

I stayed at my grandparents' for a couple of weeks, drinking and snorting through my embarrassment and frustration—and only making it worse. You'd think I'd know better than to run away, but I didn't, I guess. I didn't hear from Ritch or the Oilers once during all that time. It felt like the NHL had forgotten all about me.

Then one night I was watching TV and the phone rings. My grandma answers, then she calls out, Hey Brantt, some Glen guy is on the phone.

Jesus, Grandma, that's the GM!

I pick up the phone. Hey Brantt, Glen here, pack your bags, we just traded you to the Flyers. Good luck.

5

I shouted out with joy. I was going to one of the best teams in the league, not to mention they had guys like Eric Lindros, Paul Coffey, and Ron Hextall, guys I really looked up to. And the Philadelphia Flyers had a reputation as the Broad Street Bullies, so I figured I'd fit right in. Plus the coach was Wayne Cashman, who'd been my assistant coach in Tampa; I really liked him. And I liked the type of player he was, tough as nails. The guy had also played with Bobby Orr—not bad for anyone's credibility as a hockey player.

Shortly afterwards I received a call from Bobby Clarke, the Flyers' all-time legend and the GM of the team. He said, Brantt, you're not going to start with the big club. You haven't played a game in over two weeks, so we're going to send you down to our minor league team for a couple weeks to get in shape, play some games, and get up to speed. See you soon.

So I fly in to Philly—and since their minor team was in the same city, it was pretty easy to get settled in. I played three or four games with the Phantoms, then our coach, Bill Barber, called me into the office. Hey Myze, he said, you're going up to the big club.

The first thing I did was buy a plane ticket that day to get my dad to Philly for my first game. We were playing the Colorado Avalanche.

When I walked into the dressing room, the first guy who came up to me was Paul Coffey. Hey pal, he said, I heard you were from Edmonton?

I said yeah.

He was like, Man, I just loved playing there.

I had to let it register for a minute that I was on a team with Paul Coffey—in my opinion the best defenceman to ever play the game, the guy I'd watched break Bobby Orr's records in Edmonton (also not bad for a hockey player's cred). The next guy to come up to me was Dan Kordic. We'd had a couple real good fights when I was with Tampa so I wasn't sure how it would go, but after a few words we were laughing our heads off.

Then I looked up and saw Eric Lindros coming to introduce himself. They called him the Big E back then. Eric was the perfect combination of size, skill, and fitness. There just wasn't another player like him in the NHL. He did what he wanted.

And he made me feel right at home. One of the first things Eric said to me was, Well, big fella, it's sure nice to have you on our side rather than having to deal with you chasing me and our whole team around when you were the opponent. Here was this hulk of a man, acting like a little kid, always laughing and joking around. But he had this serious side to him, too: he was very aware of his surroundings, and he didn't let too many people into his little world. And rightly so. He had a massive image to live up to—not only was he the face of the team, but the face of the NHL.

As I was getting dressed for the game my nerves took over and I was sick to my stomach. I knew I had to fight, and got even more nervous when I saw who was on the other team. His name was François Leroux, six-foot-six and 235 pounds. I had my work cut out for me—and I needed to make an impression asap. I hadn't even practised with my new team yet. But no teammate could help with what I was about to do.

I walk out for the game and twenty thousand people are going crazy. Philly fans are insane! The game starts, and the building is rocking. Remember, the Flyers and the Avalanche were two of the best teams in the league at the time. Colorado was lighting everyone up and Philly was running everyone over. But the game had hardly settled in before I hear Cash say, Myhres, you're up.

I jump from the bench to the ice and right away I see Mr. Leroux on the ice as well. I skate over to him and say, Come on you big bitch, wanna go?

Our gloves were off and I threw as hard and as fast as I could. At one point he started to cover his face and turn away. He might have been looking to square up and reset, but I wasn't going to let him. I closed in on him, threw one more real hard punch, and the fight was over. Down we went. When I stood up I had a million chills going through my body. I could hear the crowd going nuts as I skated to the penalty box.

A lot of guys hate fighting, but it's mostly the days and hours before a fight that gnaw at you and drain away the pleasure in everyday life. The minutes right after, though, can be euphoric. Even just knowing you've gotten it over with can be just as awesome as a few Percocets when you're banged up. And a big win in front of a home crowd, especially in a rink like Philly—that's as good as any drug. You are adored. You are bulletproof. For a few minutes, you're the guy everyone in the building wishes they were.

Let's just say I was pretty happy with my first game in Philly. Especially when I'd been close to giving up back in Cold Lake only a few weeks before. My dad kept saying, I can't believe my son's playing for the Flyers. He was like a little kid, full of excitement.

As the year went on I became good friends with Eric. We were both single and about the same age. We also had cold beer in common. We just clicked: we'd sit next to each other on the plane during our card games and we'd hang out on the road. I think Big E liked having tough guys around him. He was a very private person when it came to trusting people outside the Flyers circle. We were both just big happy teddy bears.

One day he came up to me and said, Hey Knuckles, wanna go to *David Letterman* with me? He was about to be interviewed on the show. We were playing Florida the next day, but I thought it would be a great experience, so I said sure. We got picked up in a limo and off to New York we went.

I asked the limo driver to pick up a case of beer on the way, so by the time we got there I had quite a buzz on. While Eric was getting interviewed by Letterman I was in the green room watching. It went good, and when it was all over I got to meet Dave himself. What a nice guy.

We were on our way back to Philly when I picked up another case of beer. By the time we got there I was smashed, so I figured I'd hit the bar and check out the scene.

I ended up meeting a couple of twins; at one point we decided to leave the bar and go back to my place. Now, while all this was going on I was saying to myself, Brantt, you need to stay away from the drugs tonight, you have a game tomorrow, be in bed no later than one a.m. I kept telling myself that. That's what I truly wanted to do.

When we got to my place that little voice said to me, Hey, just get a little coke, not too much, maybe a few lines, that's it. Next thing I knew I was in the bathroom with both girls doing lines.

Around six thirty a.m. we all went to my bed to try and get some sleep. I had to be up at seven thirty to go to the rink, so of course I didn't get a wink in. But when I went out to my truck, my tire was flat, so I ran back in and said, Girls, where's your car, I need a ride to the practice rink.

I jumped into this little piece-of-shit car with the two girls in the back, flying to get to the rink. I dropped myself off around two blocks before we got there just so that no one would see me. Then I went into the dressing room to my stall and started putting on my gear.

Paul Coffey sat down next to me.

Holy shit, Knuckles, you stink like booze big-time and your eyes look awful.

Long night, Coff. I'm not too sure I can make it out there in practice.

Listen, if you can't skate out there, just say you pulled a muscle and get the hell off.

So I went out on the ice and could not skate. I did one lap then left the ice, telling the trainers that I must have strained something. Then I took my gear off, went to the washroom, and puked my guts out.

I doubt I fooled anyone, though. That afternoon Cash called me into the office.

Brantt, I just wanted you to know that when I was playing in the NHL I had to stop drinking because it was ruining my career. I've now been twelve years sober. If you need someone to talk to, you can talk to me. But let me tell you, if you keep up this lifestyle it's going to bury you.

I was like, Thanks Cash, but I'll be just fine.

And I believed it, too.

But as the year went on I started calling the coke dealer on a regular basis. Whenever I had a few in me I made the call. So those long nights and early mornings were coming quite often.

I was an animal on the ice, racking up 170 penalty minutes in just twenty-three games—on pace to break the NHL record. But it was like I was in this daily tug-of-war with myself. I hated the role of being a fighter; it made me sick to my stomach every day. And yet I loved being in the NHL, and I didn't want to ever give that up. Still, it meant selling my soul to do it. I'm not saying I felt sorry for myself. I knew I was lucky. I would have done anything to stay in the league.

Anything but stop drinking.

It's hard to say what it's like to have what you think you wanted only to discover you're miserable. It's not self-pity. It's more like homesickness. It was as if I missed something I'd never even known. I was living the life I'd planned out for myself, the life my grade six teacher said I'd never have. But it felt as if it didn't count. Or it was like it turned out to be someone else's dream—one that was only slightly different from mine, but different enough that it felt wrong. Or maybe it was more like lovesickness, being in love with someone you know you'll never have but have to see every day.

The thing that got me by without going crazy was knowing I could go out after a game and get wasted. Then and only then I wouldn't think about what I did for a living—what that kid who dreamt of playing with

Gretzky was doing for a living. It was a fucked-up way of thinking, I see that now, but then it seemed normal.

Eventually, though, things got so bad that even I could see it. The thing is, if I could see it, so could everyone else. One morning I showed up to the pre-game feeling the worse for wear. Cash blew the whistle and I skated to centre ice along with everyone else. But when I tried to stop I blew a wheel and flew right into Cash's leg.

He looked at me and said, Myhres, get the fuck over here right now . . . I don't know what the hell you were doing last night but you *better* be ready for the game tonight. Go back and get some sleep.

Talk about embarrassing.

My opponents could probably figure it out too. I was so out of shape that my fights were lasting only twenty seconds before I would tire out.

We were playing in Colorado one night, and I knew François Leroux would be coming for me, since I'd gotten the better of him in Philly. Sure enough, I was skating back into my end when I got a tap on my pants. As soon as I turned around, *whack!* He punched me right in the nose. I saw stars. My nose felt like it was crushed and my eyes started watering, but I knew I needed to start throwing punches. So I threw a few lefts and we both went down. I had to skate off the ice and go straight to our dressing room. I could feel that my nose was on the left side of my face.

The doctor came in and said, Oh boy, you have two options here: one is surgery in the next few days, or I try and put it back into place.

I'm not having surgery, I said, so let's put it back.

He grabbed my nose and gave it a wrench. Nothing happened. It wouldn't budge. It hurt like hell though. He tried again. It still wouldn't go back into place.

Fuck it, I said. I'll just leave it the way it is, Doc.

A few weeks later we went to Vancouver to play the Canucks. I remember the game was on New Year's Eve. I was a bit nervous 'cause I knew I'd have to tangle with Brashear again.

We were winning like 6–1 in the third period when we lined up against each other. Anyone who's watched more than one hockey game knows that a lopsided score is the signal for the winning team to settle some beefs, knowing that the game is in hand, and for the losing team's tough guys to send the message that while they may be losing the game, they can still win the battles. Everyone in the rink knew that Brashear would be looking for me.

We score another goal, so now there's a faceoff at centre ice. My coach says, Myze, get out there. As I jump the boards I see Brashear skating to the faceoff circle as well, so now we're lined up against each other. At this point I don't have to fight him, the score's 7–1 for us, but I really want to gain some respect back from getting my ass kicked the first time.

I look at him and say, Well, Brash, round two?

Yes Myhres, I'll go you again. Just wait for the puck to drop.

My heart started racing a million miles per hour. We gave each other a shot and the gloves were off. I came in and right away he pulled me in real close. That's what Brash did. He would tie you up, tire you out, then rag-doll you. I remember thinking, Holy fuck, this guy is strong! I tried to throw a few punches, but he was overpowering me and I couldn't get going. Then he opened up some space and fired at my head until I went down. As I got up to skate to the box, I was saying to myself, Wow, I've never been beat up this bad before. I wasn't hurt, but my ego was crushed.

It's not just that I got beaten in front of thousands, which is bad enough. I mean, losing outside a bar is bad enough. But remember, my job wasn't really to beat people up. My job was to be the big dog pissing on fire hydrants. It was to make everyone on my team a little taller and a little cockier, just by letting some confidence rub off. That's what a tough guy does.

But you can't do that if you're so out of shape you're getting your ass kicked.

We flew into Pittsburgh one night, but I was a healthy scratch. It was hard not dressing for that game since my other childhood idol, Mario Lemieux, was on the other team. I knew that as a tough guy, you're not going to play in all the games, but I was getting scratched from games more than I'd like. Having said that, though, it was also a relief when I wasn't in the lineup, since it meant I got to eat some popcorn and just watch a hockey game without the feeling that came with getting ready for battle.

Anyway, in the second period Eric had the puck and was flying down the left side when Darius Kasparaitis comes out of nowhere and cranks Big E in the head so hard that he's out cold on the ice. I leave the press box and go down to the dressing room. When I get there and ask where E is, they say, He's fucked up. We're worried about him—he's standing in the shower with all his equipment on, including his jersey and skates. So I go into the shower and there he is, standing there with everything on as the water pours over his head.

Hey Big E, how are ya, buddy, are you okay?

He looks at me and says, Who the hell are you and how did you get into our dressing room?

I knew at that point it wasn't good. Understanding what it was like to be drilled in the head, I had sympathy for him big-time. He was one of the best players to ever play the game, and unfortunately, that was the start of many concussions to follow, which ultimately led to a shortened career.

There was a big part of me that felt bad I wasn't in the lineup that night. Maybe just my presence on the bench would have made Eric just a little bit safer—maybe Kasparaitis would have thought twice before laying that crushing hit? My job was to prevent those hits from happening. Kasparaitis played to scare guys, and my job was to scare him. Hard to do that if you're so out of shape you're sitting in the stands.

It was Christmastime, and I'd decided to fly my two best friends, Blake and Sean, down for a week to watch a few games and celebrate the holiday. They were big hockey fans, so it was a huge thrill for them. I knew that Blake was way more of a hockey fan than Sean, so I asked Big E for a signed stick for Blake. They were both blown away by the city, just how big it was and how massive our arena was. I always felt so good showing off to my best two buds—it made me feel on top of the world to share those moments with them.

We decided to hit a bar that night called Egypt's. Around two p.m. I had a couple girls who wanted to get out of there, so I said, Boys, time to head back to the house. I have to get the valet guy to bring my car around, so meet you outside.

As I was standing under the marquee, I heard these four guys yelling at me. I learned later they were off-duty bouncers. They said, Hey Myhres, you think you're pretty fucking tough, hey?

Hey guys, I said, nothing's going on here tonight. I'm on my way home. I don't want any trouble.

Next thing I know I get punched in the back of the head, so I back off to the street, take my suit coat off, and say, Okay, boys, one at a time here.

The first guy came in and *whack*, down he went. The second guy came in, and the next thing I know, I was kicked in the head from the third guy. I went down, and when I was down I noticed that my buddies were lying on the pavement, knocked out. Then I heard cop sirens coming around the corner. They pulled up and said, Brantt, are you okay? What happened?

I said, Yeah, I'm fine. I got jumped but I just want to go home.

The next day I went into the dressing room, and there was a letter on my stall saying that I needed to see Clarkie in his office. I went in and sat down.

So, where were you last night?

I was at Egypt's for a while and then went home.

Did you get into a fight?

Yes—these fucking guys jumped me and my two buddies. I had no choice.

Brantt, you can't be drinking anymore. You can't be going out to the bars. Everyone knows you in this city—you can't get away with anything. Plus, I heard that you and Eric have been going out quite a bit. Listen, he won't be the one leaving. Eric makes $8.5 million. You make $450,000. You hear me loud and clear? It'll be you if I hear of another incident.

Yeah Clarkie, I hear ya.

I knew he meant business. Bobby Clarke is an intimidating man. He's not a very big guy, but everything about him says *Don't fuck with me*. I respect Bobby Clarke. But I also knew that I wasn't going to stop fucking around. Nobody tells me what to do. Maybe I just thought I could outsmart Clarke.

It was Christmas Eve and Coff had a big party at his house. I drank a bottle of Jack that night and got into my truck to drive home. I had a girl with me from Edmonton, who said, Jesus Christ, Brantt, you're driving on the wrong side of the road!

By that time I saw the cherries go on, and I pulled over.

This time for sure I thought I was finished. The cop came up to the window and asked me for my licence and why I was driving on the wrong side. Just then my teammate Luke Richardson came up to the cop; he must have been right behind me. He pulled the cop aside for a couple minutes. Then the cop came back and said, Okay, I know you've been drinking and you only live a block away, so go home and park that thing. Merry Christmas, Brantt.

I could not make a right decision if my life depended on it. I could feel the edge of the cliff coming, but I wouldn't take my foot off the gas.

We were flying into Edmonton to play the Oilers. We were a scary team to play against. Our first line is still remembered as the "Legion of Doom": Lindros, LeClair, and Trent Klatt were three huge guys. But our fourth line was even scarier: me, Dan Kordic, Dan Lacroix. We were called the Lefty Line, for obvious reasons. We were terrorizing the league.

Meanwhile, the Oilers had this new rookie tough guy named Georges Laraque. No one had really heard much about him, other than me since I knew him from my time with the Oilers. Saying that Georges was big was an understatement. He seriously looked like a linebacker for an NFL team. The day of the game I told my dad I'd buy a private box (meaning suite) for all the family, so bring them all. It cost me around $2500.

The game starts, and we get out to an early lead. The coach then sends out the Lefty Line—and I'm lined up against Laraque. He says to me in that French accent, Hello, Brantt, I have to fight you now.

Seriously, Georges? Can't we fight later?

No Brantt, we need to do this now.

All right, big fella—let's do this!

We start throwing punches as soon as the puck dropped. I'm doing pretty good at this point till Georges pulls his left arm out of his jersey and hits me with a big punch. It doesn't really connect, but I end up slipping and going down to the ice.

The game ends and we win. I'm in a great mood, getting ready to go out. That night my sister Cher asks if she can come out with me and the team, and I say, Sure, sis, meet us there. When we get to the bar, I'm hanging with Big E when Cher walks up. I could tell Eric was right away pretty friendly with her, but I didn't really think too much about it, to tell you the truth, since my sister had been exposed to my hockey buddies for years and never took the bait.

That night we all got really hammered and went back to the Westin hotel. I said to Paul Coffey, Hey Coff, what room are you and Eric in? I'll come meet you for a drink. So I go up to their room, and it's just Coffey and Lindros in there. I was just chillin', chatting with Coff on the bed, when I got up to hit the bathroom, and I see Lindros grab an unopened beer can and throw it at my head! I duck at the last second, look at Coff, and say, Did you just fucking see what he did?

Now, if I wasn't so loaded I would have just questioned Lindros on what the hell that was for, but since I was twisted I ran up to him, grabbed him by his neck, and pushed him back against the wall. I said, Listen here you big fucker, I could care less that you're a star in this league or my teammate, you ever disrespect me again like that, I'll end you!

Sorry, Knuckles, he said. I didn't mean it that way. We're both pretty drunk here, so let's cool down.

As I went back to my room I couldn't believe what had just happened: here was my good buddy, tossing a beer can at me. I knew there was really no excuse for that, but on the other hand I'd just wrapped my hands around his neck, almost leading to a fight in the hotel room. When I talked with Eric the next day on the plane, he said he was just tossing me another beer. Talk about feeling like a complete asshole. My closest friend on the team grabs me drink, and I take it as if he's trying to hurt me. What the fuck was happening to me?

Somehow I held it together until the end of March.

The fact that the team was in first place probably helped. I was feeling pretty good about my life, in fact. I knew I wasn't in control. But when had I ever been in control? And just letting myself get carried along to wherever I was going seemed to be working. I'd fucked up, sure. But I'd also lucked out. I was getting paid to play for the best hockey team in the world. I had the swagger of someone who made a living intimidating grown men.

And sure, the odd threat came my way from management, but no consequences. So one night I decided to head down to this watering hole for a couple drinks. Fuck Bobby Clarke. It was dark in there. Only ten or so people leaning up at the bar. I had my hat pulled down and took a seat in the corner, had three or four beers, then got up and went home.

My phone rang at seven a.m. It was Coff on the other end, saying, Did you read the paper today, Knucks?

No, I'm just getting up, why?

They put you on waivers . . .

No way, you must be joking.

No, it's true, grab a paper.

This was bad. Getting put on waivers means your team doesn't want you around. Anyone who wants you can pick up your contract. If anyone wants you.

I got into my car and drove down to the rink. There was a sign in my stall saying Go see Clarkie. I walked up to Bob's office with my heart pounding, and sat down.

You wanted to see me?

Have you been drinking lately?

No Bob, I put down the booze a couple weeks ago, not a drink.

Really? Well that's funny, one of our head scouts was at a lounge last night having a beer and said he saw you drinking. I told you, Brantt, I wasn't messing around here . . . I put you on waivers, and if you clear you're going down to the minors.

My whole world felt real small at that moment. I was in shock. The swagger was gone. I was more like the kid in grade six.

I cleared waivers and went down to the minors. How do you think that went? If you can't keep it together when things are good, good luck when the wheels come off. I was a train wreck.

Within two weeks they took me aside.

Brantt, you haven't stopped drinking. You're becoming a major distraction to the team. We've released you. We don't want you anywhere near the team. Pack up your stuff.

I'd never stopped partying when they sent me down, and they said Clarke had called and told them to tell me to go home, that I was a cancer to the team. It was horrible. Because the Flyers' minor league team won the American Hockey League's (AHL) Calder Cup that year. I felt like such a failure.

When I got into my car to go home I started crying.

For a long time I felt so lost that I didn't know what to do. Finally I picked up the phone, called the NHL Players' Association, and asked if I could talk to someone about alcohol abuse. Within ten minutes a guy by the name of Dan Cronin called and talked to me for half an hour.

At one point he said, Why don't I fly down there, pack up your house with you, and then me and you can fly to Los Angeles and get you into rehab?

Rehab? What's that all about? How long will I have to be in there for? Will it tarnish my name?

Slow down, Dan said. Don't worry about anything. It's all going to be okay.

PART II

WHISKY, BLOW, REPEAT

6

I got to know Dan Cronin pretty well over the years. But back then I knew nothing about him except that he was a counsellor for the NHL. I'm guessing he figured me out pretty quickly, though.

The first thing I told him was that I was finished drinking, that I thought I'd hit rock bottom. The Flyers had just released me and my career was hanging by a thread. If he could help me I'd really appreciate it. I had no clue what "help" even meant at that point.

Dan said he'd be flying into Philadelphia in the next day or so, and to just hang tight. He also told me to start packing up my apartment. The league would send someone to come clean it. We'd be flying to Los Angeles, where I'd be checked in to a rehab centre, located north of Malibu. I'd be there for twenty-eight days.

Again, I knew nothing of this man. But I stayed tight for the next day or so. Then the doorbell rang and it was Dan. He seemed like a decent guy, but what did he really know about professional athletes? He'd never even skated before. Still, I was pretty desperate, so I was going to give him a chance.

When we landed in L.A. Dan said, You'll stay at my house tonight, then we'll drive out to rehab tomorrow morning.

I called Ritch just to get some reassurance. All he said was, Brantt, it's time you address this. Your reputation in the league isn't the best right now, but you can rebound. Stay strong.

———

Before we'd gotten on the plane, Dan put a contract in front of me. I would have signed anything at the time, but I definitely regretted it later. It was going to change my life forever. The NHL had me lock, stock, and barrel. Basically, if I didn't follow their every direction, they could make it so I'd never earn another fucking dollar playing hockey. The contract laid out four stages. This isn't a direct quote, but it's pretty damn close:

Stage 1: The player will have to enter rehab for a determined amount of time. The player will receive full pay while suspended. The player can go back to playing hockey after he is cleared by the NHL and NHLPA substance abuse doctors.

Stage 2: The player will have to enter rehab for a determined amount of time. The player will not receive his NHL salary while suspended. The player can go back to playing in the NHL after he is cleared by the NHL and NHLPA doctors.

Stage 3: The player will be suspended for a six-month period and will not receive his NHL salary while suspended. The player must write a letter to the commissioner of the NHL, Mr. Gary Bettman, and ask for reinstatement. Once cleared by the commissioner, the player may go back to receiving a salary while playing.

Stage 4: The player will be suspended for a minimum of a full calendar year and will not receive his NHL salary while suspended. The player must write a letter to the commissioner of the NHL, Mr. Gary Bettman, and ask for reinstatement. Once cleared by the commissioner, the player may go back to receiving a salary while playing.

You might think being confronted with a rehab contract when I was hoping for one from the NHL would have been a sobering experience.

But my first thought was, So there's four strikes? That means I've got three left. I can work with three.

Stage 5: There is no Stage 5. Lifetime ban.

When I left for L.A. with Dan, I felt for the first time since I'd started drinking that I had direction, that there was a way to quit the drinking and drugs. I didn't know what that looked like, but I was willing to be open. In fact, for those first few days, it felt like a relief. It's a lot of work being hungover all the time, not to mention the hours devoted to drinking and chasing coke. It takes effort, and it consumes your thinking. For the first time in a long, long time, my thoughts were busy with something other than the question of where the next drink was coming from.

Not that I was seriously considering breaking up with booze. I still loved it. We just needed a little time apart. When I started thinking about stopping forever, my imagination hit a brick wall. I couldn't fathom that concept. Sure, I could admit I had a problem with drinking *too much* and doing coke *one too many times*. But *never* having a beer again didn't seem possible. I was only twenty-four, for god's sake. And you're telling me I can never even have just one?

I'd have to worry about that later. In the meantime, I was willing to see what this rehab thing was all about.

The place Dan took me to was called Steps Recovery. I remember that it smelled like a hospital, and that the folks in there didn't look like my teammates in Philly. The people I hung out with were athletic specimens. But there were people in Steps who had holes in their skin from shooting dope, and it freaked the shit out of me. I instantly started thinking, Fuck, I'm not this bad. I was actually embarrassed to be in there. For the first time in my life I felt defeat, and I hated it.

When I walked in they went through all my stuff. And they laid down the rules. One phone call a day. I had to make my bed. And I had to hit these things called AA meetings each day. What's AA? I asked.

They said it stood for Alcoholics Anonymous, and that it involved meetings where you go for support.

That sounded like a bunch of crap to me, but I said, Well, I'm only in here for twenty-eight days, so whatever.

More rules: No leaving without being signed off. And no contact with the opposite sex. I felt that one was going to be a hard one to keep.

Every day we had this group counselling session for two hours. I picked a chair in the corner and crossed my legs. Our counsellor, Ed Pringle, told us he'd been sober for close to twenty-six years. I thought he was lying. No one could go twenty-six years without getting fucked up. Not possible.

When it came around to me, Ed said, So, Brantt, what do you want to do with the rest of your life?

Well Ed, all I want to be able to do is buy a house on the lake, have a ski boat, and enjoy a few beers now and then.

So you don't think you're an alcoholic?

Hell no, does it look like I have a paper bag? Do I live under the bridge?

He just looked at me and smiled, saying, We'll get back to you real soon. Just sit back and listen.

I went to my first AA meeting that night in Malibu. There were probably close to two hundred people there, some who had suits on and were dressed to the nines. But what was I thinking about? I was checking out the draft picks. When I noticed a few very pretty girls, I thought, There's pretty girls out there who are sober? Can't be. Every hot girl I've ever met at least drank.

My perception of AA altered a bit that night. When they said to stand up and say your name, where you're from, identify yourself as an alcoholic, and if you've been sober for less than thirty days, I freaked out. First off, I didn't like the word *alcoholic*, and second, I didn't think I was one of them. When it came to me I stood up with a little smile on and said, Hi, I'm Brantt, I'm from Canada, and I'm an alcoholic.

When I said the word I cringed inside. It sounded awful. *Alcoholic* takes all the fun out of drinking. It means that what you're doing isn't fun.

It isn't partying. It's a disease. Now, instead of my drinking and drug use feeling free and fun, it's become a chore of checklists and guilt. I had to start introducing the other Brantt: the Brantt who was going to have to start lying, start altering drug tests, start acting like I enjoyed this sobriety thing.

Who wants the best thing in their life to be a disease?

I remember one night, sitting on my couch with Bon Jovi playing. I had a few candles lit. I also had a bag of coke. I would light a smoke, lean over and do a big line of blow, reach for my Jack Daniels, take a swig, then lean back. I had literally just found heaven. If there was a heaven, then this must be it 'cause I'd never felt more a part of the world than in that moment.

If someone had shown up just then and said they were going to make me a famous actor in Hollywood, put fifty million in my bank account, give me the perfect wife with the perfect child, and all I had to do was quit alcohol and drugs, with every cell in my body I would have said no. There was no way I could ever give up this feeling.

Getting fucked up made life livable. It was way too painful to be sober. I had to actually sit with my feelings. I had to deal with that anxiety, the kind that makes you feel as if your life sucks. Booze was a solution to a lot of problems. The word *alcoholic* took that solution away.

So no, I was not a huge fan of AA.

Not that I hated rehab entirely. The doctors set up a training schedule: I did a lot of boxing and spinning, and I spent a lot of time at Gold's Gym in Venice hitting the weights. All this sounded like hard work, but I felt I might as well do it so that I could get the hell out of the nuthouse for a while.

I would drive to Venice, which took at least seventy-five minutes on a good day, work out for two hours, then drive back in time for dinner and an AA meeting. On other days I'd go boxing and spinning. All this working out was real new to me, but I loved how I felt afterwards. It was giving me this rush of endorphins that wasn't all that different from drinking or doing drugs. I was falling in love with it.

Not that I wanted to hang around rehab any longer than I had to. I'd heard that the NHL doctor Dave Lewis was going to be meeting with me at the end of my time there. I'd spent some time with Dave in the past few weeks. He had this energy that was like, Don't fuck with me or any of my decisions—I hold your future in my hands, Brantt. Almost like, I run the show here. So I played along with his game.

We had a group meeting on the twenty-eighth day, and then I packed up my stuff. I was ready to go.

But then Lewis showed up and said I wouldn't be leaving yet—that I needed more time.

I freaked out, saying, What the fuck are you talking about? I was told around twenty-eight days. I don't care what you say, Dave, I'm out of here.

Brantt, if you leave without being cleared, you won't be able to ever play hockey again.

Are you serious right now? I won't be able to play unless you clear me? Okay then, Doc, how much longer do I have in this fucking place?

As long as it takes. Let's re-evaluate after the next month and see where you are. You'll have to finish up to Step 5 before you leave, though, so talk with Ed and get going on it.

What the heck is Step 5?

Just talk to Ed.

I found out from Ed that there were actually twelve steps to this program thing. Five didn't sound too bad. I moved my stuff back into my room.

After working out for five weeks, I was lying in the grass outside looking up at the sun, just chillin', when my T-shirt lifted a bit in the breeze and I noticed that my gut was flat with my belly button. I'd never seen that before. Working out and laying off the booze was actually changing my body.

But I wasn't all that different. So when the day came that a cute blonde walked into the facility, my first thought was straight out of the old playbook: How can I wheel this pretty little thing?

Then the thought came in: Brantt, if you get caught you're going to get kicked out, and your career is done for sure.

Within three days we hooked up.

How could I put my career on the line for one meaningless toss? It didn't matter whether it was one girl or one line, I had no control.

It's funny. I probably learned more from that girl than I did from all the counselling. The AA program has a lot to say about powerlessness, but if there was one thing I thought I had, it was power. I did whatever the fuck I wanted. That was power, as far as I was concerned.

But not when it came to women. I was a puppy chasing a tennis ball. Maybe that's powerlessness?

Still, not exactly the end of the world to a twenty-four-year-old guy. If that was powerlessness, I wanted more of it, not less. Most guys would kill for that kind of problem.

They had a family day when a relative could come visit and you'd get some counselling together. So I flew my dad in for a couple days. I don't know what I was hoping for. My dad wasn't the type to sit down with a counsellor and open up.

When he got there, I could tell he looked at where I was almost as a joke: How the hell could his son be in this nuthouse? His son didn't really have the types of issues these people had—he wasn't using a needle to shoot up, he wasn't living on the streets, he still had money in the bank. The funny thing is, my father was saying the same things I'd been thinking when I arrived, but when he said them, all I could think was that he had no clue what I was really going through.

For sure, that was partly my fault. No way would I have admitted that I was an addict. I swore up and down that I'd just hit a streak of bad luck. I could drink again; I just needed to be a bit smarter.

He'd never had a problem with alcohol and would say the same things to me as others had: Why can't you just quit, Brantt? So now, sitting in rehab, I could tell my dad wasn't too proud of me. I embarrassed him.

That's not an easy thing for a son. I'd always wanted my dad's approval. I mean, what son doesn't want to make his father proud? I *needed* to make my father proud. Going on without his approval was going to be difficult.

But that wasn't even the hardest part of sitting with him in rehab, so far from the cold rinks of northern Alberta. The hardest part was that I realized he embarrassed me, too. My father had never been a good example of how to live your life in any honest manner. He was a corner cutter and lived only for the day.

I began to lose respect for him the older I got, so our downward spiral was no surprise. I think somewhere inside I felt like I was way more of a man than my dad. He was a good preacher, but he never followed up on any of it. He went from being a hero of mine to someone I didn't think much of. The fact that he was so quick to point out the problems in my life but would never look at how he lived his own really made me realize that I didn't have to take him as seriously as I always had.

Losing a hero can be devastating. I'd never thought he was perfect, but I'd relied on him for years. Now I was beginning to realize that the support I'd always assumed was there maybe never was, and certainly wouldn't be in the future.

In other words, I was alone.

The two-month mark came, and I thought for sure that this time I'd be going home. I was wrong. Doctor Dave walked in and said, Brantt, you're not ready to leave yet.

You've got to be fucking kidding me. Are you serious?

Yes, very serious. Let's re-evaluate in the next month and see where you are.

At this point I was boiling inside—I wanted to grab him by his glasses and punch him out. So for the next month I didn't talk to anyone; I never really got engaged in anything other than doing my steps up to 5. Which were bogus. AA might work for other people, but there was no way it was going to work for me. It was for people who had a problem maybe, but what I had was a solution. It was for weak people, maybe. But I was strong. My counsellor was trying to get through to me, but I was having none of it. I felt lied to by the doctors, and once you break my trust, fuck you.

That seemed to do the trick. When I was almost at three months we were in the room with Ed. He said, Well, congrats Brantt, you're all finished here.

When I stood up to shake his hand, he walked over to the chair where I'd sat every day for ninety days and moved it to the corner. When I asked him why he did that, his reply was, I'm saving it for you when you come back.

That day I called my best friend in Edmonton, my cousin Sean Brady, and said Braids, I'm flying you to L.A., then we're going to drive home to Edmonton together.

But when I told the doctors what my plan was, they said, No, you're not driving, you're going to fly. And when you get to Edmonton you're going to go to five AA meetings a week.

I said, There's no way you're holding me back from driving anywhere. I'm driving home and that's the end of it. They didn't like it, but there was not much they could do.

They say that one of the problems with the prison system is that putting all the criminals in one place just hardens them. Rehab kind of works the same way. I met a guy in there who used to be a coke dealer. He'd gotten out a month before me. The day I got out I called him and asked if he could get me an eight ball of cocaine. I mean, I did have a thirty-hour drive coming up.

I picked up Sean at the airport, and off we went north. Then, around thirty minutes outside of L.A., I said, Well, what are you waiting for? Chop up a few lines, bud.

The next thing I knew he was shouting at me to pull over—we were going the wrong way on the Golden Gate Bridge. I was so high I'd had no idea. We never slept a wink on the drive north.

7

Just as we crossed the border into Canada, my phone rang. It was my agent, Ritch. He said, I have some amazing news for you. The San Jose Sharks just called, and they're offering you a two-year one-way contract worth $1.3 million.

I really could not believe my ears. My first one-way contract, meaning I was guaranteed that $1.3 million no matter where I played. There was only one condition: an out clause stating that if I got suspended for any reason related to the program, they could void the contract.

It turns out there was a price tag attached to sobriety. Now I knew my price. I was willing to go clean for $1.3 million. I decided right there to go sober.

When we rolled into Edmonton, I had to go to Ritch's office to sign the contract. As we were sitting there afterwards he looked at me and said, Oh yeah, the doctors called and there'll be a urine tester here in one hour.

I almost puked in my mouth. I knew that if I pissed I would fail. It had been only two days since my last line of coke.

I'd read somewhere that Visine would dilute urine enough that it wouldn't show the cocaine. The trick was to drip it off your finger into the sample. So I got up and said I'd be right back. Then I went downstairs to the drugstore, got the Visine, and came back to find the tester waiting in the lobby. He said, Hi Brantt, can I see some ID, then let's go to the bathroom.

When we got in there he said, Okay, Brantt, take your right arm and put it above your head. Now take your left hand, grab your shirt, and raise it above your head.

Well, there went my plan. I was fucked. The tester left with a vial of coke-laced piss without a drop of Visine in it.

Five days went by, and I thought I may be in the clear when I got a message to meet the doctors in Los Angeles. There was no mention of drug test, so I thought it may just be a checkup or evaluation.

When I get to L.A., I take a cab to the Ritz Carlton and meet Brian Shaw, the head doctor for the NHLPA.

We sit down and chat for a few minutes. It all really seemed like a nice breakfast. So inside I was like, Wow, I've got nothing to be worried about here, it's just more of a checkup meeting.

Then he says, Brantt, let's cut to the chase. You had a positive test for cocaine.

I instantly started to beg him to please not suspend me, that I'd made a foolish mistake, that I swear to never do it again, I'll go to an AA meeting every day, just one more chance.

Talk about powerlessness. I was grovelling.

Well, I came here to suspend you, Brantt, but something inside is telling me you're serious this time. I'll give you one more chance. Don't mess it up.

It was time for me to go to training camp in San Jose. I showed up in great shape—I'd lost about twenty pounds of fat and looked like a different guy. I was flying out on the ice and got into a couple of scraps in the exhibition season. I did very well.

Darryl Sutter was our coach. I remember one day I was sitting in the stands watching some training camp games when he came up and said, Hey, mind if I sit down? No, coach, grab a seat. He went on to talk about how he'd coached certain players who struggled with the same things I was, and how he was going to be there for me to support me in any way he could—that he didn't care about Brantt the hockey player as much as he cared about Brantt the human being.

And that type of support came from all my teammates as well. They were all very aware of the fact that I'd just gotten out of rehab. Owen Nolan, our captain, and Dave Lowry, our assistant captain, were the two guys who really stuck out in terms of having my back. I had a ton of respect for both.

I was about two weeks into camp and was feeling restless. I wanted to be able to go out with the boys and have a few beers. Just a few. It's probably the same with any sport. Hockey makes beer taste great. No beer ever tastes quite as good as the first three after a skate. Maybe it's that your metabolism is racing and you're in a great mood from getting your heart rate going. It's a great buzz, even euphoric. There's a reason why hockey players drink a fair bit.

It also feels good to be one of the guys. You can get addicted to booze, no question. But camaraderie is pretty hard to live without too. Anyway, we all went out to the bar that night, and I ordered an orange juice with two shots of vodka so that no one would know I was drinking.

The next thing I know I have the bartender by the throat, and then I'm getting kicked out.

The following morning I get back to the hotel after practice and there's a letter on my bed saying the doctors want to see me for breakfast in L.A. the next day. Again, no mention of the fight in the bar, so I thought things were going to be okay. But when I showed up for breakfast, doctors from both the NHL and NHLPA were there.

They started out by saying that the owner of the bar I was at last night was good friends with Doug Wilson, the assistant general manager of the Sharks. Boss knew the whole story.

There wasn't much I could say. Sorry doesn't work twice, at least not twice in a row. Brian Shaw, Dave Lewis, and Dan Cronin said, Fly back to San Jose and pack your stuff. You're going back to rehab in L.A.

How long will I be going for?

Don't even worry about the time frame. You just worry about getting better and on track.

I'd been gone from Steps Recovery for only two months. I walk into Ed's office, and guess what he does? He walks over to the chair sitting in the corner and says, I had a feeling I'd be seeing you soon. Grab a seat.

Stage 2 suspension meant I'd have to go without my salary. Those screwdrivers were really screwing me. Even I could see that I was screwing myself. I'd dreamed my whole life about that contract with the Sharks, and now every day I was in rehab was a day subtracted from that deal. I was pissing away my dream for the sake of a few cocktails. Well, more than a few.

Anyone who's had too much to drink knows the feeling of self-loathing that comes with the realization of what you've stupidly gone and done. Imagine how stupid you'd feel if you'd thrown away years of work. It's sickening. So sickening you want to knock back a drink to take the edge off that disgust you feel for yourself. Only you can't do that anymore. You're just stuck with that feeling for the time being. The emotional sickness of a hangover is worse than the physical sickness. I had that feeling every day. Life was a hangover for a while.

At this point my dad hadn't called. We'd basically stopped communicating, which was fine by me. Like any child, you want some type of love from at least one of your parents, even if it means not ever telling the truth about how you really feel about them. That was the case with my dad. I mean, from the age of twelve until around twenty-three we were probably closer than any two on the planet—we spent every minute together, and when we couldn't, we'd be on the phone daily.

You don't love someone because they're perfect. You love them because they're part of your life. Sure, I'd been disillusioned about my dad for a while, but that didn't mean I didn't miss him. It probably made me miss him more. I was lonely, but if he turned his back on me because of my first rehab, I figured I knew how he'd feel about my second.

My grandparents were my rock. No matter what happened to me they always stood by my side. My sister Cher would call from time to time to check in. I never heard much from my brothers, par for the course, I guess.

Then came the day when another pretty little blonde got admitted. Oh boy, here we go again. Brantt, you got away with it the first time, no way you can put it all on the line again, no way.

The next week we hooked up.

During this time I was still training down in Venice and going to AA meetings every day. I felt I was opening up a little more, but I still didn't feel comfortable in there. I was embarrassed. I fucking hated standing up with all the other infected people and saying the word *alcoholic*. And to this day, I swear the only thing that kept me going back to the rooms of AA were the pretty girls. I don't think I heard one speech. I was too busy looking for some girl to fill this lonely fucking void, one I've had my whole life: someone to take care of me, someone to protect me, to stand up for me. So I kept pretty much to myself. I'd watch the San Jose games on the TV and get sad that I wasn't playing but excited that I'd be back in the next couple of months.

One day I received a call from the front desk letting me know that I had a visitor. Doug Wilson, the assistant GM of the San Jose Sharks, had shown up to see me. We went for a long walk on the beach. I told him it meant the world to me that he'd come to visit when no one else had. He said I was still a big part of the team, and that they wanted me back as soon as I was healthy enough.

Hockey culture can be pretty hard-ass. At least back when I was playing, coaches and GMs had pretty much one way of doing things: the way they'd always been done. If you didn't like it, you could sit it out. Want to rock the boat? You'd be in the stands. But on the other side, those same hard-asses would be your biggest supporters. They expected a lot, but they would give a lot. Maybe that's why I always loved hockey. The expectations were always clear, and there was always love, even if it was tough love.

Weird to think that all along what I was really drawn to were the rules. I guess that's maybe why, even though I hated dropping the gloves, I'd fight so willingly—mess with my teammates, and you're messing with my family. I never had anyone there to stick up for me, so I took real satisfaction in sticking up for teammates who needed it.

Anyway, I wasn't surprised that a guy like Wilson would come by. And after he left, I felt this real commitment to the organization, an obligation to not let them or myself down this time.

The three-month mark hit and I was out of there, on my way back to San Jose. I felt like I was in a different head space. Ed Pringle was never so positive, though. I could tell that when we met the day before I left: he had this sad, lopsided smile on his face, almost like, This kid's not done yet, and I can't do a goddamn thing to stop it from happening again. But there was a part of me that really enjoyed being sober, and probably more important, that really liked not having to hide anything. I was guilt-free for the first time in my career.

The agreement between me and the NHL doctors was that I live with an ex-player, Dave Maley, who'd been sober for eight years. Dave had once played for the Sharks and was now a big part of its alumni. I must admit, living there felt like I was back in junior again, being supervised by others, except that now I was twenty-five years old and making $500K. It felt like ever since the day I signed that substance-abuse contract I'd pretty much signed away my freedom. They had total control of my situation. It felt like a life sentence without the bars.

When I walked back into the dressing room all the guys on the team came up to me and extended their hand. They said things like, We'll be here for you if you need us, Welcome back, and Welcome aboard. Everyone on the team, and there was not one exception—they all gave me their support. But I'd say our captain, Owen Nolan, was my closest friend through all of that. My teammates really meant the world to me, and to hear them being so positive about having me back made me feel wanted. I guess to do that job, I needed that feeling on a daily basis. I wanted to keep it all together for them, and for my coach.

That would be Darryl Sutter. He was an Alberta boy like me, with a reputation for being a real hard-ass but a straight shooter. I liked that, and could see after our first practice that he was in complete charge of that team.

I'd never had a coach who demanded so much respect—and I'd never had a coach who didn't give two shits what came out of his mouth when he was ripping into someone. I also think some of the players thought this tough-ass farm boy could lay a beating on them too if they got out of line. I mean, at times he could seriously scare the shit out of you. But he had this way of rewarding you in little ways—mostly with ice time, or in the team meetings when he'd call out your name and say something positive. And after I'd fought, he'd come into the dressing room during a period intermission and always say, Myze, great fucking job out there, way to get the team going.

My first game with San Jose was against the Washington Capitals. Before the game the assistant coach, Paul Baxter, called me into the office.

So I'm sure you know why we brought you in, right?

Yeah, you guys want me to play physical.

Yes, very physical. Don't be afraid to kick someone's ass tonight.

Now, I'd played a lot of games by that point, and I'd never really had anyone be that forward with me. You don't tell a fighter when to fight. He knows his job better than anyone in a suit and tie. That's the kind of respect tough guys get. Everyone trusts them to do the right thing for the team. That's because it's a brutal job. You can't ask a guy to do those things. He can do it only when he feels it's the right thing to do.

So I was like, Beat it, Baxie. I made it to the NHL as a fighter. I don't need you to tell me what my job is. I'll take care of it.

I was sitting in the dressing room right before the game and could hear the fans going crazy already. I was really fired up—I knew that in my first shift I'd be going after someone. I went to the bathroom, put some Vaseline on my face, and went out to the ice.

Sutter: Myhres, you're up.

I jump the boards and skate right after Brendan Witt.

Witter, let's go!

We had a good fight, but as I skated to the penalty box I was thinking, I need one more tonight.

Third period I went out on the ice and there was a scrum in front of our goalie. I grabbed the first blue sweater I saw. It turned out to be

Peter Bondra—a fifty-goal scorer and the best player on the Capitals. Not a small guy by any means, but not someone I needed to worry about. I guess he was feeling pretty angry about something—or he didn't know who I was. He shook off his gloves and threw a punch. I spun around and said, Fuck you. Then I dropped my own gloves, gave him an uppercut under his visor, and down he went.

Their team was going crazy: I'd just given their star player a black eye. I was laughing—what did Bondra *think* was going to happen? If you drop your gloves with anyone in the league, you'd better be ready. And if anyone wanted to do something about it, they knew where to find me. As I skated to the box the crowd showed their appreciation by going into a frenzy. San Jose fans are really loud. They love their hockey. They called it the Shark Howl after I would fight and then scream my way to the penalty box.

Anyway, my first game was a success, in my opinion. When we played Colorado shortly afterwards, I knocked out one of their players named Cam Russell. Things were really rolling along—we were winning and I was feeling confident. Not that I was in the clear by any means. The doctors from the league wanted me to get a urine test a minimum of three times per week. It was a bit of a pain in the ass, but I was sober so I didn't mind doing it.

I attended AA meetings when we were home. I didn't really like the meetings, but I put a smile on my face just to keep the peace. About a month after I got there I decided to go down to the Lexus dealership and buy myself a nice sports car. It was my first nice car, and I loved it. Things were good.

Or, pretty good. Living with Dave kept me on the straight and narrow, but that was a road I wasn't very familiar with. I didn't love it, I can say that much. I felt like a little kid, and having a roommate was not my thing. I like to be alone, so I was getting a bit on edge.

I believe it was around January, and we were going to L.A. to play the Kings. Ten minutes into the game we're on the power play and Alexander Korolyuk, a skill guy, got just smashed against the boards by one of the Kings players—their captain, Mattias Norström. No one did a thing about it, so I decided to jump the boards and chase him down. By the time I got to him he was stepping into his bench. I ended up on their bench too, and when I went in, the butt end of my stick hit him right in the eye. Then I had Rob Blake on my back punching me in the back of the head. Finally, the refs broke it up. I got kicked out of the game.

The next day I got a call from Dean Lombardi, the GM of the Sharks: Brantt, you're going to have to fly to New York and have an in-person meeting with the league for coming off the bench. We're going to stand behind you on this, but be prepared to get suspended.

For how long?

Probably three or four games, but we're not too sure.

So I flew to New York with Dean. We arrived at the NHL head office and went up for the meeting.

Our case was that I was changing for another player—that is, I didn't come on to fight; I was going on anyway. But it didn't look that good when the head of league discipline, Colin Campbell, called me into his office.

Brantt, first off I wanted to commend you for cleaning up your life. Keep it going. We'll make our decision tomorrow.

Colin, how many games am I looking at?

I can't say for sure, maybe six, but let me sleep on it.

The next day we were all on our plane getting ready to leave for Phoenix. I remember seeing Dean outside on his cell phone, shouting into it. He walked onto the plane and said, Myze, come here. They gave you twelve games.

What?! He told me around six! That fucker! He said he was going to sleep on it, must have had a fucking nightmare.

Twelve games was considered a pretty big suspension. I believe I cracked the top ten in all-time most games suspended at the time.

Even though I was making $500,000, I was still going to lose about five or six weeks' pay, so $50K before taxes. That was a huge kick in the balls.

As always, when things turned against me, I started to turn against the whole world. I could feel the itch to get fucked up coming on. I mean, hey, I was playing in the NHL, making real good money, single, and now had some time to kill.

One of the coolest moments of my career came when we got back to San Jose. I walked into the dressing room, and there were twenty-three cheques waiting for me. Made out to me by each of my teammates to help with the suspension. It was an amazing feeling to have the backing of your team. Now, this wasn't even legal in terms of the collective agreement, but the players did it anyway, something I'll never forget.

I wasn't allowed to travel with the team on road trips, but I still had to go to the rink every day and practise when the team was playing at home. I worked out like an animal with our trainer—I still did everything as part of the team; I just wasn't allowed to play in a game till the suspension was over.

So, as I said, with all that time off, my head started talking to me again, finding excuses for maybe just having one or two cocktails. But by then I'd been sober for about four months and things were going really good for once, so why would I mess with a good thing?

Good question. I'm not saying it makes any sense. But I was fucking mad that I'd been treated differently from everyone else. A big part of me really hated fighting. I'd always wanted to be a hockey player, but I wasn't even really playing hockey anymore. My last year of junior was the last time I really played. I'd have people come up to me and say, Hey Brantt, what's it like to play hockey in the NHL? I'd be like, I have no clue. I know what it's like to get sick from nerves the day before a game because I knew I had to fight. I know what it's like to play three to four minutes a night, maybe none some nights.

I know what it's like to get healthy scratched because the other team didn't dress their tough guy. I know what it's like to put Vaseline on my face to help with getting punched. But as far as knowing what it's like playing the actual game of hockey . . . I have no clue.

Still, I didn't let those thoughts get to me. I didn't have a single drink.

When I got back to playing we flew to New Jersey to play the Devils one night. The game was real chippy and Scott Stevens was running around crunching guys, so I went up to him after the period was over and said, If you don't stop running around, Scotty, I'm going to put you to sleep.

Yeah, Myhres, go fuck yourself. Why don't you go have another beer, you alkie.

Our team captain, Owen Nolan, heard that and freaked out. He started giving it to Stevens, saying, Real class act, Scotty, your defence partner just got out of rehab and you're saying that shit?

After the game the reporters were all by my locker asking me about Stevens. I told them what had been said, word for word, and reminded them not to worry: we'd be playing the Devils in a few weeks in San Jose, so I'd have a talk with him then.

The morning of that game the headline in the San Jose paper was "Myhres Going to Address Stevens' Comments." Now, most times I would have gone out there and tried to take his head off with my fists, but before the game Darryl pulled me aside and said, Myze, let's get him back by beating them on the scoreboard. We need these two points, so no stupid penalties—just go out, finish your checks, and play hard.

When Scott got out for his first shift the jumbotron zoomed into his face, then put a picture of a donkey's ass next to it. The crowd went nuts. That in itself was enough for me. A few days later my real good friend Sheldon Souray, who was playing for the Devils at the time, called me and said, Hey Myze, someone wants to talk to you. Scott grabbed Sheldon's cell phone. Hey Brantt, I'm really sorry about what I said back in New Jersey. Won't happen again.

It's water under the bridge, Scotty, I told him. No big deal.

It was the all-star break in San Jose and we had a few days off, so I decided to fly my buddy Sean down from Edmonton again. I knew it was a bad idea. But that sort of realization had never slowed me down. Plus I probably didn't think about it too hard. I was never one to second-guess myself.

I knew the day he arrived at the airport that I was going to relapse. When he showed up we went right to the bar and started drinking. It didn't take me long before I was hammered, since by then I'd gone over four months without a drink.

I could feel the booze lighting up every cell of my body, sort of like the way a few Percocets would make everything okay when I was in physical agony. But alcohol is different. It's more like jumping out of an airplane. It's euphoria. And once you make the decision, it's out of your control. It pulls you along where it wants you to go, just like gravity.

And it feeds on your emotions. It will tell you whatever you want to hear. I was pissed off at the world. I was pissed off at the All-Star Game, which was supposedly not for guys like me. I was pissed off at all the people who were following me around like bloodhounds, waiting for me to make a mistake. Every drink was a fuck-you to all of that.

One thing I was definitely not thinking about was the group of guys who'd left a wad of cheques in my stall.

And once I was in that state, I started looking for cocaine. I found some off a guy at the bar, picked up a girl, then headed home. We stayed up all night drinking and doing coke. It was about eleven a.m. before I lay down to try and get some sleep.

We had our skills competition that afternoon. Each guy on the team had an event to do. I was in the hardest shot competition. I showed up still mangled from the night before, thinking to myself, How the hell am I going to be able to even find the puck in this condition?

I got on the ice and they lined up a puck for me to shoot. I stepped into a slapshot, which was clocked at forty-one miles an hour. Now, for those of you who don't know much about the average shot of an NHL player, it should be at least double that. So for shits and giggles our goalie Steve Shields grabbed a hockey stick and gave it a try. He was clocked at sixty-five mph. Talk about embarrassing.

The next morning when I showed up at the arena our trainer said, Myze, the doctors called and there's going to be a urine tester here at one p.m. Once again, I knew that if I pissed I'd test positive for cocaine, so I skipped out of there at twelve thirty, saying I was sick.

Two days later I got a message saying that I had to have breakfast with the doctors at the Hilton hotel, nine a.m. I knew they couldn't suspend me since I hadn't tested, so I was wondering, Why the meeting?

When I showed up they said, So why did you miss your test the other day?

Well guys, I was sick as a dog and had to go home.

We don't believe you, Brantt. Did you bring your chequebook?

No, why?

You're going to have to go home and grab it 'cause we're going to fine you five grand for skipping a test. The next time you miss, it'll be ten grand, and so forth.

This is a fucking joke, you guys. What's with this program? Okay, no problem, I'll write you a cheque and drop it off, have a good day, you pricks.

I mean, that had just pissed me off even more. Yes, I was counting my lucky stars that I'd dodged another bullet, but I was still so angry about even being in this position. I felt it to be a jail sentence—why couldn't these guys just leave me the fuck alone? It always felt like, Fuck them, they were ruining my youth years, the so-called best years of my life, NHL or no NHL.

The season ended and I was going to try and get myself back on track. So I decided to go to L.A. to train down in Venice at Gold's Gym for the summer.

My first day of training I went in and my trainer said, Hey Myze, go warm up on the bike and say hi to your new training partner for the summer.

That's when I met Bob Probert.

When I walked up to ride the bike and saw Probert riding his, I was like a little kid in the candy store. Big Bob was my idol. He'd made the all-star team, scoring close to thirty goals one year with Detroit. He was what every tough guy wanted to be.

Hey Probie, nice to meet you, name's Brantt Myhres.

Oh, hey bud, nice to meet ya, can't believe we have to ride this fucking thing before we work out. Let's just get right to it, hey?

Of course I agreed with every word that came out of Big Bob's mouth. He could do no wrong in my book. I kind of felt like his little brother or something.

I was in shock being assigned as his workout partner. We hit it off right off the bat. Bob was really the nicest guy I've come across—hard to believe he was the toughest guy to ever play the game. At that time he'd been eight years sober, which really made me like him even more because I wanted to be sober but couldn't see a path to staying that way. So hanging out with Bob for the next couple months really helped me, just 'cause I didn't want to look like a failure to him.

After a week of training together, he invited me to his house in Marina del Rey to have dinner and meet his wife Dani and the kids. I just remember going into his fridge to get a diet soda and seeing about twenty-five non-alcoholic beers.

As we were having dinner we were talking about being sober, and Bob said, As soon as I'm done playing I'm going to line up some vodka shots in front of the league doctors, give them the finger, and pound back the shooters.

At that point I knew it was only a matter of time before Big Bob starting using again. The crazy thing was that there was this little voice inside me saying the same thing—I too couldn't wait for my career to be over with to tell them all to fuck off—so I completely understood where Probie was coming from.

It's weird when I think about it now. Two guys, living the life they'd dreamt of, counting the days until it was over.

But I crashed long before Bob did, as I've already related. I relapsed not long after that dinner, and just about destroyed his Harley when I did.

So I was already having a really shitty day when I went riding with Probie, Jeremy Roenick, and Chris Simon. I hadn't slept, and my mouth felt like the inside of a hockey glove. I was pretty much alone with my thoughts as we rode up to the top of the canyon in Malibu. Even the bike I was riding was a reminder that I'd been an idiot and had disappointed someone I looked up to. Someone who'd trusted me.

It was really cooking when we got to the top, like 110 degrees. We all decided to turn off our engines, take off our helmets, and just coast down the twisting roads. Chris Simon was the only one who didn't want to take his helmet off. Plus he'd met this girl at the bar the night before and she was on the back for the trip.

Chris was leading the gang, winding down the switchbacks, when I heard this awful sound, a sound of tires screeching against the pavement. Chris lost control of the bike and ran head-on into the side of the mountain. The bike flipped up in the air, the girl he'd just met smashed her face on the rock, and Chris was screaming to get the bike off his leg because it was still going—the tire was chewing up his leg.

We all dropped our bikes as fast as we could and ran over to him. The girl stood up and had blood pouring down from her face. So did Chris. We found his helmet in the ditch, completely bent in half. Jeremy Roenick's wife went to help the girl, but when she saw what type of shape she was in, she passed out and fell straight back, hitting her head on the pavement.

It was a real shitshow going on, and I was still foggy from the night before. Chris had to be rushed to the hospital—he ended up needing ten staples on his head from the pressure cut. Crazy how this world works: he was the only one who'd said no to taking his helmet off. He would have died that day if he'd followed our move.

———

I was still getting tested two to three times per week. There was no way to duck it. I remember taking this girl to Hawaii for a seven-day vacation. The minute we checked into the hotel there was a note saying the urine tester would be there in an hour. Really? An hour into our vacation in Maui and I've got to piss in a cup? Anywhere on earth you went they had a tester waiting.

When we got back to L.A. I was supposed to get tested by this guy who owned the testing company that the NHL and NHLPA used.

He showed up to get my urine, and asked how I liked getting tested three days a week.

It sucks, I said. I feel trapped.

Well, Brantt, if you ever find yourself in a bind, call me the night before. I have good urine in my fridge—just make sure to give me the heads-up. There'll be no questions asked.

Talk about a green light! The rest of the summer I had no worries: I'd party till eight a.m. then text him, telling him to bring the good urine. It worked every time.

So yeah, I'd liked being sober, because being sober meant getting paid. A clear conscience was nice. Improving my fitness didn't hurt as a professional athlete. But I wasn't sober for sobriety's sake, and playing by the league's rules and being treated like a child was truly exhausting.

Not that the league was wrong to doubt me.

8

I had a different feeling heading into that season.

A feeling of doom, one like I'd never had before. That little voice was telling me I was running out of chances, but of course I paid no real attention to it. I bought this new Cadillac Escalade, bought a new Harley, and rented a house in this gated community called Silver Springs, a very nice place. I think I was paying about four grand a month in rent. Scott Hannan was a rookie on the Sharks that year. I told him he could stay at my house, thinking I was going to be a good guy and all.

And of course I had to get a urine testing schedule set up. So one day my doorbell rings, and when I opened the door what I saw was a mirror image of Fat Bastard from Austin Powers. This guy was huge! He walked in and the first thing out of his mouth was how he and his son were real big fans.

I said, I'll tell you what, you just give me that urine cup and let me go to my room, and I'll make sure you and your boy get to come to the games for free, deal?

He opens his bag and says, Okay, go do your thing.

At that point I knew I had a free ride again. Was this really happening? It seemed all too crazy to have these guys hired by the league acting so shady. Still, I don't think it reflected on the league—I mean, there's always a bad apple in every cart, right?

Our first game was against the Chicago Blackhawks. I flew my grand-parents in for a week to stay at my place. During warm-ups I was skating around and all of a sudden I see Fat Bastard standing behind the glass with a big GO MYHRES sign. Shit! Now I have my urine tester cheering me on during the fucking game! I felt so uncomfortable seeing him there—how the hell did I get myself into this mess?

The game starts and one of their Russians sticks me in the balls, so I punch him in the face. Doug Zmolek comes in to help him out and we square off. I hit Doug real hard with a few lefts and he goes down. As I get up from the fight I look at the crowd, throw my head back, and howl.

The Blackhawks bench didn't like it that much, and my buddy Bob Probert was playing for them. When I get out of the penalty box and skate right to the faceoff circle, I see only Probie jumping the boards to skate up next to me.

Fuck, Myze, you have to stop running around, you're making me look bad. My coach sent me out to fight you, but fuck him for that, so just settle down.

No problem, Probie. Let's just play the game for a bit here.

As soon as the puck drops the same guy I'd fought in my first NHL game, Mark Janssens, cruises up to me wanting to fight, so the gloves were off and away we go. He tied up my left hand real good this time, so I thought to myself, Why don't you try throwing a right hand since you can't throw your left? I pulled back with my right hand and threw a couple, but it felt like I was throwing pillows for punches, so I switched back to my left. The fight was over; the linesmen come in. So now I'd had my second fight of the game, I'd already had an assist, and it was only the second period. I was pumped.

It was always nice to contribute to the scoresheet, even though it didn't happen that often. The next shift I start to skate out of my end, but when I look back I see by our net that it's a shitshow, everybody grabbing each other. So I skate into the pile and try to fight someone.

The linesman grabs me and pulls me out of the pile, my jersey coming off as well as my undershirt. Then I notice their goalie just standing at centre ice, so I break free a bit, skate over, and punch him right in the face. Next thing I know someone punches me in the back of my head and

I go down. It was a complete circus going on, and all I could think about was what the heck my grandparents were thinking.

I ended up getting third star of the game.

Not that it did me much good. Darryl pulled me aside before the second game and said I wasn't going to play. I was a healthy scratch. I'd worked all summer to get ready, played great in the season opener, and still I got scratched? Then Game 3 came and again I was a healthy scratch, then Game 4, same thing. The only way I knew how to deal with resentments was to drink, so after our fifth game I went out to really "show them."

While Scotty stayed home I headed to the bar, where I picked up a couple girls. We jumped into the Escalade to go back to my house—by this time it was about one a.m. and I was twisted again.

When I forget to hit the button to open the gate to get into my community, *bang*, I run right through it, laughing the whole way. Then we pull into my garage and I don't hit the brakes in time, *bang*, my truck goes right through the wall. Scotty runs into the garage, freaking out, thinking there's some kind of war going on. I get out and say, Ah, it's all good, bud, I'll get the wall fixed, no big deal.

One night I was at my house and decided to tie one on again. Higher than a kite, I picked up the phone and gave my dad a call. I was pretty sentimental. I opened up my heart to him. I wanted to know why we were on the down slide. I wanted to make things better. I wanted a dad.

He really laid into me. He called me a loser and a poor excuse for a son.

My dad had a way of digging really low when he talked to me, and I couldn't listen to it anymore. It's hard to explain when your father calls you down like that, almost as if you were a piece of shit, you feel the lowest of lows. I was already in a downward spiral. I had to cut the tie. Part of me really wanted to kick the shit out of him, not just for that moment but for leaving me as a child, not taking responsibility as a father.

Where were you, Dad, when Brad was kicking the shit out of me and Cher when we were just little kids? Why didn't you come rescue us when you heard there was violence in the household? You think it was okay to see me only a couple times a year? Why did you have to lose everything when I lived with you for the first time?

My grandparents had told me that he didn't pay any child support. I'm not perfect, but I figure that taking care of your kids is the bare minimum if you want to call yourself a man. My dad told me himself that he'd never paid child support. Why the hell would I pay anything, he said, when your grandparents have lots of money?

My mother was no better. I never really had a lot to do with her after I was taken in by my grandparents. The men she would choose made me puke—low-lifes to say the least. I heard through the grapevine that my mother was in trouble with the law. The cops broke her door down and found a hundred pot plants growing in her basement. She later had issues with stealing, and then mental health issues.

So the topic of my parents is a pretty sore one. We don't get to choose who we call Mom and Dad. What I do know is that if it weren't for my grandparents I would not have survived, never mind made it to the best league in the world. They gave me the two things I believe every child in the world yearns for: love and safety.

We were boarding our plane to go to Colorado when I looked up and saw this angel staring at me. I could not keep my eyes off her. She had blond hair and these deep blue eyes. What attracted me to her the most was that she looked so innocent, not like the bar stars I'd been hanging out with for years.

The whole flight I was figuring out what to say to her. How could I get her attention? Should I invite her to our game? But I couldn't do that. I wasn't even playing, hadn't played in a month. I didn't need her asking why. I'd have to lie to her. In the end I asked the PR guy to get her number.

I should have known I was in trouble when I couldn't even talk to her.

The flight comes to an end and I go up to the PR guy and ask if he got it.

No Myze, he says, I'm not allowed to do that, so I'm going to have to be sneaky about this one. I'll let you know in a couple of days.

For the next two days I could not stop thinking about her. It had been years since I'd felt that kind of joyous torment—not since Brooke.

I was at home after we get back from our trip and my phone rings. It's our PR guy.

Hey Myze, I got it for you. Don't tell anyone about this, okay?

Sweet, thanks, pal!

I'll call her Megan. I dial her number and she picks up—right away she had this sweet voice on the other line. Hi Megan, it's Brantt. I got your number from someone who works for us. How are you?

We talked for close to an hour. We just seemed to really connect. I had this sense of, Oh shit, this could be a girl I end up having some serious feelings for.

Feelings I hadn't had in years. Even a feeling of love, something that was foreign to me. Of course, I wasn't going to let all my depressing secrets out of the bag—I needed to come off as a guy who really had his shit together.

At the end of the conversation I invited her to a game in San Jose, and we arranged to meet afterwards. She lived in Sacramento, about five hours away. Of course, the Why aren't you playing tonight? question came up. I just said I was nursing an injury. No way was I going to tell her I'd been suspended from the league twice and that I had a major drug problem. I mean, this girl looked like she'd never even heard of the word *cocaine*. I was not about to burst this image I needed to build in order to be loved by her.

So we meet after the game, go out for dinner, then back to my place for a drink. I don't think Megan liked the fact that I smoked, but it went hand in hand with my booze.

After that we started going out. I managed to keep it together around her, just drinking, but that still meant having to get a piss test three times a week. I knew that the rule of thumb on booze staying in your system was an ounce every hour. So I needed to fill up some pop bottles with good urine for backup.

Megan made me feel like no other girl ever had. She had this innocent motherly love thing going on. She was making me feel like I was
a real catch. All of a sudden I felt better looking, funnier, all the ways
falling in love can make you feel. Yes, I was still living a double life, but
she was receiving the "better" half of Brantt. I didn't know what speed
to take this all in at—all I knew was how I felt about her, so stepping on
the pedal was the only speed I knew.

A little later on Megan and I decided it was time for me to meet her
father. He owned the private charter airline the Sharks were flying on,
and had a contract with another eight teams as well as the NBA. When
I got to Sacramento for dinner at his place, I could tell right away by
how big and beautiful his house was that I was already out of my league.
I mean, I came from Grand Centre, and here's a girl I'm falling in love
with whose dad is this real big deal in Sacramento. Greg oozed power and
wealth. His education was obvious. Our first meeting was probably not a
good time to tell him I hadn't finished high school.

As we were sitting at dinner, he said, So, Brantt, how much money do
you make?

I was taken aback by the question.

Umm, $650,000, sir.

Well, you know, these days it's not that much money after taxes,
about $450,000, so you better be careful with every penny.

I thought, Holy fuck, I make more money than a brain surgeon, bud.
I may not be making as much money as you, or other NHL players, but
I'm doing pretty damned good.

Needless to say, we hadn't started off on the right foot. When I mentioned to Megan on the drive back to San Jose that her dad had been
pretty hard on me, she just said that he was really protective of her, but
that deep down he was a teddy bear. I guess I was mostly bothered by
the fact that I was really feeling like a loser around him. I mean, if he
only knew what I'd been through, how I'd grown up, how I'd misman-
aged my money . . . There was no way in hell I could ever live up to his
expectations.

———

Darryl Sutter was the best coach I ever had. There was something about him that made you want to give it your best every shift, literally go through a wall for him. He would drink a whole pot of coffee before the game, so he'd be bent over with his hands on his knees just vibrating back and forth. Talk about intense! Darryl would talk to me about alcoholism from time to time; I believe it ran in his family. And when he talked to me, it really seemed out of true concern for Brantt the human, not Brantt the hockey player.

I never had a coach who could inspire me to do anything to get his approval—except Darryl. Was he a hard-ass? Sure, but I also knew that he stood by his players no matter what. It almost felt like another father figure, but this father figure I really respected. It made the thought of fighting on the ice not seem so bad 'cause I knew I'd get that little punch in the gut afterwards from him—when you got the punch you knew he appreciated what you'd just done.

We called him Big D—he'd really give it to players if they hadn't put in a hundred percent effort. Darryl didn't hold back anything: every player got it, even stars like Owen Nolan or Jeff Friesen were made an example of if they weren't playing their asses off.

We had a player on our team named Joe Murphy. Murf was a good guy, but really was on his own agenda. I guess you could call him a tad on the odd or weird side, but I liked him 'cause he was a bit crazy. We'd come into the dressing room and in our stalls would be a stuffed animal. My stall would have a tiger, someone else's would have a monkey or a shark. He'd look at me and say, Myze, tonight you're a fucking tiger, no one's going to touch you. Fries, you're a tiger shark, go eat 'em up, buddy.

Darryl and Joe would butt heads from time to time, and it wasn't pretty. One night we were in L.A. playing the Kings and Joe didn't get a shift for the first period. Big D walked by Joe and said, Murf, you're up next. Joe paid no attention to him and just sat there. Darryl walked by again, this time putting his hand on his shoulder. Murf, I told you, you're up! Joe looked at him and said, If you ever put your hand on me again, you fuckin' pig farmer, I'll throw you in the tenth row! I put my head down to hide my snickering.

Darryl came back a few minutes later and said, Hey Murf, I'll grab you a deck of cards so you can go sit with the backup goalie and play some fuckin' solitaire, 'cause you're not seeing this ice tonight.

I put my jersey over my face 'cause I was laughing so hard.

Joe's time came to an end not long after, when we were playing back in San Jose. It was the middle of the game when Ron Stern stood up on the bench and said, Hey Murf, get your ass going out there, pick it up.

Murf stood up on the bench a little way down and said, Ronnie, go fuck yourself!

Yeah, why don't we go in the dressing room and settle this, you cock-sucker?

Sure, meet you in there.

They both stood up and went off while all the guys were like, Are you kidding me? The period ended, and as we walked into the dressing room we saw Ronnie on top of Joe, pounding away. Darryl walked in, looked at them, and said, Ahh, let 'em go.

Then he walked out of the dressing room. So no, Big D was not a kindergarten teacher who wanted kids to play nice.

One of the craziest things I've ever heard come out of a coach's mouth was from Darryl one night when we were actually winning the game at home. During the second-period intermission we were sitting in the dressing room when he walked in and then went down the line, just rip-ping into each player, one by one: So-and-so, you fucking suck, where are your balls? So-and-so, take your shit off 'cause you couldn't even play for a women's hockey team, you lazy fucker.

It went on and on till there was no one left to lay into. Finally he leaves the dressing room, then five seconds later pops his head in and says, One more thing—you better pray we win this game or you'll wish you get hit by a car on your way home.

Then the door shut and we were all in shock. Finally someone said, Well, who's going to order the limos tonight? We all started cracking up, which eased the tension in the room.

That was Darryl, though. Did he really mean it? God no, he loved us like family. But he was just so emotional that stuff would spit out of his mouth from time to time that made you go, Did I just hear that correctly?

The culture has changed, in the game and in society in general. But while Darryl was a legendary hard-ass, it was never puppy dogs and rainbows behind closed doors with any coach I ever played for. It was loud and aggressive. It was war, because back then we really did go to war together as a group. That was how we thought of it.

You could only imagine what was said in those dressing rooms. In the culture we live in today, it wouldn't fly. The things we said on the ice pretty much every shift would get you a full-year suspension in today's world. It was racist, sexist, and downright dirty.

Even when I was a teenager: I remember playing for Lethbridge when I was eighteen against a junior team from Russia. We abused those Russians so severely, verbally and physically, that they almost had to stop the game. Thank god there was no social media back then. There would have been more lawsuits than goals scored.

People call that kind of thing hate today, and I agree it can be pretty awful. But I'm not sure it's *hate*, exactly. We thought of it as a kind of love. It made us brothers. We were in the trenches together. We did battle as comrades. Anyway, that was the kind of love I knew.

In the hockey world, where aggression is pretty much the only emotion guys know how to express, carving a teammate is love. Fighting for your teammates—that's love. I needed that love, maybe more than most guys. That was not a bad thing at all in my line of work. If I thought one of my teammates needed some backup, I was probably a little more enthusiastic than most players when it came to providing it. I expressed my feelings by beating the shit out of people.

I had life all figured out when it came to the dressing room and the ice. It was the rest of the day I was wrestling with.

———

Out of all the games I played in the NHL, the night we were in New York playing the Rangers was my most memorable. January 4, 1999. They had quite the lineup that night—Wayne Gretzky, Mark Messier, Brian Leetch, and Mike Richter, to name a few. There was something about playing in Broadway that was just amazing, and lining up against my childhood idol 99 made it unforgettable. Some guys don't like the idea of being role models—they say they just want to be hockey players. But they don't really get a choice. If someone grows up admiring you, then you're going to be linked in their mind with all the good things from their childhood. So if you remind people of what they always wanted to be, you're letting everyone down if you unintentionally show them it was all a fraud. That's the way it was for me, anyway. Wayne will always stand for the best I could dream to be.

The Rangers had a tough guy named Darren Langdon. He wasn't that big, but I'd say pound for pound he was one of the best fighters in the history of the game. He had amazing stamina, was very smart, and would never really get hit.

So I get out for one of my first shifts and start chasing the puck down in the Rangers' end. I throw a huge bodycheck, their player goes down, and the whistle blows. All of a sudden I see Darren come over the boards. Oh boy, here we go. Darren ends up right next to me. We talk for a second.

Wanna go, Myze?

Hey, Langer, I'm a bit tired bud, I've had a long shift, maybe we can go later?

Nah, Myze, let's just get this over with.

I didn't really want to fight at that moment, but when you've got a guy staring you down holding your jersey, you can't really say no.

Sure Langer, okay, let's do this, then.

Our gloves are off. I throw a punch that just misses his head, the momentum of the punch brings us both down to the ice, and now the linesmen are on top of us.

We both said, Well, that sucked. I guess we're going again as soon as we get out of the box.

Our roughing penalty ended, and there we were, in MSG's centre ice, squaring off for the real deal this time. We came together and I started throwing left hands as fast as I could, uppercuts, every punch I could think of. Darren was doing a good job blocking them, and I was starting to tire out. After about a minute we ended up going down with no one getting hurt. Great fight.

I got out on my next shift, and for some reason I was on the ice with Gretzky and Messier. I went to chase the puck down by the penalty box. Gretzky had the puck and I went in there to rub him out, but the next thing I know I get a stick right in the neck—I guess his buddy Messier hadn't liked that too much. If only he'd known that Wayne was as safe as a kitten around me.

In the second period, Tony Granato had the puck and I skated right to the net. He took a shot that went off my ass and into the net. Yep, I got credit for the goal, my one and only goal with San Jose. I ended up getting second star of the night in a game I'll never forget.

After the game I asked my good friend Kevin Stevens if he could grab me Gretzky's stick. I'd met Kevin in rehab that summer when I visited him the first day he arrived in treatment. We'd go golfing from time to time and train together down in Venice. We became pretty good friends, so I didn't hesitate in asking him to talk to Gretzky and get his stick. He got Wayne to sign it for me, dated 1999—the year he retired from the game. That stick meant everything to me.

Me and Megan were still going strong. We were spending so much time together, and being with her just felt right—I respected everything about her; she was so much that I was not. As the days went on I was feeling more and more vulnerable. I'd finally found a girl I connected with, someone I felt real love for, or at least what I thought love felt like. I started talking about marriage. That word seemed impossible, but I would seriously bring it up, and Megan was up for the discussion as well.

Things were going pretty smooth until one day when she was getting out of the shower at my place and yelled my name. I ran into the bathroom asking what was wrong. She pointed at the top cabinet. What the hell are those pop bottles filled with? I told her I liked warm apple juice, I was so embarrassed. The bottles were my store of good urine from when I'd had some clean time. I kept them in the bathroom for when the tester would come and I'd otherwise be caught with drugs or booze in my system.

That's not apple juice! It looks like piss . . .

Come on, honey, why the hell would I have piss in pop bottles?

Well, it's not apple juice, so tell me what the hell it is!

Are you calling me a liar?

Yes I am!

Well, get the fuck out of my house then.

She then storms out crying. I know I've just lied to her, and that I'm about to really fuck up the best thing in my life. So I chase her outside of the house, yelling, Megan! Please come back; let's talk about this, babe.

Brantt, you know you're not being honest with me. Why don't you just tell me the truth? What the hell is going on?

Inside I was dying. I'd been caught in a lie, and the only thing I knew how to do was stick with that lie no matter what. How the hell could I tell her I had these flaws? She wouldn't love me anymore. Even worse, did she really love me now, or just the impersonation I was doing of a successful, sober person? And, god, what would her dad think of me now?

My only solution was to keep pretending that piss was apple juice.

She probably never believed it, but two people can tell each other the same lie if they need to.

We smoothed out that situation. It was never really brought up again until we moved to L.A. for the summer.

It was around March 2000, and up to that point I'd played only fifteen games. I was staying out of trouble. Dating Megan really helped: no drugs, just drinking from time to time. Fat Bastard was still helping me with my urine tests, so I never worried about getting busted. My contract was up that year and there was talk from Ritch, my agent, that they were going to offer me a long-term deal.

So when the call came to see Dean Lombardi in his office, I jumped on my Harley and cruised down for the meeting.

Brantt, he said, you've been a trooper through all of what's happened during the year. I know you didn't play much, but we'd like to offer you a contract extension. It's a three-year deal worth $1.5 million.

I thought for a second and did the math. Since I was making $650,000 that year, it meant a $450,000 decline over three years. So I told Dean I needed some time to think about it, and then called Ritch for advice.

Well, he said, you've played only fifteen games this year, so for them to offer you that was pretty incredible. I think you should take it.

But I think if we wait a bit we can at least get them to $600K a year.

Okay, Ritch said. Let's go back in a week with the counter-offer.

A few days later I went into this pub thinking no one would be there of any importance. Little did I know, Dean's wife was standing at the bar. She noticed me and told me to come over. I had a double vodka and orange juice, so it didn't look like I was drinking alcohol. She was telling me how proud she was of me for staying sober.

As the night went on, though, I was getting loaded.

God knows what I was thinking. I had to have known I was taking a huge risk, boozing in front of my boss's wife. Did I want to provoke a crisis with Dean, just as I had with Megan? Was part of me cringing from the possibility that Dean would never have offered me a contract if he'd known what I was really like? I mean, he respected the fake Brantt, just as Megan loved the fake Brantt. Who knows what an alcoholic is actually thinking as he drinks his future away, but I can't help wondering if maybe I wasn't just being stupid. I think I was tempted to show Dean the real Brantt.

I'm pretty sure his wife realized after an hour that it wasn't just orange juice in my glass. A few days later I got another call to see Dean. I went into his office and sat down.

Brantt, I've just put you on waivers. If you clear you'll be going down to the minors.

What are you talking about? What about my contract extension?

I've got more important things to worry about than your fucking contract.

If you've never lost $1.5 million in one conversation, I'm not sure I can convey what I was feeling at that moment.

I went down to the minors and hated every fucking minute of it. I was away from Megan. I missed her a ton and needed to see her, so I flew her to Kentucky to stay with me at the hotel for a week. But the feeling of embarrassment was weighing heavy around her now that I wasn't playing in the NHL and was just a minor leaguer. It killed me that she was flying around guys in the NHL, and there I was in the AHL. It turned me into a jealous freak, always asking if players were hitting on her, did she give her number out, did anyone ask how I was doing on the Sharks?

Even though I was making $650 grand in the minors, I wanted to be back in the NHL so bad. Everything about the minors is, well, the minors.

You go from playing in front of twenty thousand fans to maybe four or five thousand; you go from private planes to riding the bus for hours; you go from the best hotels on the planet to average hotels. You go from having every game televised on TV to none. Not to mention that the pre-game meals were ten times better in the show, or at least they tasted better.

There was no fucking way I was going to fight down in the minors. I had a hard enough time doing it in the show. I fought for my team-mates, and I didn't want to think of these guys as my teammates. No offence to any of them. I'd been in the minors before. I didn't think I was too good for them. But my teammates—the guys I would bleed for—were the Sharks, not these guys. I was just down and out. With only a month left in the season, I just wanted to ride it out.

When the season finally ended I decided to take Megan and head south to L.A. to regroup. I was a free agent and needed another con-tract, so I was going to give myself the best shot at earning one. Not to mention that I was already in Stage 2 of the substance abuse program and that Stage 3 looked real ugly: a six-month suspension without pay and Mr. Gary Bettman having to reinstate me to play. I did not want to go down that road.

Looking back, I always wondered why Lombardi didn't rat me out to the league for drinking again. I should have really been in Stage 3, and yet for some reason not a word was mentioned. But the NHL doctors once said something that had always stayed with me and that probably applied to this situation as well. They'd said, Brantt, you know what? We don't have to bust you again. You'll end up busting yourself.

That summer was very peaceful. I confessed to Megan about my prior two suspensions, but I still made it out to sound like they were trying to fuck me, not let me have any fun. I could tell she liked me better when I was sober. I worked out all summer, ate healthy, and was just waiting for Ritch to swing a deal with one of the teams.

Around that time, the NHL and NHLPA substance abuse doctors thought it would be a good idea to bring in the guys who were in the drug program. To Los Angeles of all places. Here's who was invited:

Bob Probert: They'd actually had to start the NHL and NHLPA pro-gram because of Big Bob.

Chris Nilan: Well, his nickname, "Knuckles," sort of tells you he's not a professional dart thrower.

Billy Tibbetts: The Pittsburgh Penguins signed him to a contract after he was released from prison for sexual assault. He spent two years behind bars. Since then he'd been in and out of prison for various other offences.

Jere Karalahti: He was caught smuggling heroin into Finland.

Then there was me.

Let's just say it wasn't the kind of group who preferred to remain in their hotel rooms playing cards.

We were staying at the Sheraton in Santa Monica. I get into the lobby and Dan Cronin says, Hey Brantt, you'll be rooming with Big Bob.

Deadly! How cool is this? I get to room with my idol—I mean, he doesn't know he's my idol, but he was. We were all in the lobby just sort of staring at each other, like, What's next?

Probie said to all of us, Okay boys, let's meet here at six and then go for dinner at this place I know.

As we were walking towards the elevator, Chris Nilan said, Hey Myze, make sure you're not drinking or anything else tonight. The doctors have trusted me to be the one who tests all of you tomorrow morning at eight, so behave yourself. I have a connecting room to yours as well, just so you can't get away. He laughed when he said that last part.

I was okay with it, since I was actually fine with just hanging with the boys. And Probie—well, I thought Probie was on the straight and narrow. I didn't know much about the other two guys, Billy and Jere, just that they had reputations as animals.

As me and Probie are chilling in the hotel room, I'm thinking to myself, How the fuck is a kid from small-town Alberta rooming with his idol in Los Angeles? It felt crazy to be there.

So now it's six p.m. and we're all heading over to this awesome little restaurant. The bartender comes over and says, Hey gentlemen, what can I get ya?

Brantt: Ah, I'll get a Diet Coke please.

Nilan: Just an ice water please.

Probert: Budweiser, big fella.

I looked at Nilan. He just shrugged and said, Not much we can do. Probie's got that look in his eye tonight.

We all head to this other bar around ten, but at eleven I say to the boys, I'm out of here.

I knew Chris would be testing us in the morning, plus the doctors had said we had to do a bike ride at nine a.m., so I wanted to be fresh.

I yell at Probie, Yo, bud, see you back at the hotel.

Sure thing, Myze, I won't be too long!

At two thirty a.m. I can hear someone banging on the hotel door. Myze, open up, it's Big Bob!

Fuck. I get up and open the door.

Hey Myze, what's shakin'? I could see that Bob's eyes were big as saucers.

Not much, Bobby, I was sleeping. I go lie down in my bed and he comes and sits next to me. He pulls out his pack of Marlboros, shakes one out, and pours cocaine on it.

Hey Myze, do you mind if I do a line?

Not at all Probie, but I got to tell you something.

What's that?

Well, you see that connecting room?

Yeah, so?

Knuckles is staying in that room, and at eight a.m. he's going to be drug testing all of us.

You've got to be fucking kidding me!! Shit man, I'm fucked!

He starts pacing back and forth in the room, and finally says, Okay, Myze. How long till this shit gets out of my system?

Well, Probie, I usually wait four days for sure. I've waited three days and I've been busted, so four days should be good to go.

Hmm, okay . . . How long does it take to drive to Chicago?

Umm, about four days.

Okay, well I'm going to just tell the doctors that I had a family issue back in Chicago, so I had to drive asap. That way, they can't urine test me if I'm on the highway.

Yeah buddy, that's your only way out of this.

Probie pours the coke back in his little baggie, grabs his backpack, and gives me a hug. Later, Myze!

I found out afterwards that Probie just went down the street to a different hotel and never even left L.A. But as I was lying there, all I could think about was how I wished I was in his shoes. He'd stayed sober for eight years, and now he was at the end and wanted to let off some steam. Who was I to say no? I mean, I wanted to be right next to him doing it too, but I still had some years left in me to resurrect my career.

I couldn't sleep at all that night. All I could think about was Probie's well-being, hoping he'd be okay—not to mention what the docs were going to say when they found out he was driving back to Chicago.

9

It was August and I was getting a bit nervous. Nothing had come to fruition.

But the day came when my phone rang, and it was Ritch.

Brantt, Nashville just called. David Poile, the GM, is offering you $500 grand one-way money. They have no tough guys and they want you to be theirs.

Do you think we can get more if we wait a bit longer?

After what just happened in San Jose, do you really want to walk on that thin wire again?

Hmm, go back to them and say we want $550 grand. If they agree, let's wrap it up.

Okay, I'll give them a call. Wait by your phone.

My phone rings ten minutes later.

They said if you don't take the deal at $500K they're going to sign Reid Simpson in two minutes—

Fuck! Call them back and say okay, okay, we agree.

They only want you to do one thing before they sign on the dotted line.

What might that be, Ritch?

David wants you to fly to Nashville today to check you out—to have a one-on-one talk and make sure you're the one.

I jump on a plane and head to Nashville. Five hours later someone from the Predators picks me up at the airport and takes me to the arena. I walk into David's office, and he tells me to take a seat.

So, he begins, one of the first things I wanted to say was that the deciding factor in us having interest in you was that you've been sober for over a year, so congrats.

Sober? Me?

Umm, yeah, David, it's been great staying sober, my life has never been better, wouldn't change it for the world. At that point I felt like a piece of shit, but what was I supposed to say? I couldn't tell him the truth; if I did there'd be no NHL contract.

The meeting ended, we shook hands, and I got back on a plane to L.A. But as soon as it landed I turned my cell phone on and there was a message from Ritch.

Brantt, Nashville just called and they want you to get back on a plane and have a meeting with the owner of the team.

Ritch, Jesus, I just flew ten hours! Okay, I'll head back.

When I landed in Nashville, the Predators' coach, Barry Trotz, picked me up. We had a good chat on the way to the arena. Barry was a pretty intimating presence, but you could also see a soft side to him; he reminded me a lot of Darryl. He seemed excited to have me aboard and made it clear that help was there if needed.

I met with the owner, lied my face off again about being sober, then flew back to L.A.

The next day I get a call from Ritch saying the deal was done.

They liked what they heard, he said, and think you're a great guy. Congrats.

Looking back on my behaviour, I'm ashamed that I lied to decent people. But really, at the end of the day, the one I really let down was myself. This was the year when I'd have a fresh start, when things were going to be different. That was the plan, anyway.

Me and Megan grabbed our dog, Daisy, and started the drive to Nashville from L.A. Soon after we arrived I got set up with a psychologist, since the NHL doctors had made it a requirement to see these guys at least once every two weeks. I'd walk in there, cross my arms, and say, So Doc, why don't you tell me about me . . . I'm all ears! Knowing full well that I wouldn't listen to a fucking word he said.

I mean, please, what do you really know about me? You just met me there, Doc, and you want to assess my life in thirty minutes for $200 an hour? I've got better things to do with my time than listen to a guy who's probably never been beaten as a child or squared off with men 250 times face to face and with your job on the line if you lose, so spare me the bullshit. Trust me, you have no clue what makes me tick.

Regarding that analysis of yours: it was that feeling of authority that I despised, maybe because some of the stuff that was presented to me about myself was true, and I didn't want to dig that deep because the truth hurt too much. All that anger was coming from a place of feeling I was alone in this world—and that if I built a wall, then I couldn't get hurt too bad.

So if you were going to give me advice on the way I conducted my life, then you sure as hell better have known me for longer than an hour.

Meanwhile, things didn't go so good in training camp. I got hurt pretty early on, so I missed most of the exhibition season. As a result they wanted to send me down to the minors for a couple weeks of conditioning. I wasn't too keen, but I had to go.

When I got back we played Chicago. My first shift I fought Ryan VandenBussche. He was under six feet tall but you couldn't hurt that guy no matter how hard you punched him in the face. Still, my state of mind was that I wasn't about to fuck this up. I had to prove to my team and the league that I was a full-time NHLer. But it was becoming pretty apparent that the Predators had other plans.

After about ten games I'd had only two fights. I just wasn't feeling like fighting anymore, partly maybe because I was sober. When I was drinking I was playing on the edge all the time. When I was sober the true Brantt came out, which was a guy who never wanted to fight. It took a lot for me to play that role without any substances in my body.

———

I was feeling antsy, and it was starting to affect my relationship with Megan. The term "dry drunk" was creeping in now. I could feel my NHL career slipping away, and the only natural thing to do in my mind was to quiet those voices.

She flew her dad in for Thanksgiving. We played at home that weekend, against Colorado. After the game I told Megan I was going over to a buddy's house to play some cards. He was our trainer for the team, and he liked to get after it from time to time. She said okay, but please don't be too late. She didn't want me to show up late when her dad was there, plus we had Thanksgiving dinner to get ready the next day. Of course, honey, I said. I'll be home no later than one.

When I got to my friend's house all logic went out the window. Within an hour I had hundreds of dollars' worth of cocaine dumped on the table. It felt as though the party had just started when there was a knock on the door. When it opened, it was Megan standing there in her bare feet. She'd somehow found out where I was.

Time to go, she said. Get your ass off that couch away from the drugs and let's go home.

I said what any loving partner would say. No way, there's still lots of coke left and I'm not leaving till it's all gone, so get *your* ass home.

She started crying and slammed the door.

It's now nine a.m. and I can barely see straight from all the coke. I get into my car and drive home. When I walk into my house there's her dad, reading the newspaper on the couch. He looks up at me and says, So it looks like you're going to ruin another holiday, hey Brantt?

Yeah, whatever, I'm tired, I'll see you when I wake up.

I go up to my room to find Megan there crying, trying to talk to me about what's just happened. I told her to please get the hell out of our room, just let me sleep this off and we'll talk later. After she left I got up and locked the door.

Just as I was about to fall asleep I hear this noise coming from the other side of the door. She had a drill and was taking the screws out of the door so she could get in. All of a sudden the door falls over and she comes flying in and tries to smack me in the head. I grab her arm and say, Okay, it's time for Daddy to book your flight and take you back to California.

You're losing your fucking mind . . .

Ya think?

Dating you has been the worst decision I've ever made! You're a drug addict and you're about to lose everything you've ever worked for, can't you see that?

The plan was that Megan would return to Sacramento for a couple weeks to see if we could get things back on track. But I knew I'd gone too far. Or, part of me knew. There was still a part of me that would only ever want to go further.

I loved her. I never doubted that, and don't now, but it wasn't nearly enough to make things right.

One time, when it was snowing and freezing cold outside, I'd grabbed her and tossed her outside with no socks on while I was sipping on a Jack and Coke. She had to call one of my teammates to let her inside where it was warm. Who does that?

I've been through rehab enough times that I've learned how to talk about my feelings. I really didn't have a choice. But I still don't understand what happened with Megan. It boggles my mind that I could have treated someone I adored so atrociously.

Even at the time I understood that I was sinking down to a place I'd never been before. Cruelty was new to me. I'd certainly been a thoughtless jackass before. I'd been selfish. But any twenty-year-old guy with money in the bank and no responsibilities other than showing up to the rink on time and beating the shit out of other hockey players is going to act badly. Not to make excuses. That's just the way it's going to turn out.

But what happened with Megan was something different. With other girls, with Brooke, I was an asshole because I didn't give a shit about anyone but myself. With Megan, I was an asshole *on purpose*. I loved her,

I really did. But I went out of my way to be cruel to her. Like I said, I don't understand it to this day.

I mean, why did I even pursue her when the agony of faking who I was should have made it clear that it couldn't end well? My own father despised me. Did I really think I was going to convince *her* father of something my own dad couldn't see?

Did I pursue her because she should have been unattainable?

Was part of me *disappointed* when she agreed to see me, when she first kissed me, when she returned my feelings? Did she let me down by falling for a guy who didn't deserve her? She couldn't have been as good as I thought she was if she stuck around with a clown like me.

I mean, my own mother didn't seem all that interested in me. Why on earth would this angel, this sophisticated, well-educated, wealthy, beautiful woman, who could have had any guy she wanted, put up with me?

You'd think I'd have been grateful, that I'd have kissed the ground she walked on. And I was sometimes, and I did. But it also made me angry. You don't have to be a psychiatrist to figure out that I was angry at myself. Even if I was from a trailer park in northern Alberta, even if I hadn't finished high school, even if my mother didn't talk to me—still, I *could* have been someone who deserved her. In fact, I'd come close. I'd come close several times, because I'd had dozens of second chances. I had it in me. But I hadn't ended up as that guy. That would make anyone angry.

I had cost myself the love of the woman of my dreams.

It shows you that love can be a cruel thing. Megan was the one who kept fixing things, and I was the one who kept smashing them. Even my love was flawed and dangerous. I guess in the end she really was unattainable, even if I did convince her to love me, and even if I loved her. Even when we were together, even when she was in my arms, I knew she could never be mine. She could never really love me, not if she knew me. I could never really deserve her, even if she swore otherwise and seemed to prove it by forgiving me again and again.

I hate to say it—I hate to admit it. But the darkest of those days gave me a flicker of sympathy for the asshole who used to beat up my mother.

I could see I wasn't all that different from the guy I'd despised more than anyone in my life.

And it gave me a glimpse into the unknowable mind of my mother, whose choices in life had made me shudder since I was a little kid. Now I could see what she had in common with the woman I was treating so badly.

All of this only made me more contemptible in my own eyes.

And I had only one way of taking the edge off my self-loathing.

Megan packed her stuff and went back to California. It started to get real dark after she left.

I was beginning to get healthy scratched more and more often. So with that came more drugs and alcohol. It was January 2001 and we were in Calgary playing the Flames. After the pre-game skate I got pulled aside again to tell me I wasn't playing. They said that during the game they wanted to me to take stats: power plays, penalty kills, shots on net. I went back to the hotel, had some lunch, and took a nap. The game started at seven but it was now only six o'clock. So I had this great idea to walk down to the strip club, have a bite to eat, catch the game on the big screen, and take stats from there.

I ordered a steak and a beer, and watched the first two periods while I got a girl sitting on my lap. After that I got into a cab and headed down to the Saddledome for the third period.

The next morning we flew to San Jose. When we got to the hotel our coach Barry Trotz said, Hey Myze, can you come up to my room?

Sure Trotzie, I'll be right up.

We sat down and he started asking me questions about the game, like, What did you think of our power play in the first period? What did you think of the way we played four on four in the second?

I knew something was fishy but I couldn't put my finger on it.

Finally, he said, So, where did you watch the game last night?

At that point I knew I was fucked.

Umm, at the strippers, Trotzie. Can I ask you a question?

Sure, what is it?

How the hell did you know I was watching it there?

Well, after the game the coaches got into a cab. The driver asked us what we did for living and we told him we coached the Predators. He said, Really, no way? I just drove one of your players from the strippers during the game, his name was Brantt.

Busted.

Myze, we've done all we can for you, but you're fucking up every time you turn around. We can't make excuses for you any longer . . . We're going to put you on waivers, and if you clear you're going down to Milwaukee to the farm team. I really hope you go down there and clean up your act.

Through this whole time I'd had the doctors calling, asking if I was using again. Of course I said no—that I just felt down because me and Megan had broken up.

Well, that's not what we're hearing in Nashville, they'd say. And you know what happens if you get another dirty test, right?

Yeah, yeah, I know.

While I was in Milwaukee I kept it together pretty good. I wanted to get out of the minors so bad that I put the booze and drugs on the back burner. And during that time me and Megan worked things out again, so she was with me there. I had a way of talking my way out of anything. After she left Nashville during that Thanksgiving nightmare, I'd thought our relationship was finished. So it was just me again needing to feel as if someone loved and cared for me, even if it was all fake from my end. There were moments when I really did think I was insane.

We were shopping in Chicago one night when my phone rang. It was Ritch at the other end.

Hey Brantt, make sure you say hi to Peter Bondra when you get to Washington. You've just been traded to the Capitals.

What? Really! Yes!!

I was so excited to be traded. My time was obviously up in Nashville, and now I was heading to a team that had a real shot at the Stanley Cup. Not that I'd be playing in the playoffs, but it was still a positive move for me. And their coach was Ron Wilson, who was a pretty straight shooter.

So Megan and I packed up and headed to D.C. When we checked into our suite at the hotel, Trevor Linden called and asked if I wanted a ride to the rink. You bet I did—I'd watched Linden when he was with Vancouver. He was an all-star, so it was pretty cool to be playing with him.

Not long after, when we got on our plane to fly to Pittsburgh to play the Penguins, I sat right next to Peter Bondra.

Hey Peter, I said. Ritch told me to say hi to you.

Oh, I remember you, Myhres, you were the guy who gave me a black eye in San Jose . . .

Ahh, sorry Bonds. Heat of the moment, big fella.

No worries, it's all good, we're teammates now.

We both laughed about it. I was really looking forward to this game since number 66, Mario Lemieux, was in the lineup. Other than Wayne Gretzky, Mario was my favourite player in the world. I couldn't wait to hit the ice.

The game started and their tough guy, Krzysztof Oliwa, skated to centre ice, looked over at me, and shook his gloves—was he serious? I was still on the bench, not even on the fricken ice yet, and he wants to fight me. I looked at Ron, and once Adam Oates came off, he gave me the nod. So I left my gloves on the bench and the fight began—and within ten seconds it was over, job done for the night.

Then all of a sudden the healthy scratches were coming, like, every game it seemed. So back I went to drinking vodka and orange juice. I had my year-end meeting with the Capitals, who had the right to re-sign me in the summer, but after playing only a handful of games I wasn't counting on it. I'd just have to wait.

———

At the end of the season I was saying to Megan that I'd always wanted to have a house on the lake, so let's start looking for one in Alberta, one close enough where friends and family could visit. We searched for a couple weeks, then one popped up. It was absolutely stunning—a big place on Sylvan Lake with a huge yard, two pillars in the front, and a deck that wrapped around the whole house. I was in love with it. I made an offer and sealed the deal the next week. That house would turn out to be the most famous on the block, and not for good reasons. I knew it was going to be a rodeo when I asked the realtor what my address was and she said, it's 69 Ravenscraig Crescent.

Pardon? Did you just say my house number was 69?

So now that I had my lake home, I needed a real nice wakeboard boat. We drove to Kelowna, dropped $65,000 on a Malibu, then drove back to Sylvan Lake.

The doctors called and said, We found a urine tester to come out to the lake, so when he gets there, figure out a testing schedule that works for the both of you.

Then I see this Chevy truck come rolling around the corner, and in walks this farmer. He seemed like a good guy, but the only thing I cared about was whether he was going to watch me piss or not. We had small talk for a minute, then he pulled out the cup and said, Okay, go do your thing.

Bingo!

The only thing I have to do is to somehow warm up the piss I'd stored so that the temperature gauge would show I was human.

After moving in, I felt like I needed to share this awesome purchase with all my family and friends. Before the party started, though, I put in a call to my dealer for a bag of cocaine. We arranged to meet in town, so I told Megan I was going into Sylvan for something I needed for the boat.

The night starts out with me cutting up a big line of cocaine, snorting it back, then heading upstairs for some Jack Daniels. I hear the toilet flush downstairs. Then Megan walks upstairs and says, You think you're so sneaky, hey?

Did you flush that bag of coke?

Yep . . .

You fucking idiot! I paid five hundred bucks for that, fuck me. Well you'll be going home on a plane tomorrow for that dumb fucking move.

I made another call to my dealer. Then I jumped in my X5 and headed to downtown Sylvan, population five thousand.

The first time I tried coke, I loved it. I never imagined that one day I'd be buying it as an act of revenge against someone who loved me.

I'm wasted at this point, driving a hundred kilometres an hour down the back roads. I come up to the highway going way too fast, slide into the ditch, then fly over the highway into the other ditch. Somehow I made it back onto the highway, then rolled into the parking lot at McDonald's to wait for the coke dealer, a guy from Edmonton. I knew him from my days growing up in Grand Centre, so just for the peace of mind that came with knowing him personally, I'd offer him an extra two hundred dollars to deliver it to Sylvan.

As I'm waiting I see a cop car pull up right across from me. It parks, and sits there idling. I'm wondering what's going on when I see my buddies come around the corner and pull up beside my now scuffed and battered SUV. Myze, they say, come on, buddy, let's go home. If you try to drive out of here, that cop is going to bust you.

I get out of my car, then head home with my buddies, more pissed off than ever. I was going to make up for the lost coke by pouring Jack down my throat as fast as I could get it into me.

The next thing I remember is I'm rolling around naked on the floor puking everywhere. I can hear people laughing in the background. All I'm able to do at that point is lie on my stomach and pray I don't choke to death.

I wake up the next day feeling just terrible, and when I'm hungover like that I'm a total prick, so I took it out on Megan. That poor girl had been through the wringer. All she did was cry in our room during those times, and the more she cried the angrier I got at myself, and the angrier I got at myself the more I needed to take that out on someone else. She just happened to be in the way again.

Megan flew home the next day. And now that she was gone, all I could think about was really ramping up the party.

My neighbour's name was Bob; he had two daughters aged ten and fifteen. You could literally walk fifty feet to his door, we lived so close. At the beginning I'd go over there for a beer, shoot the shit, but after a few weeks he changed his attitude towards me. I had this stereo system that had speakers in every room. It cranked, and believe me, it drove everyone on that block crazy. Around ten thirty p.m. I could count on two people coming to my door: the first would be Bob and the second would be the cops.

Bob: Brantt, my little girls are trying to sleep and you guys are acting like animals! Please keep it down.

Cops: Brantt, the noise bylaw here is ten p.m. Please turn the music down and keep it quiet.

Once they both left I'd crank the music back up again and start partying.

I bought a hot tub for the backyard. And since it had a lot of lights, everyone could see what was going on in that hot tub at night. I'd go to Red Deer, grab a few strippers, then head back to the house. The strippers always wanted to snort a few lines, so we got along perfect.

One time, it was about five a.m. and I was wearing only thong underwear and a cowboy hat when the doorbell rang.

Holy fuck, Brantt, what the hell are you wearing, and why are you sweating so bad?

Hi Bob! You wanna come in for a beer, bud?

Fuck no, I came over to ask you to please shut down the party—you've got naked strippers in your hot tub having sex and my little girls can see everything!

Bob, are you telling me I can't have sex in my own backyard? Don't make me smack you upside the head, Bobbie boy.

I slam the door shut and go back to partying.

The next day the piss tester was going to come at one p.m., and I had no good piss, so I was freaking out. I called a friend in Edmonton.

Hey man, how are you?

Good Myze, what's up?

Umm, hey, can I use some of your piss?

What did you just say?

Listen bud, I've got this piss tester coming in three hours. I did a bunch of blow last night, and if I don't have good urine, I'm fucked, I'll test positive.

This sounds crazy, Brantt . . . All right, meet me at work and I'll piss in a bottle for you. Last time, though.

So I drive an hour and a half to Edmonton, grab the good urine, and head back to Sylvan Lake. Then, as soon as I see the Chevy come around the corner I take the good piss in a metal cup, run to the bathroom, and put it under hot water for thirty seconds. I knew that would heat it up enough to hit the mark on the temperature gauge.

The tester walks in.

Hey man, how are ya? How's the farming going? Give me the cup and I'll go get you a sample.

I take it into the bathroom, pour the good urine in, and thank god the temperature gauge hit the mark. I'd escaped another one.

But that's not to say I escaped unscathed. I bled a lot that summer.

The first time wasn't all that bad. I was wrecked by seven one night. My grandparents were visiting, but I was out of control. We ran out of firewood, so I tried to pull up some landscaping to keep the fire going. I yanked and yanked at this tree, pulling as hard as I could. When it finally comes out I go flying headfirst into the dirt. Blood was coming down my face as I walked back to the fire.

Now my grandpa opens the door and tells me to get my ass back in the house. When I walk up, my grandma sees that the skin has peeled right off my forehead and she starts to scream. My sister runs out into the living room to give me shit, I head-butt her for a laugh, and she reels away wailing.

But the joke wasn't funny anymore. Now I'm in a drunken haze, telling everyone to fuck off and get out of my house. My sister and my grandparents leave to get a hotel in Red Deer twenty minutes away. I somehow make it to my bed.

I wake up with blood all over my pillow and my memory rushing back like nausea. I call my grandma. She's so disappointed with me that all she can do is say, Brantt, you need help again. You can't keep going on like this, or you're going to die. We love you, but we can't handle watching this.

Then I received a call from Dan Cronin. It was the next day, so I have a feeling my grandparents called the league behind my back.

Brantt, are you okay?

Yeah, of course, why?

You can tell me, Brantt. I'm only here to help. If you get another dirty test they'll put you in Stage 3, and at that point I won't be able to help you . . .

Dan, I don't know where you're hearing this from, but everything is great, I'm sober as a judge.

But the whole neighbourhood knew better.

One real hot day I thought I'd take my new ski boat out for a rip. I invited about ten people, friends from Edmonton as well as a few buddies and girls from Red Deer. It was around noon, and I'd finished a case of beer. Just getting warmed up. About two minutes from shore, I think getting naked while I go for a wakeboard would be a great idea.

I take my clothes off, jump in the water, and away I go wakeboarding on Sylvan Lake. I try to do a 360 and fall flat on my face. As this happens I hear the police sirens going off, so I swim my ass off to the boat, jump in, and wrap a towel around me just as the cops pull up to the boat.

Hey Brantt, how are things? Any booze on this boat?

Yes, officer, about fifty beer . . .

Well, you know the drill, Brantt, no booze allowed. So why don't you give me that beer, and I'm going to have to dump it out. You still living on Ravenscraig Crescent?

Yeah, you bet.

Okay, I'll bring the empties to you.

That kind of took the fun out of boating. So we load the boat on the trailer and head back to the house. I ordered a bag of coke to get the party started up again, but all of a sudden I hear everyone say, Shit, the cops are here, turn the music down!

I'm so high at this point that I walk right up to the cop and tell him to roll his window down. Then I grab him by the back of his head and give him a big kiss on the cheek.

Boys, why don't you get out of that cop car and come for a hot tub!

Jesus, Brantt, you know we can't do that. Even though your party looks like it would be a riot, we can't. Here's your empties. Maybe you should take a break from the booze?

Good idea, boys, I'm going to shut 'er down for the rest of the night.

As soon as they leave I round up four girls and we head to the hot tub. I get naked and grab my cowboy hat. Then, after my bottle of Jack is finished, I get up to go grab some more booze. All I remember is falling back out of the hot tub and rolling all over the beer bottles on the cement.

When you're rolling around on broken glass, you're pretty drunk.

I get up not knowing or feeling any pain, until one girl screams, Oh my god, look at his leg!

I look down and notice that my thigh is cut about an inch deep and ten inches long. You could see right into the meat, the slice was so deep. My buddies lay me down on the ground, grab a towel, and tie it around my thigh so I won't bleed to death. I had no sense of how much time passed before the ambulance came. I lay there getting groggier by the minute, with blood seeping out of me onto the deck.

I woke up the next day with fifty staples in my leg and the humiliating memory of the sound of laughter and music as I was getting hauled out of my own party on a stretcher. As usual, I swore I would never drink again.

———

Hangovers are a gift. Those agonizing hours when you see yourself through the haze of physical pain and the ache of mortification may be the only honest moment in a drunk's life. Honest in the sense that for a few hours you know that booze only makes things worse. That whatever it was you were feeling the night before wasn't really happiness. For a short time, you can see that laughter and hilarity as nothing more than a fraud.

It was all a fraud. I had everything I thought I wanted. I was an NHL player. I had the house and the ski boat I'd always figured would complete my happiness. Thing is, I'd used that boat only twice—because I slept most days, because I'd been partying all night. There were a couple of new quads sitting on my lawn, too. But I was miserable. It's confusing to be miserable when you've gone and done exactly what you think you needed to do.

In moments like that I would pray to God to help me. Yeah—strippers passed out in my house, empties on every horizontal surface, sniffling from all the coke that had passed through my sinuses, and I'd be praying.

If only I could hold on to those hangovers. Maybe if I could stay miserable a little longer, I'd do something about it. Maybe I'd do something about whatever it was that was leaching all the happiness out of my life. But that's a hard thing to do. Grabbing another eight ball and a bottle of Jack is a lot easier.

Megan was gone. My friends were closing the door. If they were even my friends. And I still didn't have an NHL deal, even though it was well into August now. I was getting pretty nervous about the whole thing but figured it would all turn out, just as it always had before. Ritch called and said, Brantt, do you know how much money you spent last month?

No Ritch, please tell me.

You spent $120 grand . . .

Yeah, and your point is? Listen, I pay you to be my agent, not my babysitter. Talk to you later.

I know. Hard to believe I was running out of friends.

I end up going to the liquor store, grabbing a shopping cart, and filling it with booze. A typical night of booze, girls, and drugs would cost me two grand, and I was doing that about three times a week, so my funds were running a bit low. By this time I'd had already received seventeen police reports from the neighbourhood on my partying. The cops warned me that if they had to come to my house one more time because of a complaint, they were going to charge me.

That night, the party was going strong again. I knew I was getting tested the next day, but I thought I'd just call my buddy and things would be okay. Even though he said he wouldn't do it again.

I'd been warned by the cops. I'd been warned by my agent, by my grandparents, by my friend, by the woman I loved, by the league. What can you say about someone who knows where the train is heading but won't get off?

I was in my bathroom that night, having sex, when I hear my buddy saying, Myze . . . Myze . . .

Yeah, what, I'm busy . . .

You may want to look behind you.

I turn around and there are two cops watching me having sex with this girl on my sink.

Mr. Myhres, please put some clothes on and then come downstairs, we need to have a talk.

I threw on a pair of shorts, churning with a nauseating cocktail of emotions I knew only too well. Embarrassment, for sure. And anger. Some fear. Some resentful pride. But maybe also some relief. I wasn't going to stop myself. Maybe someone else would do it for me.

Listen, Brantt, I really don't want to charge you, you seem like a nice guy, but a nice guy with a drinking problem. Why don't you get some help?

Little did they know I'd been in rehab twice before. I told them I would for sure get some help, but I already knew I was bullshitting them. I was just trying to get them out of there.

Good luck with that, Brantt. I hope we never have to come to this house again.

You won't, I promise.

The next morning I was a complete wreck. The sun was too bright, and I was so hungover my hands hardly worked. But I couldn't sleep it off, because the urine tester was coming in an hour. Soon enough, the familiar Chevy pulls around the corner and I run to the bathroom to put some water in the good piss to dilute it a bit. Easy-peasy . . . Or so I thought.

When the doctors called, my gut dropped.

Brantt, do you have anything to tell us? We're only going to give you one chance to tell us the truth.

As always, I stick to my guns.

No, what are you talking about?

When we tested your urine you had so much H_2O in it you should be dead. No human has that much water in their urine. We know now that you altered it.

I'm thinking, Fuck them. If they can't legally bust me, then fuck off.

Turns out they could bust me. I was on to Stage 3: six-month suspension without pay, and having to be reinstated by the commissioner of the NHL before ever playing again.

Brantt, one of the doctors said, listen. This may be too hard for you to do. Maybe you should just call it a day and get another line of work? What you'll have to go through is going to be long and hard, not to mention that the commissioner has to reinstate you, and there are no promises that he will.

Guys, this is my life. I have a grade nine education. Ever since I was five I wanted to be a hockey player. I don't know what else to do. I promise you, from here on in I'll put the booze and drugs down. I'll do anything it takes to make it back to the league. I know it's going to be a long road, but as I said, I'm prepared to walk that path.

Okay, Brantt, you're going to have to get on a plane and head to Vegas for treatment.

Vegas?

Yeah, Vegas. There's this good spot there that we're going to try out. Be prepared to spend at least three months there, then three months of after-care.

Ritch called me three days later.

Brantt, you owe me and my family a trip to Disneyland.

What?

That's the agent fee you'd have had to pay on $500,000.

What are you talking about, Ritch?

I just got off the phone with the Anaheim Ducks. They offered you a one-way contract at $500K, but I had to tell them you were just suspended. For the love of god, Brantt, go to rehab this time and get healthy. Your nine lives are running out.

Don't worry, Ritch, this time is different. I want to finally turn my life around. I'm so tired of this roller-coaster ride, I just want to get off once and for all.

PART III

TOUGH GUYS DO CRY

10

Something had changed in me. Maybe I knew that if I made it back from Stage 3 it would be my last chance. No one ever made it to Stage 4. That really scared me. Since I'd been sober, me and Megan had gotten back together once more. I'd promised the world to her, and she wanted to believe there was that true side of me really wanting to change. I would eventually start losing respect for her, knowing she would always take me back.

I was living with her in Sacramento now. The only job I had was to stay sober, which included going to five AA meetings a week. I even needed to get my AA form signed stating I was there. Meanwhile I was still getting my urine tested three days a week, but that was a piece of cake when I was sober. You want me to piss when? You want me to piss where? No problem, give me that cup. The season ended and I was still in California.

Nine months passed, and then it was time to write that letter to Mr. Bettman asking for reinstatement. At this point I was absent from alcohol and drugs, trying to look at the big picture of what it took to make it back. I felt good physically, but mentally the tug-of-war was ramping up. I also couldn't stand those fucking doctors. It felt like they were parole officers—it made me sick having to talk to or even look at them.

When I flew back to Sylvan Lake to visit some family for a week or so, I got a call from one of the NHL doctors, Dave Lewis, saying he'd be in Edmonton for a meeting and wanted to see me for a review before I asked for reinstatement.

Sure Doc, where should I meet you and what time?

I'm staying at the Westin hotel. Why don't you come to my room at nine a.m.?

Sounds good—see you then.

As I was sitting there on my couch in Sylvan playing some Tiger Woods golf, I thought that since the meeting was at nine the next day and I lived an hour and a half away, I should just go to Edmonton that night, get a good night's sleep for the big meeting. So I drive to Edmonton and get a room at the Westin, thinking it would be convenient.

Oh great, now I've got that little fucker on my shoulder again, talking to me.

Hey Brantt, as long as you don't do any drugs tonight, it'll be fine. You're pretty anxious about the meeting, so just go out and have two or three beers, that's it.

Anyone who's stayed at the Westin knows the mini-bar is always stacked with some pretty cool beverages. As I open it up I get this rush of excitement—I can hardly wait to crack open a little bottle of whisky. Again, the deal I've made with myself is two or three drinks, then hit the sack. I'll be meeting Dr. Lewis at nine just down the hall, so there's no fucking way I'm going past that. That meeting will be worth about $650,000; it'll be worth all these months of complying with these assholes; it'll be a chance to get back in the show.

I call my friend Danny to meet me in the lobby. Now we're heading downtown to have one or two drinks. I believe it was at the four-drink mark when the only thing on my mind was buying some cocaine—but only one gram. I needed to be responsible, and one gram would be just the right amount to be in my bed and sleeping by midnight. It's now two a.m., and I'm having the coke dealer meet me in the hotel lobby for another two grams, since there's none left—and I'm feeling like there's more time to party and still be coherent for the big meeting at nine.

By eight thirty the next morning there were two girls in my room, chopping up what was left of the cocaine.

Danny looked at me and said, Myze, holy shit, don't you have a meeting in thirty minutes with the NHL doctor?

Why yes, I do. Don't worry about me—I'm going to take a shower then rub cologne all over my neck. He won't know a thing.

Myze, there's no fucking way he won't know—your eyes are shot and you're sweating like a pig. Just call and cancel!

I can't cancel, bud, this is my review meeting for reinstatement. I have to go.

After getting out of the shower I put my clothes on, do one more big line of blow, then throw a piece of gum in. I'm ready now. I walk up to the doctor's door and give it a knock.

Hey Brantt, come on in. Grab a seat, make yourself comfortable. Want a cup of coffee?

No, I'm all good for the coffee, thanks though.

It's just the two of us. The room is so quiet I could practically hear my thoughts racing.

So Brantt, it looks like the last nine months have gone really well. You've gone to all your meetings, you haven't had a skipped test, you've complied with everything we've asked. How are you feeling?

I'm feeling great. Sobriety has given me back my life. I've never been more content. Thank you for helping me.

All I could think was how much I hated that guy.

Okay, he said. Well, it's time for you to write to the commissioner of the NHL for reinstatement.

I'll head home and get right on it.

I could not believe my fucking ears. I didn't get busted! I was just mangled and got out of there with the green light. I head back to my hotel room and Danny is still there.

Myze, holy fuck, I can't believe you went. How did it go?

Buddy, you won't believe what just happened! It went smooth, he had no clue!

On my drive home I tried not to crash my car. I could barely see straight.

I don't have the letter, but this is close to what I wrote.

Dear Gary,

The past nine months have been the best of my life. I have never been so dedicated to sobriety as I am now. I have taken this opportunity to focus solely on getting healthy for once. I have attended five AA meetings a week, and have an AA sponsor I work with two times a week. I know that I have let the league and myself down before, but I promise you that I will not let you, the league, or myself down if you give me this opportunity to play in the NHL again.

Thank you for your time.

Brantt

I was drinking a case of beer while I wrote that letter.

I was completely out of my mind. I felt so low about myself that I didn't really feel worthy of anything good in my life. When I was drinking those beers my attitude was, Maybe if I get caught, this nightmare will end one day.

That may sound complicated, but it really wasn't. I may have been begging to be allowed back into the league. But once I was back, I'd have to fight. As long as I was suspended, I could live in what I tried to convince myself was peace. So the joke was that the league was trying to help me get sober when it was the league that made me want to get loaded and the league that made me want to stay suspended.

———

A week later I get a call from the doctors telling me that Gary Bettman had reinstated me. I got off the phone and yelled at the top of my lungs! I really didn't know what to expect. Let's just say I was ready for the worst.

I phoned Ritch and said, Let's get on the horn and start calling around. I'm ready to go and I've never felt better—I've been working out for nine months straight and I'm sober and loving it . . . (Not really sober, not really loving it.)

It wasn't long before he called to say that the Boston Bruins had just offered a two-way contract: $175 grand in the minors, $500 grand in the show. They'd talked to the doctors from the league and felt comfortable in signing me. Ritch knew I didn't want a two-way deal, but he made the case that all they had for a tough guy was P.J. Stock, and they wanted me to fill that heavyweight role. We didn't haggle this time. I took it.

I flew into Boston for training camp. Things were going pretty good. I thought so, anyway. I had a couple good scraps in the pre-season. I was sober and going to AA meetings in Boston, toeing the line for sure. I'd really given myself a chance at making the team. But from day one I never really got a good feeling from our coach, Robbie Ftorek.

On our last day of camp I got the call to see Robbie.

Brantt, he said, you've had a real good camp. But what's fucking you is that we have too many guys on one-way contracts—so we're going to have to send you down to Providence until a roster spot opens up.

Ahh, fuck you, I thought. I'd heard that one before. That's always the response they give when they send you down.

So I packed my bags and headed to their minor team in Providence, Rhode Island, with a sour taste in my mouth. I felt like I should have made that team. But when you're on a two-way contract, you're pretty much screwed. They don't tell you that when you sign your contract or when they talk to your agent—it's just the name of the game.

Still, when I got to Providence my attitude was, I'm going to stay sober and work my ass off to get called up. Getting wasted wasn't an option anyway, considering that the next stage was 4, and that there was no way Bettman would reinstate me one more time.

I opened up the 2002–03 season playing really well. Plus my coach, Mike Sullivan, was playing me a ton. So I just kept thinking that I'd soon be getting the call back up to the show. I was dusting guys up when I fought, so that wasn't an issue. And Megan was coming to visit me for a week or so each month. We always got along when I was sober.

One night we were on our way to play the Portland Pirates when I had this thought to call Rogers—before I left Canada I'd gotten a new phone and signed a new contract with them: $200 for two thousand minutes of talk time. Or so I thought.

Mr. Myhres, they said, we notice that your phone bill was very high last month.

Really? What was it, like three hundred bucks?

No, no, three thousand.

What the fuck are you talking about?

Sir, you've been averaging three thousand minutes a month at ninety-nine cents a minute. The last six months has cost you fourteen thousand.

Are you kidding me?

You see, at the end of the day, that was my fault. It was coming off my Visa, and I never check my bills. I was so irresponsible at the time that I never paid attention to that financial stuff.

But that phone call threw me off. I almost puked on the bus.

So now I'm skating around in warm-up and I'm pissed. Someone's gonna get it tonight. They had two little shit disturbers on their team: twin brothers Peter and Chris Ferraro, who would do things like stick you in the back, then hide behind a teammate. All game they were acting like rats. Then Peter two-handed one of our guys across the chest with his stick, and then after that, when our guy got out of the penalty box, Peter elbowed him in the head, and down he went.

I'm on the bench going crazy, looking over at their bench and giving them the death sign across the throat. Then I looked at our coach and said, Okay, Sully, you need to put the five toughest guys we have on this team out next shift. It's going to get nasty.

Myze, he said, are you sure you want to do this?

Yes, Sully, they're going to pay. Put the boys out and let's go to work!

So Sully put out five of our toughest guys. I don't tell anyone what I'm about to do. The puck drops and it gets shot into our end, but I skate as fast as I can the other way, right up to the other team's goalie, who must have been wondering what the hell I was doing. And I punch him right in the head, then keep pounding on him when he goes down.

It's not quite as crazy as it sounds. For one thing, goalies are pretty well protected. And for another, guys like the Ferraros need to know that when they run around like idiots, their own teammates are going to get hurt. But still. It was pretty crazy. It was a zoo out there. I was kicked out of the game.

But I was in the lineup the next night. And we'd be playing the same team. Word was their tough guy, Garret Stroshein, would be coming after me. Meanwhile our other tough guy, Steve Parsons, was back in Providence with a broken hand. I'll never forget the call he made when we were on the bus going back to Provie after the game.

Hey Myze, it's Pars. I'm playing tomorrow.

What the hell are you talking about, Pars? You have a cast on your hand.

I don't give a shit, Myze. Put Sully on the phone.

Okay then, bud. I give Sully the phone and he looks stunned.

They agreed that Steve would play.

The next night during warm-ups I see Garret staring at me, smiling. Oh great, here we go. I head to the bathroom to put Vaseline on my face, getting ready for a fight with this six-foot-seven, 250-pound monster.

We get out for our first shift. Well Myze, Stroshein says, we doin' this? You bet, Strosh, let's go.

But when I went in I lost my balance and fell back. Then, while we're in the box, we looked at each other and said, Let's go again. When we get out we drop the gloves again—and this time we start teeing off on each other. It was a great fight. Everything was back to normal for both teams.

I never did get my phone bill sorted out, though.

11

It was about middle of November when I got the call to go back to the show. I had to get a flight out to Buffalo to play the Sabres that night. I was so pumped—all the hard work had paid off and I was back in the NHL. The word was that Eric Boulton needed a shit kickin' because he'd broken P.J. Stock's face earlier in the year. They also had a tough guy named Rob Ray, a long-time killer in the NHL, so I knew it was going to be a long night.

When I got to the rink some of the excitement started to wear off. I was too nervous to really talk to anyone. And now that I was about to go out onto the ice and fight a couple of monsters in front of twenty thousand people, I realized that the guys I was sticking up for weren't really my teammates. P.J. Stock wasn't my friend. It's one thing to go into battle to defend guys who would do the same for you. But I was more like a pit bull being brought into the rink in a cage.

And what was I even fighting for? I used to think guys fought because they're brave, but I realized I was fighting because I was scared. I was trapped. Lose, and get sent back to the minors. Win, and you just have the same fear the next game. All a victory means is that you get the rest of the night off.

It's one thing to fight for a reason. That's what courage is for. But when you know you can never *really* win, that's when fear takes hold.

I get out my first shift and line up next to Boulton.

Hey Bolts, we're going . . .

Myze, I got the red light to fight. So not now—maybe in the second period.

Fuck, Bolts, I gotta go now!

But he wouldn't drop them. Finally the third period rolls around, and we're up 4–1. So I think it's a great time to address Mr. Boulton. I skate up to him. Okay, now we're goin', Eric. No more fucking around.

He skates away, though. But now Rob Ray skates up and cross-checks me in the back. I turn around and say, Okay, Razor, I'll go you instead.

Ray won't fight either—so I skate up behind him, grab him, and throw a punch. He turtles, and then it's all hell. I get a double game misconduct and two fighting majors. Don't ask me how the hell I got that, but I did.

Buffalo went on a seven-minute power play. As I was skating off to the dressing room I hear the crowd cheer: the score is now 4–2. I get into the dressing room and I hear them cheer again; it's now 4–3. I was praying they wouldn't tie the game up, which they didn't: we held on for the win. All in all, I ended up getting thirty-one penalty minutes in that one game.

When we get on the plane to fly back to Boston, I'm feeling really good about what just happened. I stuck up for our team and made it clear we weren't going to get pushed around again. I left their two heavy-weights with their tails between their legs. When the plane lands I walk right by the coach and the GM. Nothing is said. Just another night. I was still thinking all was okay. But as I'm walking off the tarmac, the equipment trainer said, Hey Myze, here's your bag. You're going to need it when you go down to Providence tomorrow.

What? I got sent down?

Yeah, they didn't tell you?

No . . . You know what? Keep my fucking bag. Take it to the dressing room, and I'll be there tomorrow.

I was so pissed that I'd been treated that way. Talk about disrespect. They never even had the decency to tell me to my face. So I show up at the rink the next day, and my hockey bag is the only one in the middle of the room. I walk into Robbie Ftorek's office and say, Robbie, why is my bag not unpacked?

We sent you down last night, Brantt.

Well, I sort of figured that out when the trainer told me, but I just wanted to hear it from the coach of this team, not the trainer. Take care, Robbie.

At that point I was just fed up with the whole process—the way they can treat you like a piece of shit at times. I felt like I wasn't ever going to get the call again to go up.

Now my head starts talking to me again. And that guy on my shoulder was getting louder and louder.

Brantt, just have a cocktail. You need to unwind after all this shit.

You're in the American Hockey League now, not the NHL, so they won't be testing you as much.

There's no way you can get caught if you don't test dirty.

Just have one, Brantt. You'll be fine this time.

A couple weeks later, at the start of December. I looked at my buddy Pars and said, Hey bud, wanna go for sushi? I was ready to roll the dice.

Sure man, I'll meet you there.

When we sit down and get ready to order I ask the waitress to bring us six shooters of vodka along with six beers. We finished those, then we ordered our food and six more drinks before dinner. The next thing I remember I'm snorting cocaine off the bar table with the owner of the restaurant. We head to the strippers and finish the night there. I think I spent about two grand that night acting like an idiot. The bear was poked and it was full steam ahead. I was on a mission.

The next morning I realized that one of the strippers had stolen my eight-thousand-dollar Rolex. Even worse, when I got to the rink I found out they'd put the A on my sweater, meaning I was now alternate captain. The coaches thought I was still sober. They thought I was a *leader*. The only way to deal with that kind of guilt is to hoist a drink.

I was partying like an animal. It's not accurate to call it partying, though. It wasn't fun anymore. There'd been a time when booze gave me a warm rush of something like joy. It used to be easy to confuse a buzz with happiness. But by the time I was wearing the A in Provie I was chasing something I knew I'd never catch up to. It was a hopeless chase. It was work. It was something I had to do.

After I did enough cocaine one night to kill a baby seal, we pulled up to a 7-Eleven to grab some mix for our booze. As my buddy Pars walked into the store I stood outside, pissing on the side of the building. All of a sudden I see my BMW going down the road with no one in it. I'd left it in drive. I was so stoned I couldn't make a sound or even move. Pars comes flying out of the store, running down the road after the car. Stuff like that was starting to happen all the time.

The first time Megan came to visit after I'd relapsed, she said I didn't look very healthy and asked if I was drinking again. No babe, I've been sober now for over a year. Little did she know the night before I'd done coke with a girl till eight a.m.

When the piss tester would come, I found out early that I wasn't going to be able to alter it in any way. He watched me piss right in the cup, so there was no getting around it. And he was supposed to show up at seven thirty the next morning.

I woke up at seven a.m. and told Megan I had to go down to the rink to get my back worked on. Instead I went right to McDonald's and sat there reading the paper while my phone went off at seven thirty-one. Fuck that. I wasn't going to answer no matter what. Later that morning I got the expected call from the NHL doctor.

Where were you this morning?

Bad back, Doc, had to have treatment this morning. I'll try next time to give the urine tester a heads-up. Sorry about that.

———

I was able to keep it together enough not to get caught the rest of the year. We ended our season in Winnipeg playing the Moose in the play-offs. I was in the hotel room the day before our last game, a potential elimination game, and a rookie by the name of Colton Orr walks in. He'd just got called up from junior.

Hey Myze, I'm rooming with you.

No problem, Orrzie. Just to give you a heads-up, I'll be going out tonight for a bit.

Aren't you playing tomorrow, Myze?

Yeah, but I'll be back before midnight. Just going for one.

I show up at six a.m., and I'm really loaded . . . so drunk that I was in my bed and had to piss but couldn't move, so I pissed the bed. Not one of my finer moments in life. When I woke up later, Orrzie was gone. I went to the bathroom to puke before I left for the pre-game skate.

When I got to the dressing room, Orrzie came up to me.

Fuck me, Myze, you were a wreck last night. Are you okay?

No, buddy, I still feel hammered. I have no idea how I'm going to play tonight.

It was the only time in my career when I was still drunk for the game. I couldn't see the ice that well and could barely skate. I was praying Sully wouldn't play me that much.

Anyway, we lost the game. Now the playoffs were over, so we headed back to Providence to have our meeting with the coaches, pack our bags, and head out for the summer. I was told that since I was the oldest, at twenty-eight, I'd be first in line for our exit meeting the next morning at nine.

So that little guy on my shoulder said, Hey Brantt, you're not getting tested tomorrow. You can rip it up for a bit, just a bit.

I call one of our rookies on the team, a first-rounder, only twenty years old, very promising future.

Hey Sammy, wanna go to Boston with me? I have to see a buddy, then come back.

Sure Myze, I'll go with you.

When we get to Boston I buy a bag of cocaine, then start driving back. Sammy looks at me and says, Myze, I know what you're doing—you're doing coke, right?

Um, yeah bud. I didn't want to do it in front of you; I know you don't do drugs.

I've never tried cocaine before. Does it make you feel good?

Oh yeah, it makes you feel amazing! Want me to chop up a line for ya?

Sure, I'll try a little one.

Well, that little one turned into me and him smoking cigarettes and doing blow till eight a.m. I looked at him and said, Buddy, shit, we have a meeting with the coaches at nine. Can you drive?

No, Myze, I can't even feel my face!

Fuck it, I'll drive. Let's go.

When we get to the rink all the head brass are there, even the GM from the big club. And I'd just drunk a bottle of Jack and snorted three grams of blow. So as I'm taking a piss in the bathroom I'm thinking, No way I'm going to make it out of this meeting without getting busted.

Just then one of our teammates came into the bathroom. Holy shit, he said, Sammy had to sign autographs on the hockey sticks and he's bleeding from his nose all over them! Is he okay or what?

I have no fucking idea about Sammy, I said. I wasn't with him last night.

Oh boy, that poor kid hung out with me for one night and now he's got a nosebleed. I wonder what he'd be like after a week.

It's nine o'clock and now it's my turn to meet with the head brass. I walk into Sully's office and there they are, all five of them with their notepads. I try to pick a chair that's the farthest away, then I sit down and put my hand over my mouth, acting like nothing's wrong.

So Myze, Sully says, first off, we just wanted to tell you how proud we are of the way you conducted yourself this year. Staying sober must have been hard considering you were down in the American Hockey League all year. Secondly, you were just awesome with the younger guys on the team—a great role model for them.

Thanks guys for the nice words. Yeah, staying sober wasn't the easiest, but I'm glad I kept it together.

Have a great summer, Brantt. Go home and work your ass off! You're only twenty-eight—there's lots of hockey left for you.

Thanks again, guys, take care.

When I left they also handed me a cheque for $80 grand, part of my bonus.

I felt so shitty about myself—so low I just wanted to hide away forever. I drove to a Chinese restaurant, thinking I'd have a bowl of soup and a beer.

Hello, the waitress says, what can I get you?

I'd like a bowl of wonton soup and a case of beer.

Pardon?

A bowl of soup and twelve beer please.

Sir, it's only eleven thirty and you want me to bring you twelve beers?

That's what I just said, didn't I?

I sat there, drank twelve beer in about an hour, and got up to go home. I'd known I needed sleep, and that the only way I could fall asleep was to drink all that booze.

I was back in Sylvan Lake that summer, but by this time Megan had had enough. She wished me the best but said she couldn't stay around and watch me kill myself. That was really hard. I knew I'd lost a great girl, and that she deserved so much better than a lying drunk like me. Part of me knew that it was unrepairable—that deep down I'd wanted her to leave. I mean, how could I expect her to keep trying to believe in the good side of Brantt?

I thought the Bruins would make me an offer by July 1, but they didn't. I was now an unrestricted free agent in more ways than one. I was on the phone quite a bit with Ritch, seeing if there was any interest out there. He said it was still early, and that he thought someone would step up to the plate.

The partying on Ravenscraig Crescent was still going strong. I literally could not be alone, so I always had someone over who was on the same demolition course I was going down. And since I had a free pass with the urine tester, who never watched me piss in the cup, I was drunk all the time. By now I'd spent almost all the money I'd made over the years. It didn't help that I hadn't collected a paycheque for almost two seasons because of the suspensions.

The $80K I'd received for a bonus was getting eaten up by my two-thousand-dollar nights. I decided to sell my ski boat to a friend and sell my two quads as well. That gave me about an extra $50K.

It was a typical night at my house—loud music, coke, strippers. The doctors had called me that day to say the piss tester would be there at nine the next morning. I'd run out of good urine, so I wasn't going to indulge in any booze or drugs. There were about five people at my place who were partying hard, but I was just having a few smokes and drinking some Red Bull. It was close to midnight and I had this girl begging me to have just one line of coke with her.

I kept saying, No, I'm good, no drugs for me tonight.

Come on, Brantt, just do one with me! Finally I'd had enough. I chopped up a line, rolled up a bill, then put my face next to the line and pretended to snort it, making it look as though I had. Then I gave her the bill.

Okay, now are you happy? I just did one.

At around five a.m. I was wanting to go to bed, so I told the girl she had to leave. Before she did she noticed the bottle of pills sitting next to my bed.

What are those?

Ah, I got them from the doctor when I felt like I was having a heart attack. They're called Ativan—they're supposed to calm you down in times of anxiety.

Do you mind if I have a couple? I'd say I qualify for some calming down!

Actually, you can take the bottle. I don't have any use for them anymore.

I lay down for a few hours till the tester showed up. It was one of the only times I wasn't waiting to see his truck turn the corner so that I could alter my urine. It sure felt good not to worry. Right at nine he knocks at the door.

Hi Brantt. The summer going good?

Yeah, it's been busy, but good busy. So, where's that cup? Let's get this finished—I have to work out in an hour.

I walk to the bathroom, piss in the cup, easy squeeze, all done, see you next week.

When I get home from the gym my phone rings.

It's some angry guy. Hey hockey boy, you like drugging girls?

What the fuck are you talking about, and who the fuck is this?

I'm Sandy's boyfriend. She's so drugged she won't wake up. I can't get her to even say a word.

And why are you calling me again? Why is this my issue?

I'm calling you because I'm going to come over to your house with a fucking bat and smash your knees in so you can't ever skate again. And if Sandy doesn't charge you with drugging her, I'm going to!

Listen here, jerk-off, I never put one pill in your girlfriend's mouth. She's twenty-five years old—I'm sure she can decide for herself what she takes. She was the one who asked me for the bottle of pills, and she was also the one who came to my house to get laid, so it's not my problem that you need to put a leash on her.

Well I know where that party house is, so I'll be over soon to take care of those knees.

Go fuck yourself.

Five minutes after I get off the phone my doorbell rings. I look out my window and it's the cops. The door opens . . .

Hey Brantt, we told you we weren't playing around with charging you if you didn't keep the partying at a low. Here are your papers. We're charging you with two counts of mischief. Your court date is set in two weeks.

Needless to say, the morning was getting off to a rough start.

———

But worse was yet to come. A few days after all that went down, I get a call from the NHL and NHLPA substance abuse doctors.

Hi Brantt, we're going to be in Calgary for the Olympic training camp. Can you meet us for breakfast on Friday morning?

Sure guys, I'll be there. It'll be good to see you.

This really did seem like a routine meeting. There was no way they could prove I'd relapsed. Maybe they heard from an outside source that I was using again, but they needed proof, which they had none of, so I felt at ease this time.

I get to Calgary and pull into the Westin hotel to park, with really no anxiety about the meeting. I mean, what could be so bad? I'd stayed clean the past week or so.

They'd wanted to meet at Starbucks, just down the road from the hotel. When I sat down, I could see that this was not routine at all.

Brantt, we're going to get right at the point of this meeting. You tested positive for cocaine again. What do you have to say for yourself?

What do you mean positive for cocaine? I haven't done any cocaine in over a year.

The tests don't lie, Brantt. There were traces of cocaine in your system. Want to tell us the truth for once?

I swear to you, I never did any cocaine! It's impossible for this to be happening.

Okay, Brantt, is there anything you have left to tell us before we make our decision on your future in hockey?

Okay, okay, I'll tell you exactly what happened last week. I had this girl over at my house and she was begging me to do a line of coke with her. I told her all night I wasn't going to be doing any drugs, so lay off. She kept bugging me, so I finally grabbed the straw and pretended to do the line of coke.

What?

It's the truth, I swear . . . Out of all the times I lied to you in the past, I promise you, this time I'm telling the truth!

Brantt, it really sounds like you're losing your mind if you expect us to believe you *pretended* to do cocaine. We've just made the decision to suspend you, Stage 4.

This is so fucking wrong. I'm telling you guys the truth!

Listen, Brantt, this stage, no one's ever been in it, so we don't know what that looks like at the end. We suggest that you take some time for yourself, take time to reflect on what you want to do from here on in.

What do you mean "what I want to do"? I want to play hockey, I don't know what else to do, you guys.

Brantt, we can't see you making your way out of this, and even if you did complete the full-year suspension, we're not that sure the commissioner would reinstate you after he just reinstated you a year ago. Not to mention that we've spent more money on you and your rehabs than anyone else in the NHL. It's time you just walk away and call it a day.

I got up from the table with tears in my eyes. I was walking back to the hotel to get my truck when I saw Eric Lindros walking towards me—the Olympic team must have been staying at the same hotel. I turned around and started walking in the other direction. I didn't want him to see me in that condition, I was so embarrassed.

When the coast was clear I jumped in my truck and called my grandma. I always called her when I was going through a rough time in my life. I cried to her on the phone for two hours.

Grandma, I just got suspended for the fourth time by the league, I'm so screwed, I feel like dying right now.

Now, now, sweetheart, you just worry about getting sober. You've been doing this long enough. It's time you start to turn your life around for good before you do die.

Later I called Ritch. I told him what had happened and that I was willing to do whatever it took to make it back from Stage 4.

Brantt, I've talked to the doctors. They recommend that you get a job and forget about hockey.

Ritch, there's no way I'm going to give up as long as there's hope . . .

Okay, well, I've stood by you this long. I'll let them know in a week or so. It's still really fresh for everyone, so let's talk in a week.

I was so down when I got back to my house. I had two thoughts running through my head: one, if I kept drinking I'd end up killing myself from the shame, and two, get my ass to AA and start turning my life around. I picked up the phone and called the AA hotline. They told me about a meeting in Red Deer that night.

When I got there I was pretty bummed out. I had my head down the whole time. I was sitting next to this guy named Rob. We started chatting, and the more we talked the more I realized all that we had in common. He'd been sober for seven years, he told me, and went to a lot of meetings. He shared his story of having everything going for him—great business, lots of money—but how the drugs and booze had brought him to his knees.

I left that meeting feeling so much better. I'd felt totally defeated, and the only thing that helped was speaking in that AA meetings in an honest way. It took a huge load off my shoulders. I made a decision to hit meetings with Rob during the next week.

The day came for my court date. As I stood in front of the judge, I explained that I was an alcoholic, that I was truly sorry about what I'd done, and that I intended to get help. He said that if I committed to going away and getting help, he wouldn't convict me. Instead he would ask that I pay a thousand dollars to a charity of my choice. And sell my house.

Sell my house?

Yes. All your neighbours want you gone. So put your house on the market as soon as possible.

Of course, I agreed.

I decided to go home to Cold Lake to spend a few days with my grandparents. I really felt hopeless. I couldn't see a way out. Hockey was gone. Megan was gone. My house and boat—gone.

I headed to a bar to ease the anxiety. At midnight I was snorting cocaine on the hood of a car with this girl. We decided to go to her house to continue the party.

Me and the girl went upstairs to do more coke. By the time it was all gone it was about seven a.m. and I could barely talk from being so stoned. I walked downstairs. There was a guy sitting in a chair in the hallway smoking a small pipe. I asked if he had any more coke.

No man, there's no powder left. Why don't you take a hit of this?

What is it?

It's hard coke, it's crack.

Man, I've never done that before, what does it make you feel like?

Dude, it makes you feel amazing. Just try it.

I grab the pipe, put the lighter to it, and pull back a hit. As soon as I blow it out, I fall to the floor. I grab the chair. I can feel my heart pumping through my chest. I get up, saying to myself, Brantt, you need to go for a walk.

As I'm walking down the road towards the beach, my hands start to drip with sweat and I can't swallow.

I get to the beach and sit down on the curb. My head starts to feel like it's going crazy. I can't process a normal thought other than this little voice saying, Brantt, if you don't go get help, you're going to die here on the street.

It's now Sunday morning about nine o'clock. I get up off the curb, walk to this house, and knock on the door. A lady opens the door. I see her husband making breakfast.

Hi, how can I help you?

I'm not doing too good. Could you help me please?

What do you mean you're not doing good?

I'm having an overdose—please call the ambulance.

She yells for her husband, and he comes to the door.

Oh my god, he says. Okay, I'll call the ambulance. Just wait on the steps, they should be here real soon.

I guess they didn't want a six-foot-four addict ODing in their house.

The ambulance shows up, and once the paramedics have checked me out, they help me into the back. As the driver pulls out he glances in the rear-view mirror and says, Brantt, is that you?

It was my grade seven teacher, Mr. McKenzie.

Oh, hi Mac. It's been quite a while, hey?

So Brantt, why don't you tell me what you did last night?

I did about three grams of cocaine, smoked a joint, and took a hit off a crack pipe. How about you?

I didn't do any of those things, but when we get you to the hospital they'll take care of you, don't worry.

They'd better pump my stomach because I'm dying here.

Like I said, don't worry, they'll take care of you.

When I get to the hospital they put me in a room and tell me to take my shirt off. Soon the curtain opens, and it's my aunt. She was a nurse there.

Brantt! Are you okay?

No, Auntie, I'm having a rough morning.

I didn't know this till later, but she went and called my grandparents, who came to the ER room to wait for me.

The doctor appeared, told me to open my mouth and put a couple Ativans under my tongue. After he'd gone I lay my head down on the pillow. I was getting a bit cold since they'd taken my shirt off to run some tests on my heart.

The doctor returned about thirty minutes later and asked how I was doing.

I'm still feeling like I'm really out of it. Is there anything you can do?

Yes, open up your mouth again. He put another pill under my tongue and then left.

Within five minutes the lights went out.

I woke up six hours later feeling like a bag of shit, to say the least.

My grandparents had left a few hours earlier, so I called a cab and went home. When I walked through the door they were sitting in the living room. I walked by them and said, Please don't say anything. I know I fucked up. I just need some sleep. They were good about it and never said a word.

After that night I knew I'd missed my date with death. It was time to finally change and get sober.

When I got back to Sylvan I called Dan Cronin. We ended up talking for two hours. I told him what had happened, and that if they didn't help me I was going down a real bad path. He said he'd phone the NHL doctors and see what he could do for me.

Later that night he called to say that they had agreed to give me the opportunity to complete Stage 4.

12

This time I had to find my own rehab. I went to three or four before I stumbled across a place called Herbert House in Marina del Rey. When I walked in, there was this guy sitting at the desk playing his guitar. He looked at me and said, Hey bro, how ya doin'? If you're thinking of a place to stay, this place is awesome! I've loved every minute here, everyone is so cool. My name is Derek. What's yours?

So Derek, what do you do for a living?

I played guitar in a few bands; I'm playing in one now. I had a massive heroin addiction, but I've been six months sober. Never felt better!

That's awesome, man. I'm a hockey player, but I just got suspended for the fourth time. I really need a place I can feel safe in. If they reinstate me, it'll be my last chance—there is no Stage 5.

Well man, me and you will hang. It's all going to be okay.

So I checked into sober living. I was staying in a little room—there were four of us staying in one room. I had a top bunk.

I'd wake up every morning and go to an AA meeting. Later I'd hit the gym, then go back for dinner, and finally I'd hit another AA meeting after dinner.

During one meeting I met a guy named Joe Manganiello—one of the only guys bigger than me. After a few times chatting I asked him if he wanted to go boxing with me, 'cause I needed a partner. Joe was this big teddy bear, an actor who was on the same path as me, wanting to resurrect his career. So we hit it off pretty quick.

I got set up at Bob Dylan's boxing gym, where we'd go twice a week to train. Our trainer, David, would always say no head shots. But we were both too competitive for that, so we'd add in the odd head shot from time to time.

Each week I had to see a therapist, named Gary Fisher, who turned out to be the first therapist I really opened up to. I could tell him anything. But he was really good at calling me on my bullshit, which I needed big-time. For whatever reason, opening up to Gary felt different. I could talk to him about my underlying embarrassment over all the bad decisions I'd made. And how I felt about some of my family members—old pain that wouldn't go away. So for me this was a real breakthrough in trying to be as honest as I could.

Back at Herbert House, me and Derek would be going to meetings together; I'd also go watch him and his band rehearse. We were becoming real close as buddies.

A few months went by and things were rolling along pretty smoothly. I'd see the NHL doctors at least once a week to check in. It was an amazing feeling to meet with them and have nothing to hide or lie about. It was at about the six-month mark when I got some real bad news.

When Derek had been sober for nine months, it was his time to leave. He moved in with his girlfriend and, as I later found out, stopped going to meetings. One night I looked at my cell phone and saw that I had a missed call from him.

I checked my voice messages . . .

Hey Brantt, it's Derek. My head's all fucked up, man, could you give me a call?

I called him right away and it went straight to voice mail.

I didn't really think much of it till I got a call the next day saying that Derek had overdosed from heroin. He was dead.

I was in total shock. I'd thought he was doing so good—I mean, we'd been hanging out just a week before he left the house.

I was told that when you put anything ahead of your sobriety, you'll end up losing it in the end—and that even means your life. So when I heard that Derek hadn't been going to any AA meetings I guess it all made sense, but that didn't take away the fact that I was devastated. Part of the recovery experience is the closeness you feel with the people who go through it with you.

When I first went to AA I hated it. I hated the idea that I had anything in common with those losers. I didn't want to be a loser. But they weren't losers, and I wasn't different. We were all just people trying to figure out something much more powerful than we were. There's nothing like having your ass kicked by booze and drugs to teach you humility. None of us has any reason to think we're better than anyone else.

But the bond goes a lot deeper than that. Only fellow addicts know what we've been through together. Other people may love you, but they don't understand. It's stupid, and it's unfair, but we turn away from those who don't understand us. Maybe we feel that if our friends and family did understand us, they'd stop caring about us. That means the only people whose love means something for sure are fellow addicts. They already know the worst about you.

It's probably a bit like guys who've served together in the military. You may come from different backgrounds and be different in pretty much every way. But if you've gone through something horrible together, you're brothers. That's what it felt like to lose a guy like Derek. It may look to the outside as though we were just roommates for a while. But losing a brother like that cuts deep.

True sobriety was new to me. For once in my life I felt as if I could live without booze or drugs. Before that, it didn't seem possible. But around the seven-month mark of the suspension year, I was starting to wonder what was going to happen when nine months were up. I was keeping my mouth shut during the process, but I have to admit it was nerve-racking spending all this time in sober living not knowing what my future was going to be.

I received a call from Ritch saying that Darryl Sutter from the Calgary Flames was calling about me, asking how I was doing. I'd always loved Darryl, who'd supported me through thick and thin when I was in San Jose. Now he was saying that if I was on the straight and narrow he'd be interested in signing me. Hearing that made the last months worth every second. I respected Darryl more than anyone in the game. So at that point I was determined to do anything it took to sign on that dotted line with the Flames.

I was shopping at Fred Segal in Santa Monica one day when I went outside to get some sun and saw a guy having a smoke.

Hey man, I said, I see you're smoking Canadian cigs. You from Canada?

You bet, I'm from Halifax. Name's Eli—I'm a hairdresser in L.A. Where are you from?

I'm from Edmonton, just down here doing some work.

What kind of work?

I'm training for the upcoming hockey season.

Really? That's cool. I love hockey!

You're a hairdresser and you love hockey? That's pretty rare, pal. Tell you what, next time I need a haircut I'll book with you.

About two weeks later I got my hair cut from Eli. We just hit it off—and he was the only guy around I could talk hockey with. Little did I know he'd become my best friend. It's funny how timing is everything.

My year suspension was up and I was ready to see where I stood. There was talk that there may be a lockout in the NHL, and if that happened I couldn't afford to miss another season without playing. It was time for me to have a talk with the doctors on my status. I'd been waiting and working one full year for this moment.

Ritch called them and explained that Darryl Sutter had said he would sign me for the 2004–05 season if I received clearance from the league.

It was now one week from the start of training camp, but it looked like the league and the players' union were miles away from getting a deal done. After having a two-hour meeting with the doctors, we came up with a plan. If there was an NHL lockout they'd let me sign a deal with the Calgary Flames, but only an AHL deal, since of course you couldn't sign an NHL contract during a lockout. The NHL doctors also said that once the lockout was over I could ask the commissioner for reinstatement. I was totally okay with that—having more sobriety time under my belt would only help my chances of getting back in. And after being away from hockey a full year, I couldn't wait to get back to playing. I say "playing," but what I really mean is I couldn't wait to start getting a paycheque.

Still, the prospect of returning to hockey brought back the reality that I'd have to go back to uncaging the animal again—and that wasn't a maybe, it was a guarantee. Yes, having to spend all that time in sober living was difficult, but it was also a huge relief not having to get punched in the face either. Rehab was the only place where I didn't have to fight.

The NHL and the players' union ended up locking out, so now the players in Calgary's system were headed to Lowell, Massachusetts, along with players from the Carolina Hurricanes. I had no idea where the hell Lowell even was! I was told it was this little town forty-five minutes from Boston, and that they had a new rink and supported the team pretty good.

I pack up my bags and jump a plane to Lowell. When I get there I meet the boys. From the Flames team we had quite the lineup:

Mark Giordano	Richie Regehr
Mike Commodore	Carsen Germyn
Chuck Kobasew	Matthew Lombardi
Craig MacDonald	Brent Krahn

The Carolina players were an impressive bunch as well:

Eric Staal	Chad LaRose
Cam Ward	Ryan Bayda
Gordie Dwyer	Matt Hendricks
Colin Forbes	

Needless to say, we had a stacked team. Most of these guys would have been in the NHL if there was no lockout. Plus, our coach, Tom Roe, seemed like a straight shooter: very honest, and he liked players who played the way I did.

So when I was in the dressing room for our first practice, I had the biggest smile on my face. I was back to playing the game I love. Even though it wasn't my end goal of the NHL, I was on my way.

Meanwhile there was absolutely nothing to do in Lowell, which, looking back, was a good thing. My buddy Carsen would come over and I'd make Shake 'n Bake chicken, with those fake instant mashed potatoes. We'd play video games—*Tiger Woods PGA Tour*, or *ATV Offroad Fury*— all night long. He was pretty much the guy I hung around with the most. Since I wasn't drinking alcohol, I started chewing tobacco like it was bubble gum—there was nothing better than throwing in a big dip and playing vids. If the boys ever wanted to go out for a night on the town, we had to go to Boston. A lot of the times when we didn't play for a couple days, we'd just head in to hit a nice restaurant and a movie, then drive back to Lowell.

I was dead set on being the toughest son of a bitch in the league. I didn't want any hesitation from Calgary when the lockout ended. We played our first game against Providence, my old team. They had my old roommate Colton Orr playing for them. I heard before the game that Colton was mopping up the AHL killing guys and that he was going to be coming after me, so be ready. I was like, Yeah, well, we're good buddies, so what if I pissed the bed that one night in Winnipeg when we roomed together? He won't ask me to fight tonight.

When Tom sends me out for my first shift, I look to my right and see only Orr coming off the bench. Hmm. He lines up next to me.

Hey Myze, how are ya?

I'm doin' good, Orrzie.

Real good to see you back playing hockey, congrats.

Thanks bud.

Well Myze, I've got to go ya. When the puck drops we're gonna go, okay?

Orrzie, you don't want to play a shift or two first?

Nah, let's just go now and play after.

All right then, Orzzie, I'll go ya, but don't jump me.

The puck drops and he starts swinging away. Fuck! I can hear these bombs graze by my head, he's got a real good hold of my left hand, and everyone knows I can't throw rights, so I'm pretty much screwed. He hits me pretty hard, I go down to one knee, and the refs are going to come in, but I get up, tug my left arm out of my jersey, and start swinging hard lefts. I hit him with two or three and he covers up. Fight's over.

It was one of the first times I've ever felt like I was going to lose bad. Orr had such a good grip on my left arm that I couldn't break loose, and if it wasn't for my arm slipping out of my jersey it would have ended pretty bad for me. At no point did I think for a second that he may lay a beating on me. I mean, I was in great shape physically and mentally. But to be a good fighter, you have to want to fight. I had to admit it: Orrzie was hungrier than I was.

A couple months had passed and I was just loving playing in Lowell. I'd always hated playing in the AHL, but this time I really enjoyed it. We had such a great team—all these kids were really lighting it up.

Eric Staal was a nineteen-year-old who could practically fly. Cam Ward was a young goalie with incredible talent. These were guys who weren't far away from winning a Stanley Cup. It just seemed like we were all on the same page and clicked.

My parents weren't perfect. But neither am I. I have hurt people I have loved, so my parents' imperfections are no reason for me to judge what was in their hearts. That's me and my mother with my sister Cher on the couch up top. And that's me and my dad at the rink below. We didn't always get along, but he supported my hockey dreams with everything he had.

I went through a lot of upheaval when I was a kid, and long after I was a kid. My grandparents were there for me no matter what. They picked me up again and again. I am glad they were also there for the good times. That's grandpa and grandma with me and Roman Hamrlik, my teammate in Tampa. He was a star, and I was a tough guy. We traded a few punches in our first scrimmage, but became great buddies after that.

All I cared about was hockey. Life was complicated, but hockey made sense, and when I wasn't on the ice, I was dreaming of getting back out there. My teachers had a hard time keeping me focused in class, because I spent that time practicing my autograph for when I made the NHL. More than one told me I'd never make it.

In minor hockey, I was a scorer. In junior, I was just big. I got in a scrap my very first scrimmage, and I just kept scrapping. In my draft year, I had the most penalty minutes of anyone my age. When you're a lonely small-town teenager living far from home, you're kind of lost. On the ice, though, I was in control. I controlled the whole rink with my aggression, and I loved it. The top photo is of me in Lethbridge, getting ready to put on a show. Back then we used to take off our helmets when we dropped our gloves. And the bottom photo was taken in the dressing room in Spokane. I guess I'd had a good game.

For a while I was on top of the world. I was young, I had money, pretty much every door was open to me, and I was literally living my dreams. At the top, that's me and David Letterman. I travelled to New York with Eric Lindros in a limo when he was on the show. At the top-right, that's me during warm-ups in Philly. I played some good hockey there, and the fans loved the way I played. And at the bottom is me with my childhood idol, Wayne Gretzky. When I was a kid, I actually begged the Oilers' equipment staff for a wad of tape The Great One had peeled off his stick and tossed on the floor. I kept it by my bed. It wasn't long before I was drinking a few beers with Wayne at his brother's wedding, and talking hockey.

First square off

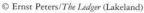

■ Tampa Bay Lightning right winger Brantt Myhres, left, squares off with St. Louis Blues left winger Tony Twist in the first period Tuesday at the Lakeland Civic Center in the Lightning's first preseason game and the Blues' second. The Lightning lost 7-1. Story, photos, 1D

© Ernst Peters/*The Ledger* (Lakeland)

Lock Monster Brantt Myhres (74) squares off with Providence Bruin Colton Orr in a main event bout at Tsongas Arena last night.

Bang-up beginning

Goals, fights, shootout – and a Monster win

© David Selenius/*The Lowell Sun*

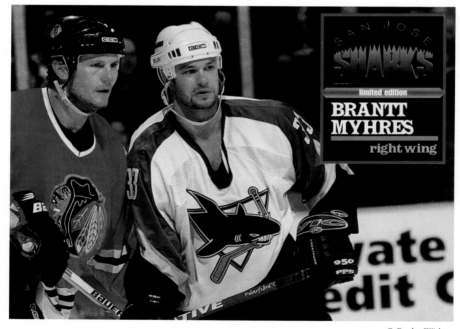

© Rocky Widner

When I was a kid, I loved scoring goals. But that wasn't my job in the NHL. My job there was to tangle with guys as big and as tough as I was. Before I even made the opening-night roster in Tampa I squared off with legendary killer Tony Twist, and when I was in the minors on the way out, I had to drop the gloves with my former teammate Colton Orr. People think NHL heavyweights are mean, but they're mostly smart, funny, gentle guys. Most hate fighting. That's me and all-time champ Bob Probert at the bottom, talking about avoiding fighting each other. We were good buddies off the ice. Bob would do anything for his teammates, but fighting took a real toll on the big guy. It took a toll on all of us.

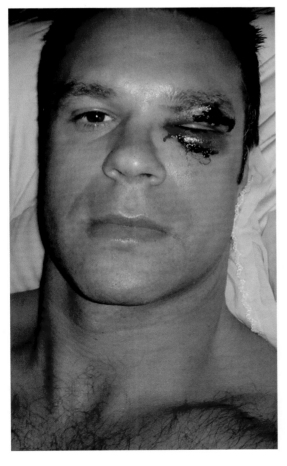

Hockey gave me everything I dreamt of. But it very nearly killed me. Not that I blame the game for my own bad choices. But violence and fear, and booze and drugs, lured me into a life that would cost me nearly everything. That photo at the top is me and a bunch of buddies raging at my summer house in Sylvan Lake. We did that pretty much every night, strippers and cocaine included, even though I was being monitored by the league's substance abuse program. Finally a judge forced me to sell the place to save the neighbourhood. At the bottom, that's my face after my last NHL fight—a broken orbital bone courtesy of Georges Laraque. Strange to say, the embarrassment hurt more than the damage to my skull.

When you're at the bottom, it's hard to clean up if you're doing it just for yourself. If there is one thing that doesn't seem worth it, it's yourself. But you can do it for someone else. I was every bit as proud to make it back to the NHL as part of the Kings' staff as I was to be drafted, and I was very happy to be able to help others where I had stumbled so spectacularly. That's Chloe and her brother with Kings' defenceman and all-round good guy Drew Doughty. The bottom left photo is me and Chloe at her first NHL game. She couldn't believe that used to be my job. On the right, we are doing my favourite thing—just hanging out together. I would fight any battle for her.

I still had to fight, though. There was a guy by the name of Jeff Paul who played for Portland, and I swear this guy was insane—every time we played each other he'd ask me to go. Go fuck yourself Paulz, I'd say. I want to play tonight.

No, no, I've got to go ya!

All right, just this once, then fuck off.

After about ten lefts to his face the fight was over.

This guy would be sitting in the penalty box with an ice bag on his forehead, looking at me and pointing at centre ice, wanting to fight again.

Paulz, are you serious, you want to fight again?

Yeah, just give me one more shot.

After we get out of the penalty box, we find each other out on the ice together. I feel this stick whack me in the pants. Hey, you ready?

Jesus, yeah, fine, let's go. Last time I'm fighting you tonight.

The same thing, ten punches to his face, down he goes. Then he has the fucking nerve to get up off the ice and say, You won this time, but we play you in five days and we're gonna go again!

I couldn't believe this guy. No matter how bad a beating I gave him, he'd always come back for more. I kind of respected that, to be honest.

It was around November and still no NHL—the lockout was going strong with no end in sight. There were rumours, though, that they'd end it by the middle of January, with just enough time to salvage half the season. Meanwhile we were first in the league, and having a blast every day going to the rink. On our way to play Manchester, the Los Angeles Kings farm team, some of the guys were talking about this George Parros guy, saying he was a Princeton grad and that he was tough.

Yeah right, I call bullshit on that one . . . You're telling me this Einstein can also fight the big boys?

Yeah, he's like six five and 225 pounds, and he can really go.

I didn't pay much attention to it. Throughout my career I've heard of lots of players who thought they were tough guys until they get knocked out a couple times, then the show's over.

I get out for my first shift and I hear this guy say, Yo, big man, wanna go? It's Parros.

You bet I do, you big fuck!

We square off at centre ice and come together. I throw a punch and he goes down. I don't think I connected with a hard one; it was more that he lost his balance. The next time we get out against each other, I find him and give him a cross-check in the chest. You ready to finish this, Georgie?

We square off again and this time I come in wanting to knock his fucking head off. I swear I must have hit that pumpkin six to eight hard bombs right in the face and he didn't go down! So I pull back and hit him as hard as I could—and immediately wish I'd missed. I could feel my thumb hanging off to the side. The refs came in and I knew I was in trouble.

When I went to Boston the next day for X-rays, the doctor said things didn't look very good. It turned out that I'd torn the tendon off the bone and needed surgery in a couple days to repair it. I was really bummed out, particularly because the NHL could have started playing again and I'd still be in a cast. That said, I'd been sober for fifteen months and back playing hockey with at least a solid chance to get back to the show.

Surgery is not something to be undertaken lightly by anyone who's trying to stay away from drugs. When they put the IV in my arm, I could feel serenity radiating from the needle—a soothing warmth that washed away the stresses of everyday life like rain erasing a child's chalk drawing from the sidewalk. I woke up from surgery remembering the same delirious relief coming over me after a long, thirsty haul from a bottle of Jack or a fat line of coke making the world seem perfect. It reminded me of laughing more than I had in the past months, wanting to love more, to dance more. In other words, the first thing I thought about when I woke up was getting that IV back into my arm.

But I wasn't a complete idiot. I'd made plenty of mistakes, but at least I'd learned that the happiness you pour down your throat or stuff up your nose is an illusion. The happiness you get from scratching your way back to your dreams may not be as thrilling as getting fucked up. But it lasts a lot longer, and it doesn't leave you feeling like a piece of garbage. I felt as though I'd faced down temptation as I walked out of the hospital. I would take the long, hard grind over the easy thrill of drugs and booze.

And I've got to be honest: a hockey fight is a pretty big rush anyway. It wasn't as though I was going *completely* clean. My line of work was probably about as exciting and dangerous as skydiving and race-car driving put together. I mean, anyone who's ever been in a bar fight can tell you it's a huge buzz. A bare-knuckle scrap against the absolute toughest guy an NHL team can find to put out on the ice, in front of twenty thousand people—that's addictive too.

Which doesn't mean you necessarily like it. But it does mean you need it. If I wanted a real rush, I needed to get back to the game. That plan never changed.

I talked to the NHL doctors and my team to see if it was okay to go home for a week, and they gave me the green light. So I flew home to see my grandparents. I'd always loved being at Grandma's when I was feeling a bit down. I still wasn't talking to my mom or my dad, and to tell you the truth, in a way it seemed to me like they were dead. I know that may sound harsh, but at that time I had so much resentment towards them that I had no more feeling left. Sure, I loved them somewhere inside this soul, but I couldn't get to it.

My father pulled some stunts that you just don't do as a father. Here's an example. I'd bought a $10,000 quad that I kept at my grandparents' garage when I played. I got a call from my grandpa saying there were people there to pick it up.

Grandpa, what the hell are you talking about?

They say you signed away the quad in exchange for a $5000 loan.

The fuck I did . . .

I know, son. It's not your signature, it's your dad's.

That was a real heartbreaker for me. I never thought my dad would stoop that low with his son. It was always money with him. My attitude was, Why the fuck are you coming to *me* for money, Dad? Isn't that a bit backwards? You're not in a wheelchair, you can work, so go work your ass off, save your money, and if I need a dollar maybe I'll ask you. How's that?

Not that I was the perfect son.

What I go back to is unconditional love. When I was in rehab my dad came to see me only one time, whereas my grandparents never gave up on me, never lost touch. I never resented him for steering me towards the tough-guy role. It wasn't all bad. I had some of my dreams come true. So I don't want to sit here and say that making the NHL was brutal. It was fucking amazing, and I wouldn't change a thing. Was there a tradeoff with the fighting? Yes. I get it. But I made it to the National Hockey League, and it doesn't get any better than that. I guess I just wanted that type of love from my father.

Two months passed. It was now January 2005, my cast was off, and still no NHL. They had weeks to salvage half the year, and if not they'd be shutting the doors for the whole season, which hadn't happened before. Now I was sort of hoping for that, just so I could recover from my injury. And as it happened, the NHL and the NHLPA couldn't come to terms and the season was cancelled. For me it also meant making $75 grand for the year—that was the AHL deal I signed. All that other stuff didn't matter. All that mattered was that I had sixteen months of real sobriety. And I was loving my time in Lowell. For once, I was really having fun playing the game.

Later that February we went into Norfolk, Virginia, to play the Chicago Blackhawks farm team. One of their players, Jim Vandermeer, was running around taking liberties with one of our goal scorers. So when the second period came to an end and all the players were skating off the ice to hit the dressing rooms for intermission, I skated over to Jim and gave him a little cross-check to the chest.

Hey Jimmy, you better stop fucking runnin' around or I'm gonna knock you silly.

Fuck you, Myze, I'm just playing hard.

I don't care how hard you think you're playing, do it again and you'll answer to me.

The refs ended up getting in there and splitting us up. It was over, so all the guys started skating off the ice.

All of a sudden I hear, Holy shit, T-Roe is in a fight! That was a nickname for our coach. I turn around and see him and the head coach for the other team, Trent Yawney, getting into a scuffle at centre ice. I undo my tiedown so that I can get out of my sweater if I need to and yell, Boys, let's go!

Now both teams are pouring back onto the ice. I get into the pile, punch someone right in the face, and next thing you know, all hell is breaking loose.

Someone punches me in the side of my head and I go down. All I remember is Shawn Thornton from the other team grabbing my hands and pulling them in—there were skates all over the place, and I guess he didn't want my fingers to get cut off. Then I hear this scream: one of the linesmen had broken his ankle in the pileup and they were carrying him off the ice.

As I stand up, all I hear is, Fuck you, Brantt, you started all this shit.

It was Yawney, standing right in front of me.

Ahh, fuck you, Trent, you pussy.

He kept giving it to me. I guess he was a pretty brave guy—he'd have to be, yapping away at someone who didn't put up with much yapping. I had to decide what I was going to do. I mean, it was just me and the coach. He was in his suit and tie, and I had my skates on. Do I hit him or just skate away?

Fuck it. I grab him by his tie and punch him right in the face . . .

down he goes. Then I get punched in the back of my head, and down I go again. Meanwhile our goalie Cam Ward was going toe to toe with the other goalie.

It was by far the craziest game I've ever been a part of. Both coaches got eight-game suspensions. I got an eight-game suspension as well. It was a night I'll never forget.

That August the NHL and NHLPA finally came to an agreement. The lockout was officially over. So I phoned Ritch and asked if he could give Darryl a call—I wanted to see whether there was interest in signing me to an NHL contract.

Ritch was like, Brantt, I think you should get clearance from the league first before we start calling teams.

True, I said. I'll talk to the doctors and get this going.

Dear Gary,

I wanted to start out this letter with some facts. I currently have two years sober, and have attended AA meetings on a regular basis over the last two years. I spent nine months in treatment, in which I gained a whole new level of respect for how to live sober and how to conduct myself as an honest person in society. I have an AA sponsor who I am in contact with regularly. I saw a therapist once a week for a full year. We worked on my childhood trauma, and why I have self-sabotaged my career up to this point. I have never missed a urine test in two years, and have always been upfront and honest with the NHL and NHLPA doctors.

Over the last two years I had a lot of time to reflect on my life and where it had ended up. Ever since I was four years old I knew I wanted to play hockey in the NHL. What I didn't know was that I suffered from a disease, called addiction. The only way I felt I could cope with life was to drink or take a drug. With that came a life of dishonesty and shame. I realize that I wrote you a letter a couple years ago to be reinstated from Stage 3. I was not in a good place back then. I was still struggling with the fact that I was an alcoholic. I couldn't face that fact.

Today I am here to tell you that I am no longer in a struggle. I accept my disease, and have taken the necessary steps to recover. I'm asking for one last chance. Mr. Bettman, I know there is no Stage 5, and that this would be my last chance. I will not let the NHL or myself down. I will make everyone involved glad they stood by my side during this journey. Please consider reinstatement so that I can play again.

I thank you for your time, and look forward to hearing from you.

Brantt

It was now September 10 and NHL training camp was about to open. I got a call from the doctors letting me know that they felt everything was going to be okay—it was just the logistics that needed to be worked out. The Calgary Flames agreed to bring me in until I was cleared, then I would sign an NHL contract.

When I got the news I was floored, totally overwhelmed with joy. It had taken me two years of hard work for this opportunity, and I'd done it all on faith—there were no guarantees I'd even play again. I'd been working my ass off in training camp waiting for that call. We'd played our first exhibition game and I still wasn't cleared, then we played our second, then third, then fourth, and no clearance. I was getting frustrated, calling them, What the hell is going on, guys? I need to play here, can we get this done?

Now I looked at the schedule and noticed we were playing the Edmonton Oilers the next day. That was the only time I prayed not to be cleared to play. They had the NHL heavyweight champ on their team, Georges Laraque, who was six four, about 270 pounds, and had a left hand that could really hurt someone. No one was able to beat Georges. I'd worked hard for months. Now my reward was to be thrown to the lions.

Still, I went to the rink the next day figuring it would be like any other day. Darryl Sutter walked into the dressing room and sat down beside me.

Congrats, Myze, they cleared you to play. Real proud of you. I hope you're ready 'cause you're playing tonight . . .

I almost puked right there. I got up and went to my truck to head back to the hotel.

I loved fighting. I hated fighting. I honestly did not know whether what I'd received was good news or bad. I was exhilarated and proud, no question. I was terrified, too. On my way I called my dad and a couple friends, telling them the good news and that if they wanted to catch the game they better get there quick.

Yeah, I called my dad. Despite everything we'd been through, I still wanted to talk to him.

When I got back to the hotel I couldn't stomach the pre-game meal. Couldn't even think about swallowing food. I just went to my room, jumped into bed, and rolled up. All I could think about was fighting Georges at seven p.m. in front of nineteen thousand people. If I lose I'm going to get cut from the team. How will I look to all my friends and family? Will I hit my head on the ice and die? I couldn't control these thoughts.

Then something happened to me that had never happened before.

I've already said that fighting is a rush. It's an addiction. The reason it's a rush is that you never know how it's going to turn out. It's like gambling. You can make all the right moves and still lose a lot of money in Vegas. You can be a good fighter and still get your ass kicked.

And when you're squaring off with Georges Laraque, chances are you're holding a bad card. It's one thing to gamble, and another to deliberately step in front of a freight train. Georges outweighed me by over fifty pounds, so that comparison is not altogether misleading.

I started shaking in bed. And not like a little shake—I could barely stay still. I knew at that time in my life that I'd crossed the edge, the point of no return. I had to stop this, but how? I hate fighting, what the fuck am I doing? Am I just doing this for the money? The prestige? Brantt, don't put yourself through this anymore, you've been fighting since you were sixteen years old and the role has destroyed you.

I lay there and shook for two hours. Then I got up and drove to the rink. On the way I stopped at Burger King to try and put a burger down my throat. It wouldn't go down.

At the rink it felt like everything was in slow motion. Everything looked familiar—and on one level I felt a sense of gratitude that I was back in an NHL rink. The luxury dressing room, the trainers and physiotherapists, the cooks and other polite staff. The tidy rolls of tape, the snacks laid out. But on another level, it felt like I wasn't even there. It was as though I was seeing all these things through someone else's eyes. Or even worse, seeing it through a camera mounted on someone else's helmet. I was there and not there. It was sickening lurching through familiar routines as though they were someone else's.

Warm-ups start and I can't even see straight. I don't remember one thing about warm-ups. It's now seven p.m. and we skate out to the ice. I have enough Vaseline on my face to fill a bathtub. The game starts and I'm shaking on the bench, everything just slowed down. I'd fought hundreds of times before. Never had I felt anything like this panic. I'd fought Laraque himself before and never felt this kind of panic.

The game wasn't even three minutes old when Sutter sent me over the boards.

Not two seconds later I heard Georges's distinctive gravelly voice: Hey Brantt, let's go.

We square off. I see he has his left hand cocked. His chin looks like it's within reach.

I decide to risk everything on one devastating left. I put everything I've got into it.

But he's backing up already. I can see that my opening salvo is going to come up just short of his chin. I reach with my right to get a hold of him, but he's still retreating.

I can't get a grip on his sweater. Now I'm off balance, leaning in, and Laraque's left is free.

Then everything goes black.

Everything is quiet, except the little voice in my head that says, Get up. Start throwing.

I get up off my knees and fire off a left. Then it all goes black again. The next thing I remember is Georges on top of me and the linesman saying, It's over Georges, let go.

My head was ringing really bad, my left eye felt like it was out of the socket. My head felt like it was in a vise. When I stood up I immediately put my fingers to my left eye socket. And I knew right away something was really wrong.

They rush me into our dressing room and put me on the medical table for the doctor to take a look at me. He walks in, looks at my eye.

Brantt, take your gear off, you're done for the night. You're going to need quite a few stitches. It's a bad cut we're dealing with.

The first player to come see how I was doing was Jarome Iginla.

Hey Myze, are you going to be okay? Man, you've got some balls.

I guess that's the reason why he was the captain of the team. What a stand-up guy.

Brantt, the doctor said, you're going to have to get an X-ray of your eye tomorrow at nine a.m. sharp.

They finish stitching me up. I take a shower, wash all the blood off, and put my suit on. My family was waiting for me. As I was walking down the hall, I couldn't see out of my eye; it was swollen completely shut. As soon as I saw my dad and my friends, I took them aside and started crying. Dad, I can't do this anymore, I'm done fighting forever, I can't handle it, it's over for me.

In case you've ever wondered, tough guys do cry. That night I was reflecting on the last two years. All that work, everything I put into getting reinstated—and what was it all for? I was on the ice for five seconds and it all was over.

When I woke up the next morning I went straight to the bathroom to take a look at my eye. I had to lift up the swollen flesh to get a glimpse of my eyeball. It was not right at all. It looked like it was sunk back. That scared me, to say the least. The hospital was only a few blocks from my hotel, so I walked there to get the X-ray.

A while after that the doctor came in. Brantt, your orbital bone is crushed: there's no floor for the eye to sit on. We need to do surgery asap. I'm going to have to put a mesh plate in under the eye.

So, what does that mean for my future?

Well, I don't recommend any more fighting. If you get hit again in the same spot, it will crush the plate.

As I left the hospital I'll never forget the feeling I had . . . It was finally over. For the last seventeen years I'd had to worry about fighting to keep my job. For seventeen years I'd had to look over my shoulder worrying about someone tapping me on the shin pads wanting to fight. For seventeen years I'd had to turn into a mean son of a bitch when I'm really just a big teddy bear.

Walking down the street, I felt sad—but also filled with joy that I never ever had to fight again. I had so many things running through my head. Then my phone rang. Caller ID said Georges Laraque.

Hey Georges, how ya doin'?

Good, Myze. I just wanted to call and see how you were doing. I heard you had to go to the hospital. You know how I feel about fighting, Brantt. It's not my favourite thing to do, but it's our jobs and we're good at it.

I laughed and said, Well, *you're* definitely good at it. Not so much can be said for me at this point.

Ah, you'll be fine. It will heal and you'll be back in no time.

It's funny how words like that can mean so much more than a punch in the face.

13

I went for surgery the next day. Afterwards the doctor told me that everything went really well. Still, I was suffering from major headaches and other post-concussion issues. That was really hard—my balance felt all over the place.

But I went to the rink the day after the surgery to have a meeting with Darryl Sutter. When I went in wearing sunglasses covering my black eye, he walked up to me and said, Take your glasses off, let's have a look.

I take them off and he says, Ah, you'll live.

Typical Darryl Sutter comment. I just laughed and said of course I will.

Brantt, we're going to send you down to our AHL team to rehab that injury. Work hard and we'll see you soon.

See me soon? I'd figured they would have just thrown in the towel after that fight. So now I thought, Well, if I can make it back in a few months to play in the NHL I'll suck it up as far as the fighting goes, but what if I get hit in the eye again? Didn't the doctor tell them that?

On the other hand, I was still Brantt Myhres, and Darryl Sutter was telling me to go to Omaha to join a hockey team. So I packed up and headed off.

Right before camp I bought a new Mercedes SUV I shouldn't have bought, considering my salary had just dropped to $75 grand. As for the fighting, I still had three or four months of rehab ahead of me. I'd figure it out.

I was still sober and feeling quite good about it—and if I wanted any chance to get back to the NHL I had to stay sober. The first month was pretty boring: go to the rink, see the team trainer, go home. I wasn't allowed to work out because of my concussion.

In my second month I was able to ride the bike for a bit, nothing too crazy. We had a team of great young guys: Brandon Prust was just a rookie, so was Eric Nystrom. Eric sat next to me in the dressing room. I tried to take him under my wing and teach him the ropes about being a pro—but the funny thing about it was that I didn't really want to be a pro anymore. I was feeling like I'd really had enough. I would talk to Prusty from time to time about my career and what it would take to get a shot, and then how to stay. He was an eager kid who had all the tools in the tool box for a long career. Too bad he was getting advice from a guy who'd pretty much done it all the wrong ways.

It was around Christmastime and I still wasn't cleared to play. I was getting really bored with everything and was at least a month away from playing. I was having thoughts of having a cold beer from time to time, but I held it together. I had a lot invested in sobriety, whether I was going to be a hockey player or not. I knew what I had to do, and I was prepared to do it.

Until Christmas Eve. All the boys were at Prusty's house for a party. They were drinking really hard and I was feeling really uncomfortable. At this point I wasn't really feeling part of the team—not playing, not travelling, just showing up to see our team doctor and give him updates on how I was coming along. I was the type of guy who loved feeling "part of," and my head was starting to say that the only way I could feel "part of" was to bond over a couple drinks. So I kept going back and forth: do I have just one? Anyway, that night we all jumped into my buddy Carsen's car to hit the bar. The music was cranked, so I turned it down and said, Hey boys, I think I'm going to just have a few beers tonight. You guys okay with that?

Haven't you been sober for over two years, Myze?

Yeah, I have, but I just feel like having a few, that's it.

Well, you're a big boy, let's go party!

When we got to the bar my heart was pumping hard. The last two years were running through my head—all the hard work I'd put in, the letter to Gary Bettman, my friends and family, Darryl Sutter.

None of that mattered in the end.

I walk up to the bar. I ask for an Amstel Light. I down it within seconds. I order another one, then another one. The next thing I remember I'm walking down the road in my underwear, freezing, trying to find Carsen's townhouse in a maze of identical townhouses. Finally I found myself standing on the porch. I pound on the door.

Carsen, it's Myze, open the door, I'm fucking freezing out here.

Nothing . . .

Carsen, I'm not kidding, open this door or I'm gonna break the fucker down!

Nothing. I back up and kick the door open. As I'm walking inside I notice that the furniture doesn't look like Carsen's. I go to the bedroom, open the door . . . and see two people in bed grab the covers and pull them over their head. Fuck me, I'm in the wrong house.

I back up and run out. Then I find the right house, walk up to the door.

Carsen, it's Myze, let me in, it's freezing out here!

Nothing. If you don't let me in I'm breaking this fucking door down! Nothing. I back up and kick the door down. This time I'd found the right house, so I get into Carsen's bed and lie down.

Then I hear the boys come around the corner, hollering the whole way. I get up and they come in.

Myze, someone just stopped us and asked if we'd seen some big guy in his underwear walking around. Was that you?

Yeah, boys, I broke into the wrong house.

My bad.

So much for having a couple of beers. My testing schedule was only about once a week, and at this point my attitude was I don't fucking care anymore, I'm a liar and a cheat, so bring whatever's coming down the pipe. I just give up. Suspend me if you want, I'm totally spent. I knew there were no more chances left. If I get caught, I get caught.

The irony is that I was back in the lineup shortly after that. Our trainer came up to me and said, Hey Myze, you're going to have to wear a visor now to protect that eye of yours.

Now, in the past I would have never put on a fucking visor—to me, that was pretty much what all the Europeans wore. But when he said that, I was like, No problem! It was a perfect excuse not to fight.

And believe me, I had every fucking tough guy in the AHL asking me to fight, to give them a chance, to make a name for themselves. All I would say is, Not tonight boys, got to rehab this eye, sorry.

I felt real bad one night during a game when I did something I'd never done in my career. We were playing the Peoria Rivermen, who had a real tough cookie named Rocky. I'd fought him before, back when I was playing for the Sharks in San Jose, and I'd dropped him with a punch. So I had a feeling he'd be knocking at my door asking for a rematch. I was on a line with Prusty, he on the left side and I on the right. We scored a goal and our coach, Gilly, sent our line out for the faceoff at centre ice.

I see Rocky coming my way to line up next to me. He taps my shin pads and says, Myze, we're gonna have to go.

Rock, I can't fight, man, for fuck sakes, I have a visor on.

I don't really care if you have a visor on, bro, let's go!

Rock, there's a tough son of a bitch across the ice by the name of Prust—why don't you go ask him?

Sure enough, Rocky skates directly over to Brandon, and next thing I see is that their gloves are off and it's on. As I'm watching the fight, I'm feeling pretty bad about what just happened—I'd just handed off a fight to a twenty-year-old rookie. Pretty easy to see where my head and heart were at regarding fighting again, especially in the minors.

And it was pretty easy to see that I was off the wagon again too. The more you drink, the more you want to drink. One beer means two, which means twenty or more. And one hangover means such a septic tank of guilt and shame that the quickest way out is—one beer. That Christmas Eve party had started a disgusting downward spiral.

One night it got pretty ugly. We had an early practice the next day but were all partying at a guy's house when I felt like I wanted to find some coke. So I drive downtown, where I see this car at the gas station.

Hey man, anywhere I can find some blow around here?

Of course, just follow me and I'll hook you up.

I start driving into a real bad part of town, the hood, as they say. I walk upstairs, follow the guy into his apartment.

I see two girls smoking crack. They look at me: Hey boy, want a hoot?

No thanks, I'm looking for powder.

The guy gives me my cocaine. I go back to my apartment and start chopping up lines before I even get my coat off. I just sat there with my elbows on the table, doing another line every time the rush showed any sign of fading. I snorted the last line at seven forty-five a.m., because I had to be at the rink at eight.

I used to sit right beside Eric Nystrom in the dressing room. So when I sit down Eric looks at me and says, Holy shit, Myze, you look like death. Are you all right?

No buddy, I've had a long, rough night. Make sure I don't fuck up out on the ice, okay?

Five minutes before practice I run to the bathroom and puke all over the place. After that, I knew I had to say I was sick and couldn't practice.

The trainer looked at me and said, Is there anything else you want to tell me?

No DJ, I just need to go home and lie down, I'm really sick.

As the season went on, I was drinking and doing more drugs than ever before. I wasn't returning the doctor's calls and they stopped urine testing me. It was clear to everyone involved that I was now in that stage of no return. My chances of making it back to the NHL were over. Over the years the only thing that could possibly hold me back had been the promise to myself that if I could get my shit together I'd have a shot at getting back to my dream. Now that the dream was off the table for good, there was nothing holding me back. I was cut off not just from the game but from the people in the game. I had nothing to live for. If you have a problem with drinking or drugs, chances are you have some experience with self-pity. You'll find any excuse to chase that rush. Could be a good day, could be a bad day. Could be that you're pumped up. Could be that you're bored. You'll take any excuse you can get. But self-pity is one of the most seductive.

I should know. I could get depressed even when I was on top of the world. So when I actually had something to be depressed about, I went straight to the bottom. I became a slave to the booze and drugs. Any light at the end of the tunnel was becoming pretty dim.

Towards the end of the season I was at Carsen's house one night when some of the boys were having a few and I got into the coke again. They all went to bed because we had an early practice. At seven a.m. Carsen walks out of his room and says, Hey Myze, you ready to go to practice?

Practice? Are you fucking kidding me? I haven't slept a wink and I'm vibrating from all the blow I just did. Tell the trainer I have food poisoning, I can't make practice.

Okay, Myze, I'll tell him.

The trainer calls. Brantt, what's going on?

DJ, I don't know, but I've been puking all night. It must have been the sushi I had last night.

Can't you at least come in to see the team doctor?

No man, I can't even move from my bed right now.

Are you at your house?

Yeah, I am, got here last night after sushi.

When I arrived at the rink the next day, our coach Gilly said, Myze, come into my office, let's have a chat. So, what happened to you yesterday?

Gilly, I was puking all night at my house, it must have been the sushi I had.

So, you were at your house all night?

Yeah, right after dinner I went home 'cause I was feeling so shitty.

That's funny—after practice yesterday I drove by Carsen's house and saw your Benz parked out front.

I didn't say anything for a minute or so.

Gilly looked at me and said, Myze, you've played a long time in this game. I know what's going on with the drinking—there were a few times we could smell booze on you during practice. I'm going to have to let the Flames know what's going on. I don't know what they're going to do, but as long as you're here for the next three weeks, please act like a pro around the guys. You're not going to play any more games, so just try and hold it together till the season is over, okay?

Okay, Gilly, I'll keep it together till we're done.

It was a horrible feeling walking around the guys with my head down. I was full of embarrassment knowing what was coming my way: the inevitable clock winding down any chance of ever playing another shift in the NHL. Not to mention that I'd blown through all my cash and had no clue what I wanted to do after hockey. I mean, with only grade nine, what could I really do? Talk about any scenario looking like a bad one.

When our season ended I didn't know what to do with myself. I had about eight thousand dollars left after making millions during my career.

I was suspended for life from the NHL.

I was thirty-three years old and without even a high school education, so finding a good job was out of the question. A payment for my Benz was due. That was $1200 I couldn't afford. I skipped that month. I had to really watch my money.

I drove home to Edmonton and called my friend Jason to see if I could stay with him for the summer. Jason was an old buddy I'd grown up with in Grand Centre; we'd been pretty tight since our teenage years. I couldn't afford to get my own place, but I didn't let him know that. On the outside I was still living the amazing life of a pro hockey player.

Don't get me wrong: I'd partied like a thousand men, had three hundred girl "friends," and had ridden my ego for fifteen years, hard. I was so ashamed of what I'd turned out to be that I couldn't let anyone get close.

By the time I was two months late on my car payment I was down to four thousand dollars. I needed to get a job playing hockey over in Europe. I called Ritch to hook something up. But I could tell he'd had enough of my act as well. I'd lied to his face so many times that he'd pretty much shut off to anything coming out of my mouth.

There was interest from a team in the U.K. called the Newcastle Vipers. They offered me six hundred pounds a week, about $4200 a month. That was peanuts really, but I had nothing else on the go and figured I could go over there and actually play hockey for once.

On the phone I told the coach, Rob Wilson, that because of my eye injury I wasn't going to fight—and that the first time I get the tap to fight I'm on a flight home. I'd heard from a couple guys that this league was a bush league, lots of fights, lots of drinking. I guess I really didn't care about that. I mean, at least it was a paycheque, and I wasn't going to ever drop the gloves. And the drinking part, well, that seemed right on par with my current attitude.

One day I came home to find my Mercedes being taken away for nonpayment. As I stood in the driveway watching it go, I went numb. By this time, two weeks before I was set to leave, I had only $1500 left in my account.

Then, with only a week left to go, I'm desperate for cash. I look at my wrist and see my beautiful Cartier Roadster watch. I'd paid $8000 for it when I was playing for San Jose. I clean it up and head to the pawnshop. They gave me $2000 for it.

There was almost nothing left of the good I'd built in my life. All I could do in times of shame was get loaded. I'd be partying, laughing at times during the night, but there was that little voice saying, Brantt, you're such a loser, look what your life has become. The way to shut that voice up was to down some Jack Daniels and snort a line. It was way too painful to address the situation. All I could focus on now was getting to England and playing some hockey.

14

After I landed in London I got on a flight to Newcastle upon Tyne. I'd done a little research on the city. *GQ* magazine rated it among the top ten places to have a bachelor party on the planet, so maybe not a smart place to visit for a guy having addiction problems.

When I got there they had one of the guys meet me at the airport. It was my first time in England, and I just remember it being overcast and gloomy, lots of rain. Still, there was some excitement to this new venture. I was focused on getting some cold beers down my throat, maybe meeting a girl or two.

As we drove I asked what the schedule was for the next day.

We practise at seven a.m. at this shit rink, the guy told me. It's cold and dark, you'll see.

Really, seven? Wow, that's fricken early!

So, what do you want to do now? The coach and a few of the guys are having a few beers at the pub. Wanna go meet them for a few?

Did you just say the coach and the guys are having beers together?

Yeah, our coach is actually like Reggie Dunlop from *Slap Shot*—he's a player coach.

You've got to be fucking kidding me.

Nope, he's our defenceman. He just says who's up before he goes out on the ice.

It sounded like a circus to me. Holy shit, what had I got myself into?

We show up at the pub, I meet the guys and the coach, and as I'm sitting there I'm thinking, Jesus Christ, Brantt, you went from playing in the NHL, the best league in the world, to drinking with the coach. I never heard of any of these guys—there wasn't one former NHLer. So this is what they meant by the end of the road. I was trying to act like I was some big deal since I was the only guy who'd played in the show, but in all reality, I was playing in a league that was way down on the totem pole.

One thing leads to another, and it's now five in the morning and I'm taking puffs of this inhaler. It's supposed to cut oxygen off to the brain and give you a buzz.

Now it's six a.m. and we're on our way to the rink for practice. As I walk in I could not believe how much of a shithole this fucking place was—real cold and real dark, with water dripping from the ceiling and creating lumps on the ice.

A guy would pass you the puck and it would hit one of those ice balls and almost smack you in the face. It was just crazy. When we played our first game I was on ice for about twenty minutes, which hadn't happened since junior. I was dead tired! It was all foreign to me playing that much. On the one hand it felt good just to play the game of hockey again without the worry of dropping the gloves, but on the other hand it felt like a fucking waste of time: there was no carrot dangling for a better outcome. I knew that in my heart, so it was real difficult to feel good about making a good pass or scoring a goal.

It felt more like a beer league than anything else—and after the game we had an actual bucket of beer on ice waiting. I had about five while I was still in my gear. Then, after I'd showered up, we headed out to the pub.

In the first two weeks I was drunk every day. It seemed to be a normal thing to do. After hockey, hit the pubs. And the women there were insane—all they wanted to do was get shitfaced and have sex. I've never seen anything like it. After the games we'd always have some event going on, the sort of thing where you'd grab a drink and mingle. That's where you'd see all these crazy English girls waiting just to talk to you, like they thought we were some kind of celebrities or something. I'd say there were about three thousand fans per game, and they were pretty loud when things were getting rough on the ice. I believe they were really only there to see shit get out of hand.

After three weeks of drinking every day, I started to get real sick. My body was run down. One morning, after having strep throat, I was in my condo when I looked down and noticed a red dot on my foot. It looked strange, but I didn't pay too much attention to it.

The next day we were heading to Sheffield to play a game when I heard rumours that they weren't happy with me. A couple players were telling me on the bus that our coach had thought I was some big NHL tough guy but that I was playing like a pussy.

During the game the coach gives me a tap on the pants to go fight. But he knew how I felt about that, so I just looked at him and said, This is a fucking joke. It also seemed like my chance to get the hell out of there and go back to Canada. I was missing home. And I knew that if I fought I could walk into his office and tell him to book me a flight home, since I'd told him right at the beginning: Don't ever ask me to fight or I'm gone.

So I go to the faceoff, look at the guy, and say, Well, my dickhead coach sent me out to fight, so what do you think? I had no clue who this guy was. All I knew was that a couple teammates had told me he was their tough guy.

We have to fight now?

Yeah bud, as in right now . . .

The puck drops and we square off. As we take our helmets off I put my fists up in the air. But all I can think is, What the fuck am I doing? I'm about to fight some nobody in some bush league with the chance of getting hit in my eye where the doctor told me it could be fatal. I reach out to grab him with my right hand and then I start throwing my left hand as fast as I can. He hits me once or twice then grabs my pants and tugs me down to the ice. I think my teammates, coach, and fans were expecting a way better performance.

After the game was over we headed back to Newcastle, smoking and drinking Jack Daniels right on the bus. I knew I was done there, since I'd told them to never send me out to fight. I mean, hey, I'd also been drunk for twenty straight days, so no wonder I was playing like shit and they wanted to skid me. Still, it was a hard pill to swallow that I couldn't even crack some low-level English league team. I'd thought I could drink like an animal, not work out, chase women on a nightly basis, and still shine as a hockey player. Well, that's not the way this world works.

The next day our coach called me into the office.

Brantt, this hasn't turned out like either one of us had planned. We're going to release you, so after today you're free to go wherever you want.

Yeah, Willy, I had a feeling this talk was coming, no problem. Can I stay at the condo for at least five more days to find a place to play?

Sure, no problem.

So there I was, released from the U.K. league. Holy shit, it just keeps getting worse and worse by the minute. I had Ritch working on finding a deal somewhere else, but there was no interest from anyone.

I started to panic. Maybe I could go play in that goon league in Quebec? There was a men's senior league there that was a complete rodeo. These guys were animals on skates—all you were paid to do was fight, and not just once but two or three times a game.

I kept saying to myself, How the hell am I going to manage that? But I thought that if the money was right, I'd do it. I was so desperate, I would have played anywhere. And when I talked with one of the teams from that Quebec league, they said they'd give me a $20K bonus as well as two grand a week cash. I was so close to taking up the offer. But in the end I said no. I couldn't play in that league—I hated fighting, my eye had a plate in it, and I couldn't imagine fighting twice a game with no insurance.

———

On the plane going home to Edmonton, I sure had lots of time to think. I was now hanging up my skates forever. A lot of the things people had said to me during my career came rushing through my head. Brantt, take care of your money 'cause one day it'll all be over. Brantt, if you stay sober you'll have a couple million in the bank to start a new life after hockey. Brantt, you shouldn't have dropped out of school—you'll need your education one day.

Brantt, how are you ever going to have a decent girlfriend with the way you've ended up? Brantt, everyone's going to say I told you so, he was going to eventually fuck things up.

When I landed at the airport I had a friend pick me up who agreed to let me stay at his house while I figured things out. Of course I'd picked a friend who liked cocaine as much as I did. He was such a great guy—he'd do anything for you—but at that time in my life I needed sober friends and I had none. My good friend Eli wouldn't talk to me anymore—he said it was too painful to watch me slowly kill myself. And I wasn't really talking to my parents or my grandparents, either: there was too much shame. I was all alone.

When I got back to my friend's house his buddies all asked why I was back so soon from playing.

It just didn't work out.

What are you going to do now?

I really have no idea.

I felt like a deer in the headlights, not knowing which way to turn. That night I counted my money: I had five hundred dollars left to my name.

The friends I stayed with also smoked a lot of pot, so every night around six I'd light up a joint. It would put me into la-la land, and eventually make me tired enough that I could sleep. You see, that was the only time my head shut off. I wanted to sleep as long as I could so that I wouldn't have to face myself.

One night I woke up and was sweating so bad that I got up and went to the bathroom. When I turned on the light I thought I was still in a nightmare: the red dot on my foot I'd first noticed in Newcastle was still there, but now I saw that others like it had spread all over my body, head to toe. It was itchy and it looked horrible. I started freaking out.

When I finally saw a dermatologist, he told me that I had psoriasis—and that it can develop when someone's really sick and rundown, which I was. This skin issue really affected me badly. I felt so embarrassed by how I looked. I wouldn't wear short-sleeve shirts; I was always covered in clothes. And no medication worked for me—it seemed to just get worse. Now I looked the way I felt.

It was a cold, snowy night and I'd been up for hours doing cocaine. At around five a.m. I finally went to bed, but as I lay down I looked to my left and there I am . . . I'm staring at myself in the mirror. What I see is a man who's scared and lost. A man who had it all and now has nothing. My beer belly was hanging over my underwear and I had to wipe the sweat off my face. I turned the lights out and rolled over to stare out the window. My friend's dog would often be in the bed with me, so there was dog hair all over the sheets. I just felt so gross about myself. As I looked up at the sky, I noticed all the stars. They looked so beautiful, and they were so far away.

That's when I had a conversation with whoever it was out there. Basically I was saying, I'll see you soon. I didn't want to be here any longer. The psoriasis was all over my body; I couldn't even look at myself; I wanted to go. I knew there was a heaven out there and that it had to be better than this place.

It was one of the first times since I went off the rails that I really came to terms with who I'd turned into. It was frightening. I closed my eyes and went to sleep.

A friend phoned to say I should give this guy a call about selling emergency equipment in Grande Prairie. After the guy offered me the job I called my dad, who I hadn't talked to in a long time, and asked if he wanted to go to Grande Prairie with me. He had an old Jeep that ran pretty good, so that's what we used.

But as soon as I got there the whole thing was shady. I mean, fuck, I was hanging out at the Hells Angels clubhouse with this guy, doing enough coke to kill a moose. It was not a good scene, to say the least.

Me and my dad were trying to put the past in the past, and to be quite honest I was just yearning for a father's love or support even though we'd had some rough patches. I ended up not getting paid, so now it was back to square one.

I moved back to my buddy's place, which was hard to do 'cause I really felt like I wanted a better life than that. For the next month I just got loaded every day. I was completely broke. But I wasn't completely hopeless yet, and I wasn't completely out of the game. I'd fallen a long way from the world of charter flights and five-star hotels, but I still knew people. I'd played with hundreds of guys and got along with pretty much all of them. So I picked up the phone and called Ritch to see if I could do anything for him. Specifically, whether I could bring him clients.

I mentioned earlier that I figured Ritch was pretty much done with me as well. He'd gone through all the stages by my side, and it had taken a toll on him I'm sure, but at this point I had nothing to lose. So I put together a list of all the players who were still playing and who I had a friendship with. I ended up writing close to a hundred names. My thought was, Heck, if I could get even 5 percent of those, how amazing would that be? I could tell by Ritch's voice that he was wary of my proposal. But hey, he's a businessman, and if he could possibly make some cash, why not?

We came to an agreement: he would hire me strictly on commission. The only thing that really helped me at that time was his agreeing to rent me a truck. (I had no way to get around other than my dad's old Jeep, and I didn't want to borrow that all the time.) If I brought a new player over I'd get a percentage of what Ritch received. That looked real far away, though. Any actual payments wouldn't be coming anytime soon, and I needed money asap.

Ritch suggested that I email the NHL's emergency assistance program, which is there for retired players who are in need of financial help. I did that the next day, but I still needed some cash. So Ritch gave me $1000 to get started. That would last a couple weeks the way I was living my life. Every day seemed like a fog. I'd get home after being at Ritch's office, make some dinner, smoke a big joint, have a few cold beers, then go to bed.

I started to notice I was putting on weight, weight like I've never really seen before, bad weight as they say. My psoriasis was still really bad, covering my body. It was so bad that I couldn't bear to turn the lights on in the bathroom. When it gets that bad you know you're in a bad place. But I wasn't done yet. I'd look at myself in the shadows of the bathroom mirror, give myself a wink, and say, Keep going.

Keeping going can mean different things at different times in your life. It used to mean hitting the gym, or hitting AA—buckling down to get back on the road to the NHL. But that road was closed to me. Now keeping going just meant getting a little more cash in my pocket. If someone had offered me money to move drugs, I probably would have done it. I understand now how people feel when they're desperate. Desperate people will do anything to keep going. They don't have much choice. And that's just when the stakes are putting food on the table or paying the phone bill. Add drugs to the equation, and look out. There was almost nothing I wouldn't have done. I saw the way those Hells Angels were living and it was looking pretty damn good. I was starting to think I'd make a pretty good biker.

But I had advantages most people can't turn to. I received a letter from the NHL emergency fund letting me know they would help me out each month for a while. That was the best news I'd had in some time! I couldn't believe they would help me, considering how they'd already spent hundreds of thousands of dollars for my rehabs. I wasn't asking any questions, though—I was just very grateful for the support. It was one of the times in my life that I wished my parents had done something with their lives and so be able to maybe help out. My grandparents would have helped, but I couldn't bear the thought of asking them. I guess that's life, though.

You may be wondering, Why didn't I just go get a job? I would have, but I was going to the office every day hoping to land a player for Ritch. Working on commission is a tough gig, I tell ya, but if you land even one, it could have a nice return.

I had a good buddy playing for the Calgary Flames' AHL team, Mark Giordano. He mentioned that he wanted to find a good agent, that his wasn't working out. Gio was one of those players who you just knew would be awesome if a team would just give him a shot. He was undrafted, basically came to camp as a walk-on. And he'd had a great year in Omaha, like real good.

So I called Ritch. Hey Ritch, you need to see this guy play—he's tearing it up, down in the AHL. It took a bit to get the two of them in the same room together, but it finally happened. The rest is history. Gio was making only $40 grand that year, so let's just say I could have maybe bought an iPod with my commission.

I was going to work each day not really knowing what else to do. I mean, now, looking back, I could have killed in that business; nothing would have stopped me from representing tons of players. But back then I was too fucked up. I was smoking weed and drinking each day, going to the office with a fake smile on my face, acting like life was just great. Meanwhile, Christmastime was coming and what the hell was I going to do for gifts?

It was the first Christmas in seventeen years that I couldn't afford to buy presents. I wasn't even able to watch hockey on TV—it was too painful a reminder of what I'd thrown down the tubes. The only thing I did was get real high on coke, go downstairs, and put in my fight tape. I'd sit there and watch that for hours. I was also having these dreams where I'd be back in the NHL for a tryout and would have only one glove or one skate and couldn't find the other one in time for the game. It drove me nuts.

———

After working with Ritch for a few months, it was clear that I needed something else for income. Then came the call.

Hey Brantt, it's Ritch. Come down to the office, I have some real good news for you.

I rushed downtown and walked into his office. What's up, Ritch?

The NHLPA has informed me that they're dispersing cheques to two thousand players who played in the mid to late 90s. It's money for using your name on hockey cards, video games, and any other things where your name was involved.

Really, Ritch? How much are we talking about?

I almost fell off my chair when he told me I was about to receive a cheque for $30 grand.

Now, what's the only thing worse for an addict than no money? Money. It fuelled my disease, with thoughts of how I'd spend it directed solely towards drugs, booze, and whatever else came with partying.

I got introduced to this guy named Arnie and right off the bat we hit it off—we both liked the nose candy and lots of booze. I finally had enough money to get my own place, so we decided to move in together. He'd work out of town for ten days, then come home for four.

The day he'd get home I'd have the house filled with booze and about five hundred dollars' worth in drugs. From the time Arnie walked in the door till the time he went back out of town, we'd be wasted, and I mean every time. And once he'd gone I'd find another guy to party with, usually Kenny, my drug dealer. Strippers were always good to have around since they were in the same boat as you. I found that hanging around other bottom feeders made me feel better about myself. And the strippers would never say, Hey, maybe you shouldn't be drinking or doing so many drugs. They were the ones chopping up the lines and pouring you another cocktail. The last thing I needed was someone pointing out what I had become.

I'd received that cheque from the NHLPA in May. By August I was down to about five grand. So I thought of the things I could do. One of the things I really liked were cars, so I put on my suit and headed down to the BMW store to ask for a job. I had a feeling I may be able to make a little cash selling cars. I mean, that's something that former NHLers do, right? I got hired the next day.

But it was one of those jobs where it's all based on commission. The base salary was five hundred bucks a month if you didn't sell anything. So it was imperative that I sell some cars. I'd already tried my hand at the Audi dealership. I hated it, but at least I sold one car there before I packed it in. A sobering moment was when the dealership's GM told me I wouldn't be selling cars on the new side, but rather on the used side. I was like, Holy fuck, I can't even crack a job selling new cars—it's over to the used side for you, Brantt.

Things were getting worse by the minute. I was going to work wasted—so sick that I'd retreat to the washroom, puke my guts out, chop a line of coke, then head back out to the sales floor where the gleaming cars I could no longer afford were lined up and the rich lawyers and real estate agents wanted to talk hockey. After a month at BMW I hadn't sold one car. I was a disgrace at it. Now I was down to about fifteen dollars. We couldn't afford to pay rent, so me and Arnie decided to pull a midnight run. I cringed to think what the clients at BMW would think of that.

Plus my cell phone had been cut off because of nonpayment. I never wanted to ask anyone for money again, but I was broke after the holidays. When I finally asked my good friend Jason for $150 so that I could get my phone turned back on, he wired it to me the next day, no questions asked. I felt a lot of shame around that. Then I ended up selling my Gretzky stick to Jason's brother for $500. Hell, sticks these days go for $250 so $500 was peanuts for a Gretzky game stick. I told him I'd sell it on one condition only: if one day I could afford it, he would sell it back to me. No problem, he said. I hope that day comes for you. I received the cash and the stick was gone.

Around that time, me and my dad had a real blowout. We basically sat across from each other and said, Let's fire away—you tell me what you don't like about me and I'll do the same. To this day I wish I'd never done that. Some of the words that came out of my dad's mouth were just horrible. I told him to leave, and then I cried for a couple hours. In my mind, after that, my father was dead to me. It was really painful.

One night I went to a Bon Jovi concert and drank so much that when I got home and lay down to sleep, I started to puke out this black blood. I couldn't move from the bed, so it was going all over my sheets. It was alcohol poisoning. I woke up at noon the next day feeling like death. There was a missed call from BMW. The message said don't even bother coming in. You're fired.

It was February 17, 2008, and I was invited to my sister's for dinner. At the dinner were her husband and their two kids, along with her husband's sister and brother. Something had been weighing on my mind for months. When I arrived around six I started drinking whisky along with straight vodka. I got to the point where I needed some blow just to keep it together.

So I texted Kenny, my drug dealer. For the last two years he'd never been late for a delivery—all I'd do is text him and within fifteen minutes he'd be there, no matter where I was. But that night thirty minutes passed, and nothing . . . Then an hour. No word from Kenny as I slid deeper and deeper into a black pit of drunkenness.

Funny. My life would have turned out very differently if my dealer had shown up.

The next thing I remember is that I had my face in the snow outside my sister's place with two cops on my neck. I was handcuffed so I couldn't move. A sight I'll never forget: I looked up and saw my sister in the doorway crying her eyes out. The cops stuff me in the back of the cruiser. At this point I still don't know what the hell I'd done.

I said, My sister, that bitch, got me arrested? What the fuck is wrong with her?

Now, now, slow down, Brantt. We asked her if she wanted to press charges and she said no, that we should just take you home.

When I woke up in the morning I saw that I'd pissed the bed—I'd been so loaded I couldn't move. I reach over and call my cousin.

Sean, my fucking sister got me arrested last night—what the hell is wrong with her?

Brantt, I got a call from Cher. You better call her right now.

And so I called.

Cher, what the hell happened last night?

Brantt, you went into a rage—you wanted to fight my husband, calling him a fucking pussy, and you grabbed me by the throat.

Then you grabbed a knife from the table and pointed it at yourself, saying, Do you want me to fucking kill myself? I might as well do it, I don't fucking care anymore. You then went over to our glass table, picked it up, and smashed it on the floor. The kids were upstairs hiding in the bedroom with the door locked. I had to call the cops—no one could settle you down. I took pictures of what you did, I'll show you. You're not allowed over here again.

The picture of what I did after I heard all that still resides in my head. I hit my knees, put my hands together, and cried. Then I started to pray.

> *Dear God, please help me, I need your help. I can't go on like this anymore. I know I haven't kept in touch lately, and I'm sorry for that, I have felt so lost. I don't know where to turn, but I know that I'm a good person and that I don't want to die. I'm going to be a father and I want my baby to be proud of me, so if you're hearing this prayer, I ask for one more chance, please . . .*

I went to a Catholic school when I was in grades seven, eight, and nine. All I ever really understood about Jesus or God was that we had to go to church once a month, take communion, and then giggle with the kids on the way back to school. I was never one for saying that there's no such thing as God, but I must admit, I never felt a connection to anything supreme in my whole childhood and adult life. I did think something had made the planets, the universe, and so on, but I didn't think too much about it, just that it was present.

At my first rehab, they'd had the spiritual side right up there with the importance of staying sober. I never had a problem praying in rehab. I didn't think it was bullshit; I did believe in God. But I didn't feel like God even knew I was alive, if that makes sense. I doubted Brantt Myhres was even on God's radar. I figured I'd be face to face with him once I died, then I'd probably get at least a couple minutes of his time.

But through the years—when I was arrested, puking blood from too much alcohol, hearing a girl was late on her period, getting caught cheating, in the back of the ambulance getting rushed to the hospital for a cocaine overdose, wondering if I'd waited long enough to pass my piss test—I did say a prayer. So yeah, I guess you could say I prayed. But looking back, it was for all the wrong reasons. And those types of cry-out prayers never really work.

It wasn't until that morning when I actually felt a true connection to something other than myself.

As I was praying I couldn't stop crying. I've cried before, but nothing like this. It was flooding out and I couldn't control it. Then I had the most serene, amazing warm feeling rush through my whole body . . . it was a feeling of You're done, it's all going to be okay, no more suffering for you, Brantt. It was the first time in my life that I felt that way, as if I knew with every cell in my body that I was done drinking and doing drugs.

It was February 18, 2008, and my life had just started.

PART IV

MY LAST
LAST
CHANCE

15

My phone rang the next day. It was Dan Cronin from the NHL.

Brantt, are you finally done?

How did you hear about what happened, Dan?

It doesn't matter how I heard. My question is, Are you finally done?

Yes, Dan, I have never been more done in my life.

Okay then. Will you commit to long-term treatment if I can get it?

Yes, yes, I'll do whatever it takes, Dan. Do you think the league will help? They told me after the last suspension they were washing their hands of me.

I'll see what I can do. I'll get back to you by the end of the day.

When Dan called back, he asked if I could get on a plane the next day. I didn't hesitate. My only question was how long I'd be going for, and Dan said it doesn't matter this time.

I said, Dan, I'm about to be a father. My daughter is going to be born in a week.

He said, If you don't get on that plane, she won't have a daddy.

I was going to a place in Oregon called Astoria Pointe. There'd be a guy named Larry there to pick me up. That's all I knew. I was just groping for a lifeline in the dark. I was blown away that the NHL was going to pay for my treatment again after all the shit I'd put them through, but I was just grateful for the chance.

I'd been given many chances over the years. But I'm not sure the emotion I'd felt was ever really gratitude. In fact, for a while, I felt *unlucky*— as though I was getting singled out for something that lots of guys were doing. And trust me, NHL players can go pretty hard.

After a while, when more chances came my way, I started to feel as though I was beating the system. I figured I was smart enough to get back to where I needed to be. But by the time I was blowing through my final chances, deep down I didn't feel I deserved them anyway. Part of me wanted to show everyone how wrong they'd been about me when they'd taken my side.

And once you've sunk so low that you despise yourself, that's how you feel about the people who believe in you. You think they're fools. You can't really be grateful if you think the people who are offering you a hand are fools for doing so.

That may sound like the therapy talking, and you can take it with a grain of salt if you want. But I know one thing for sure. Every time I was caught breaking the conditions of my rehab and got myself suspended, it meant I didn't have to get punched in the face for a few months. As embarrassing as it was to be suspended, not getting punched in the face isn't the end of the world. No grain of salt is going to change that.

In any case, second chances had always given me second thoughts. I'd never been completely grateful. But this time was different.

I didn't really understand the reason for that when I first learned it. I was in a Canadian Tire parking lot the previous summer when I got a text from this girl named Shauna. I'd met her a few years before, when I lived in Sylvan Lake. We'd kept in touch and hung out from time to time. It wasn't serious at all—when there was a party we would hook up. So her text caught me off guard:

Are you sitting down?

Oh no, is she going to tell me what I think is coming?

Yeah, I'm sitting down, what's up?

You're going to be a dad!

I almost passed out. Are you serious?

Yeah, I'm pregnant.

My first feeling was sadness. That's how bleak my life was. I'd always wanted to have a child, but not like this. I was in the worst spot I'd ever been in my life. I was broke with no real promise of a future.

But there was something inside of me whispering, This is the best thing to ever happen to you even though you can't see it now, Brantt. This child will change your life for the better. I wasn't really paying attention to that voice; the only voice I was paying attention to was shame and guilt. It took a few days for the news to really settle in. Then, as the days went on, I became more and more excited about it. And now the baby was almost here—Shauna was due in a week.

But I knew I was in no position to be a father. I mean, my own father had told me everything that was wrong with me. I was sliding deeper and deeper into a swamp of booze and coke, and the reminder that I now had one more person to disappoint did nothing to slow down my descent.

At least not at that moment. But now that a new chance had appeared out of nowhere, a new feeling came with it. I may never have felt true gratitude for myself. I may not have deserved it—and I have to think I've received more than I deserve. Suddenly, though, I had someone to be grateful *for*. This new opportunity was a chance for my unborn child. It could give that child a protector and a provider who might otherwise not be there. It could change a young person's life. It could make an innocent kid's life better.

I might fuck up my own life. But there was no way I was going to fuck up this innocent kid's.

The day was February 27, 2008. I'd been in treatment for only a week. My phone rang; it was Shauna.

Congratulations, you have a baby girl! Her name is Chloe Grace Olivia Jenkins.

I started to tear up. Really? What does she look like?

She's beautiful, Brantt, she has your cheeks and your nose. She has beautiful blond hair and is healthy. When will you be coming home to see her?

Gosh, Shauna, I have no clue. I think in a month or so.

Okay, well I'll send you some pictures of her in the meantime.

I was so excited that I went around to everyone at the facility and bragged about being a father of a baby girl. But at the same time, I was scared. What am I going to do when I get out? How am I going to support her? Then I calmed myself down. Just take it one day at a time, it's all going to work out, focus on staying sober, that's the most important thing right now; you'll be no good to her if you don't stay sober.

I reflected back on my first NHL game, back in Hartford. I'd always worn number 33, but when I walked into the dressing room I saw Myhres 27.

People around the game talk about the hockey gods. There's something about the game that rewards doing things right. You see it all the time. Rookies scoring in their first game. Guys who've been in the league for years finally winning the Cup when it seemed impossible. A lucky bounce for a guy who deserved a bit of luck.

I'm not saying I deserved anything. But it didn't seem like a coincidence that 27 became my lucky number.

I remember my first night at Astoria Pointe. I was lying in bed looking out at the night sky when I picked up my journal and wrote that one day, I wanted to give back to the NHL and NHLPA for helping me. They'd never given up on me even when I gave up on myself. I said to myself that as long as I stayed sober I'd have a chance to help another player going through the same things I went through.

This place felt like home to me. Everyone at the facility was awesome; they made me feel safe. We went to AA meetings every day, and at the meeting I'd put my hand up to talk, where before I never did. I loved being in those meetings—everyone there felt the same way I did, and they didn't judge. I think what made this one different is that the weight of that thousand-pound gorilla was off my back. In my other rehabs I'd been a dry drunk. Not now. I was actually excited each morning for my alarm to go off. It used to be, Oh fuck, not another day. Now it was, I'm looking forward to learning about Brantt, what made me really tick, what made me end up in my fifth rehab. In Astoria I never fought it once—I was just so grateful to have that fifth chance. I truly looked at it as a gift from God. But I also looked at it as my last one from God in terms of help.

When the thirty-day mark came I was freaking out a bit, wondering what the hell I was going to do when my time was up. I was still receiving that monthly financial support from the NHL. It was enough to help with child support and some other bills, leaving me with about $150. After putting a dollar every day in the AA basket, I was down to 120 bucks. So yeah, I had no clue what to expect. What I did know, though, was that it was all going to be okay, no matter what. When I first got to Astoria, I met this young guy named Wesley. He had this amazing energy for such a young guy trying to get sober. He ended up being like a little brother to me. I'm sure we were both looking out for each other. I believe he only spent two months in there, and when the day came that he was going to get released, he came to me and said, Myze, guess what?! Larry offered me to be a cook here at the Pointe! So, I'm not going anywhere.

For the eight months I was there, we hung out every day. Wes has twelve years sober now and still lives in Oregon.

I'd asked the old-timers how they got to twenty years sober without a drink. Considering I had only thirty days, it seemed so far away. But as they would say, Well son, one day at a time . . . that's how I did it. I was just so full of gratitude. I couldn't believe that I, the same guy who'd been suspended four times from the league, was getting another chance. That was another God moment for me.

I used to have that guy on my shoulder talking to me all the time about how I could get away with having just one or two drinks. Now that guy on my shoulder was telling me, All you have to focus on is just making it through the day without using. That's it.

On Day 32 I was walking around nervously, waiting for them to release me into the big old world again. The program director came up to me.

Hey Brantt, can I talk to you for a second?

Oh shit, I thought, I'm going back to Alberta. What am I going to do?

Larry just sat down, put his hand on my shoulder, and said, I think we're going to keep you for another month, okay?

Yes, of course it's okay, thank you so much.

I left there feeling so damn happy that I had at least another month of treatment.

Shauna sent me some pictures of my baby girl, Chloe. I'm sure most parents say this, but she was one of the most beautiful babies I've ever seen. She had such big blue eyes and this little blond fro-hawk. I felt so torn because I just wanted to hold her and give her a big kiss, but I also knew that I needed the treatment.

Over the course of my career I've had lots of therapists, and the only one I opened up to was the one in L.A., the one I've talked about. At Astoria we had group meetings every day for over two hours, but our therapist at the time kept falling asleep, so they had to find another one. In walked this blond lady, real bubbly girl, full of energy. The next day in group we spent the whole two hours laughing. Shelly had a way of making you not take yourself too seriously. I really started to trust her. She knew just how to handle me. And one of the things she preached was total honesty, no matter what.

But I'd lied my way through life.

What do you mean by total honesty, Shelly?

Well Brantt, first off, it's a much easier way to live your life. If you never lie you never have to remember what you said. Secondly, recovery is about building on the positive things you do each day. If you lie, it keeps setting you back. And eventually one day you'll pick up a drink because you'll have so much shame from the dishonesty.

Yeah. That rang true.

I made a promise to myself that I'd do my best to be honest with everyone, no matter what. It's been my experience that most therapists have a tendency to just sit there and wait for you to talk. Shelly was the complete opposite. She let you talk, but would interrupt you when you started spilling bullshit out of your mouth. I liked the fact that she seemed really engaged in my thoughts and feelings. I had a brain that wasn't really thinking straight, so she had a way of inserting healthy thoughts back in.

I was beginning to understand the reasons behind my behaviour. I had so much anger and resentment towards my mom for staying with a guy who beat her kids, I had so much resentment towards my father for not rescuing me and Cher, I had the most resentment towards myself for being such a fuck up. I'm not making any excuses at all for the choices I made, but there were underlying issues that drove me to try and dig that grave.

When I'd checked into Astoria, they went through my bags to make sure I didn't have any booze or drugs. I also had to fill out these forms, and to give them my weight, so I stepped on the scale. I weighed in at 256 pounds. I was fat. When I played hockey I weighed around 215 to 218 pounds. I'd let myself go. So I said to myself that first night, If I'm going to change my life, I'm going to change it all.

I made a commitment to working out every other day. And I was sticking with it. They were long, hard workouts, and I was beginning to tell the difference in how my clothes fit. Also, one of the biggest things that was happening was that my psoriasis was healing! I couldn't believe my eyes. It had affected my self-confidence so bad that I couldn't even leave the house, but now, with no booze or drugs and eating healthy, my skin was getting better.

I'd now been sober for sixty days, and was waiting for Larry to pull me aside and say goodbye and good luck.

Hey Brantt, can I have a talk with you?

Sure Larry, what's up?

He sat down next to me, put his hand on my shoulder, and said, I think we're going to keep you for another month.

Really? That's great news, Larry, thank you so much! So I had another month at least in Astoria.

I'd go to an AA meeting once, maybe twice a day, I'd have two hours of therapy, and I was eating healthy—it was the best I'd felt about Brantt in years. I'd send the doctors an email from time to time to let them know how good I was doing, but I got the feeling they weren't holding their breath. I mean, they'd heard it a hundred times before. I understood that. All I could do was stay on track and not worry a damn what other people thought. *I* knew what I was doing each day, and that was all that mattered.

I hit the ninety-day mark and was able to attain a ninety-day sobriety coin. In the sobriety world, they have milestones: thirty, sixty, ninety days, six months, a year. To get ninety days meant a lot. Not to mention that it was the first coin I'd gotten that I was truly proud of. I kept it in my pocket every day and would look at it whenever I was having a down moment.

That day they asked me to chair the meeting, meaning I'd sit at the desk and lead the discussion. It means you're on display in front of everyone at the facility. Usually there were about fifty people in there. Getting asked to do that was so good for my sobriety—it really made me feel like I was doing something responsible.

After the meeting I was chatting with a few friends, telling them it had been nice to know them all, but that I was probably going home in the next day or two. Then Larry came up to me.

Brantt, can I talk with you?

Larry put his hand on my shoulder. I think we're going to keep you for a little longer, is that okay?

Now, since I'd been in treatment, no one there had stayed longer than three months. Usually the longest was a two-month stay. So now I was on my way to four months, and up to that point I'd never paid a penny. What a gift the league had given me. I felt grateful all over again.

I knew I needed an AA sponsor, but I waited until I found a guy I could really open up to. The most important thing was that I trust him. I'd been listening to this older man talk at meetings—his name was Jack, and he sure sounded like he knew the AA program and lived it every day. Jack was in his late sixties, had a real deep voice, and wore cowboy boots. At the time he'd been sober for twenty-six years. It seemed so inspiring to me that someone could stay away from alcohol for that long, so when he spoke, I listened. I almost looked at him as a father figure, and I didn't even know him yet.

One day I walked up to him and said, Hey Jack, I don't really know how to ask this, but would you be willing to be my sponsor?

The question is not if I'm willing, Brantt, the question is if you're willing.

What do you mean?

Willing to do the work, willing to take direction, willing to be honest with me, willing to live your AA program outside the walls of AA.

Yes, of course I am. For whatever it's worth, Jack, this time I feel different and I'm willing to do whatever it takes.

Okay then, let's get to work on your steps.

There are twelve steps in the recovery program, and Jack was going to be the perfect guy to guide me through them. We'd spend a lot of time together reading through the AA book and going to meetings.

Back on that day he just said, Here's the Big Book of AA. It's going to be your bible of sobriety. Read it from page one to the end.

I'd never read a book from cover to cover before, so asking me to read one that had close to five hundred pages seemed impossible.

Oh yeah, Jack said, one more thing: grab a highlighter and highlight anything in the book you can relate to. And when you're done we'll go over it, okay?

After my workout that night I picked up the Big Book, lay in bed, and started from page one. I really meant it when I said I'd never read an entire book before, so it was a good feeling to start on my first one.

The first chapter really had an immediate impact on me. I was getting good use out of the highlighter. My baby girl was now coming up on four months old, and I'd been getting to that point of wanting to leave. I just wanted to hold her. And when I'd started getting a little frustrated, I reverted back to when I always did things Brantt's way. But this time I had to trust the process and take direction.

Jack was an angel. This man gave himself whenever he could, spending hours with me talking about life and how he'd gained strength from sobriety. He had me start working on the twelve steps. Step 1 begins with admitting that you were powerless over alcohol and that your life had become unmanageable. Well, I could definitely concur with the first part of that step. If powerless meant going to rehab four times, blowing millions of dollars, being rushed to the hospital for overdosing, and grabbing my sister by her throat while I had a knife in my hand and not remembering a thing about it, then you know what? I may just be powerless . . .

I believe that alcohol and drug addiction is one of the hardest diseases to overcome. It's the only disease on the planet that tells you, You don't have it. Hence the merry-go-round for years, the hundreds of times I swore that if I can just get out of this, this one time, I'll never . . . again.

The second part of Step 1, admitting that your life had become unmanageable, fit with the first part. But back when I was playing hockey and making lots of cash, I'd been unable to admit anything was unmanageable—and to be quite honest, a lot of my teammates were right next to me during those nights. So if my life was unmanageable, then surely theirs were as well. There wasn't one thing in my life that I was managing other than breathing. Everything had fallen down around me. I didn't see a light at the end of the tunnel, I saw a Mack truck.

At the five-month mark Larry had that talk with me again—the hand on my shoulder, the news that they'd be keeping me for just a bit longer.

Meanwhile, I was just focusing on day-to-day tasks. I went from 253 pounds to 220. There were these stairs outside of the facility, probably a hundred of them. I'd put my iPod on and sprint up to the top, do push-ups, then run back down. As I was doing those push-ups I'd be saying to myself, Keep going Brantt, things are going to work out. I'd do ten sets, and by the end I'd be exhausted.

I was still receiving emergency pay from the NHL. It was really coming in handy. I was able to give Shauna a bit of money for Chloe and make my truck payment—somehow I'd been able to get approved for a loan on a Jeep Cherokee a few months before I entered rehab. But there was still that overwhelming fear: What the hell am I going to do when I get out of here? I was coming up on the six-month mark, and surely they were going to send me home.

And I had no home to go to. So all I could do each morning was to get on my knees and pray for strength and guidance. For some reason I knew in my soul that if I continued to just stay sober, things would work out. That may sound strange, but it was the same feeling I'd had that morning when I knew I'd taken my last drink.

I never had much, materially speaking, or at least not for long, but what I couldn't buy was faith. I just had it.

At almost the six-month mark Larry came up and said they were going to release me, but not totally. They wanted me to have two months of out-patient care before I left. They even had a place for me to stay, thanks to the owner of the treatment centre, a man named Bill Dooner. He'd been sober for fifty years and was one of the best guys I've ever come across.

Everything in his life he dedicated to helping people in need. Bill had this little cabin at the top of the hill he'd use every month or two when he came to check on the facility, and that's where he said I could stay. They also said that in the next two months I could start putting together a plan for going home for good. At least now I knew when I'd finally meet my baby girl. I was so excited and yet so nervous at the same time.

While I was doing the outpatient program, they gave me a job from time to time. I got paid eight dollars an hour to cut the grass and drive patients in the van to meetings and back. It gave me a sense of purpose. I mean, the last time I'd had an hourly wage was when I was sixteen, and I got fired from that job after I stole the stereo equipment.

By the time I hit the seven-month mark I was getting worried about where I'd stay when I got out in a month. I really didn't want to live with my grandparents, but my options were limited.

A few weeks later I was talking with my friend Rob back in Red Deer, Alberta, who'd just gotten a divorce from his wife and was feeling pretty down about it all. Rob was like, Hey Myze, if you need a place to stay while you get back on your feet, come live with me. Rob had been eight years sober at the time and was involved in AA, so to hear that was such a relief. It was yet another gift. As long as I stayed sober, things would work out right. It had been eight months now, and my time at Astoria Pointe had come to an end.

They were even about to have a going-away party for me. I was the only person to stay longer than three months, so it was going to be a happy but sad day as well. That place saved my life, all the people I'd met over the eight months saved my life, and the NHL and NHLPA saved my life for giving me the opportunity to stay without paying a penny. It gave me more of a reason to stay sober and to one day give back to the league.

And by now I knew exactly how I wanted to give back. My goal was to continue on my path and, as soon as I was able, to apply to the league to be a substance abuse liaison.

They'd asked me to share my story with all the patients, so the night before I was to leave I lay in bed thinking about what I was going to say. But the next day, as I sat down in front of about sixty people, I started to break down. I had a hard time keeping it all together. I was just so full of gratitude for what had been given to me at no cost—how could such a fuck-up be given all this love?

So many things were flying around in my head—from the first day of stepping on that scale to Larry putting his hand on my shoulder and extending my stay for yet another month, to losing all that weight, to receiving pictures of my baby girl, Chloe, to Shelly helping me peel away the pain of my past, to Jack helping me for hours with what true sobriety was. It was just overwhelming to actually feel I'd completed something in my life that was positive and had meaning.

I spoke for about half an hour. Then, after my speech was done, I hugged everyone and packed my bags. I was finally headed home.

When I got to Red Deer, Rob and I had a good long talk. He said, Brantt, for the next nine months all you have to do is go to AA meetings and stay sober. The job and all the other stuff will fall into place if you do that. I won't charge you rent as long as you do those things.

A couple weeks later, I went to a meeting with Rob and received my nine-month sobriety coin. I kept that in my pocket everywhere I went.

They told me that if I ever felt like drinking, I needed to put that coin in my mouth for five minutes. After those five minutes, they promised me that the urge would be gone.

But there was no need to put it in my mouth. The obsession to use was already gone.

I called Shauna to let her know I'd be in Edmonton the next day and to ask if she could bring Chloe over so that I could meet her. We set a time of two p.m.

The night before I couldn't sleep. I was a nervous wreck—it's not every day that you get to see someone who has half of you in them. I was wondering what she looked like, and what she was going to do when we looked at each other for the first time. One hour before Shauna got there I was pacing the room back and forth. I'll never forget that feeling, looking outside to see if they were there yet.

Finally I see Shauna's car pull up. My heart started beating a hundred miles an hour. Shauna walked in with Chloe, who had a blanket over her so I couldn't see her right off the bat. We went into the living room, sat down, and I pulled the blanket off her.

As soon as I looked at her she gave me the biggest smile. I instantly had tears in my eyes. Chloe was more beautiful than the pictures I'd seen. I picked her up and gave her a kiss, then a real long hug. I then knew what it was like to feel the love that a parent has for their children. We sat and played for a couple hours. I didn't want to let go, so it was real hard when they had to leave.

I was determined to head back to Rob's and start working on a plan. Chloe was going to have a father who'd be able to be there for her no matter what.

16

My years of booze and drugs were awful. Soul-destroyingly awful. But they're not hard to explain.

When you wake up hungover and ashamed of yourself, when you have no choice but to admit you've thrown away everything you've worked for and lost the trust and love of so many people who've stood by you, there's nothing you can do that day that can make you feel better than to have another drink.

It sounds insane, but there's no way around it. Even if you know, as every drunk does, that another drink is only going to make things worse in the long run, the long run doesn't matter nearly as much as the urgent need to blunt the edge of the pain you've inflicted on yourself. The long run requires hope, and as you drink away your career and your friends and everything you've accomplished, you also drink away your hope. You drink away the thing you need to stop drinking.

You need hope, because going without booze is hard. It's more than hard. Not because it feels impossible, though it often does. It's hard because it feels pointless. What's one day of sobriety going to do for you when digging yourself out of the hole you've dug will take countless days—if it's even possible? It's hard to build a life for yourself. It's more than twice as hard to do it twice, because the first time you were young and full of ambitious energy. Now you're a drunken loser.

The only way out is hope. Hope is the conviction that you don't have to fix a lifetime of mistakes in one day. It's the belief that if you put enough of those days together they'll add up to something. And that something will be better than the rush Jack Daniels or cocaine can give you. That belief had better be strong, because the days are long and tough, and you know better than anyone how easy it is to escape the grind of putting one clean day after another.

You don't anticipate how lonely it's going to be. When things were at their worst, I could always comfort myself with the knowledge that booze and drugs could lift my spirits. Gazing at rows of identical bottles of Jack in the liquor store was actually reassuring to me. It was a bit like those "In case of emergency, break glass" signs. Navigating the world without that sense of safety leaves you feeling raw and vulnerable. It's like losing a friend.

And the shit-kicking your pride takes doesn't make it any easier. When Christmas rolled around that year, again I didn't have enough money to buy presents. So I went to Walmart and got photos of Chloe made up for my family. That left me with about eighty dollars to spend on Chloe. And yeah, it did occur to me that eighty dollars would have got me through only a few *minutes* of partying.

That's humbling. When I was Brantt Myhres the NHLer, I could pretty much do whatever I wanted. When Brantt Myhres the recovering alcoholic got back to Alberta, I was sleeping on a buddy's couch. I was nobody special. I knew it. Who wouldn't want a break from being nobody special? Every bar, every liquor store I drove by reminded me that taking a break from being nobody special would be the easiest thing in the world.

But that would have been a heartbreaking waste of the clean days I'd already put in the bank. They may have only been days, but I'd put a lot of work into them, and they were precious to me. And they started to add up.

That's hope. Once you get a bit of it, hope starts to accumulate too. On Day 1, it's easy to believe that there's nothing better than another drink. It takes a while, and it's a lonely grind, but over time it becomes more and more clear that the days you've put together prove that you can do some of the things that not all that long ago seemed impossible. Maybe all of them.

For the next few months all I did was go to meetings and hit the gym. I would travel to Edmonton to see Chloe when I could. It was hard seeing her for a couple hours, then having to go back to Red Deer. I just wanted to hold her forever.

That spring, I knew it was time for me to look for a job.

I really had no clue what I wanted to do. And what I wanted didn't really matter anyway. The question was more, What *could* I do?

Rob introduced me to a friend of his, a golf pro at River Bend Golf Course, who offered me a job for the summer. I'd be booking tee times and working in the pro shop. Sixteen bucks an hour. I instantly did the math: it worked out to $1100 a month take-home. My ego screamed *No*. It told me that I was too good to be working in a pro shop, that I'd be a loser if I took that job. Brantt, how can you go from making a couple hundred thousand dollars a year to this job for peanuts? Don't do it!

The last time I'd been in a pro shop I was an NHL player. Probably drunk. Probably chirping at the guy behind the desk. When I got to the NHL, my cheques every two weeks were $28,000. Now I'm going to settle for $1100 a month?

But a little humility is not a terrible thing. I was no longer a hockey player; I was just another human being on the same planet as everyone else. I might as well get used to that fact. I made a pact with myself that I had to start from nothing and work my way up the totem pole.

Starting from nothing sounds great. And if there's no way around it (where else was I going to start?), then you might as well get at it. But it doesn't *feel* great. When I tried to get excited about my future I'd think about my current situation and it would bring me down. I had about $25,000 in debt, my credit was terrible, and my schooling had ended in grade nine. How the hell was I ever going to get a credit card, never mind an entire life? I couldn't even rent my own place—how was I going to buy my own home? It seemed a million miles away. I thought I'd have to win the lottery for that to happen.

I may have developed some bad habits playing hockey, but I picked up a few good ones too. If you get behind a few goals, coaches will remind you that you can only score one goal at a time. If you fall behind in a playoff series, they'll remind you that you can only win one game a time. You can't do everything all at once. If you try, you'll just make things worse. Just go out there and win your shift.

I accepted the job and started at six the next morning.

I actually liked working there: getting up early, grabbing a coffee, and putting in a good day's work felt great. It took about a month before I wasn't embarrassed to stand behind the till and book tee times. I was still always looking over my shoulder to see who was coming around the corner, praying it wasn't an old teammate. I wouldn't really know what to say. On the one hand I was trying so hard to just stay in the moment and be grateful for a paycheque, but on the other I felt somewhat ashamed.

From time to time my boss, Todd, would ask me to golf a round with him and a couple of his friends. That's when the question would always come up: So Brantt, anything else planned after the summer is over? I'd always go back to hope: Yes, I'm actually aiming to work for the NHL in helping with addiction issues. It was far from a lie because I believed it with all my heart. It's just that it seemed so far away.

After a month passed I got paid for the first time—the first time since I was sixteen that I cashed a cheque from a company other than hockey.

One night I had so much pain I thought I was dying. My stomach was killing me. I fell off my bed, crawled upstairs to Rob's room, and asked him to take me to the hospital. After doing some tests they came back and told me I had gallbladder issues and that I may need surgery.

As I woke up the next morning I was getting my vitals done by this beautiful blond girl. I didn't think too much of it till she asked if I wanted a ride home. After that I decided to ask her out on a date. It was my first date in over two years. When I was using drugs I couldn't even think of dating anyone—I'd just wanted to be by myself. So this was all new to me.

For the next three months we spent every day together. Jamie was the first girl I'd ever dated who I didn't lie to or cheat on. When I'd made a deal with myself that I was going to live an honest life, I meant it. All along, though, I knew deep down that it would eventually end, since she was thirteen years younger than me. So I just tried to enjoy the time we had together.

Dating Jamie was really hard on me. I didn't have much, materially speaking, and it made me feel less than. We'd go on trips and I'd be freaking out that I couldn't afford it. But I kept going back to how I wasn't going to pretend to be someone I was not—and that Brantt the person should be enough.

We'd been together for four months when Jamie decided to book a trip to Chicago to visit her brother Paul, who played in the AHL, and watch a couple of his games. I was not feeling too good about it. My confidence was pretty low when it came to her, since I had nothing in financial terms. And now she was on a plane to Chicago to hang with guys who were making a hell of a lot more than $1100 a month. It brought me right back to when Megan was flying around with all the NHL teams, and it drove me crazy. Even though I knew it would end, I really loved her, and I hadn't felt that in the years since Megan, so I didn't want to ever let it go.

Paul had a roommate, and let's just say that when Jamie got home I knew something was not right. Today, Jamie and the roommate are married and have a child. This really took a while to get over. My therapy was to work out like an animal, go to meetings, and pray. Slowly it got better.

Working your way up from the bottom isn't easy when you have no education. A high school diploma won't get you very far, and I didn't even have that. I cringed when I remembered that I used to be in the same tax bracket as a surgeon—and definitely without the qualifications. Unless you count Hockey U. But I knew I'd have to get a piece of paper that showed I could be useful.

I'm not an easy guy to intimidate. But applying to school scared me. I mean, the real thorn in my side, day in and day out, was the reminder of all the opportunities I'd squandered. Enrolling just made it official. I was at square one.

Better than being in an alley somewhere, though. If that was the alternative, I was ready to go to school.

There was the discouraging matter of tuition, however. I had about $150 to work with each month. Tuition was going to come to about $9000. I couldn't make the numbers work. I came to understand money in a whole new way . . .

I flashed back to my parents and how they'd thrown in the towel at the age of around forty, living off the government each month with pennies to spare. It creeps into your head that, well, maybe it's not that bad of a thing to just scrape by in life; both my parents have done it, maybe that's my path too? Each way I turned it seemed the easiest thing to do was throw in that towel. You can talk about hard work and taking responsibility all you want. But without enough cash to get the process started, a lot of hardworking people will never get ahead.

I'm lucky, I know it. I'm part of a brotherhood. If you've played NHL hockey, you're in, whether you deserve it or not. I'm not saying I deserved the league's support. But in the end I got it. That's right. I called Dan Cronin again. Only after I'd tried every other way. I hated the idea of Dan seeing my number come up and rolling his eyes. When someone has done so much for you, the last thing you want to do is ask for more.

On the other hand, I had to either call him or give up. And there was no way I was going to give up. Dan helped me out. Of course he did. He set me up with a guy from the league named Brian Lewis, who walked me through the steps. After submitting my paperwork, I waited by the phone for a couple days. Finally the phone rang and it was Brian.

Brantt, he said, the committee has agreed to fund your courses. Please keep all receipts and submit them when it's over.

It was another moment in my life when I couldn't deny it: these were the gifts of staying sober. How else could you explain it? Or maybe the gift wasn't so much that a break had come my way. It was that I was no longer too drunk and selfish to know what to do with it.

So I packed my bags and headed to Calgary to go to school. I'd been accepted into the Continuing Education program at Mount Royal University, where they offered a certificate in Addiction Studies. That certificate, I hoped, would bring me closer to my goal.

As I checked into a hotel not far from campus, I was feeling torn again. Shit, I'm going to look like an old man walking in there! I showered, put on some nice clothes, and walked into class—only to find that I wasn't the only thirty-something there trying to improve their life.

Now comes the part where I'm receiving books to study for quizzes they'd have at the end of the day. I couldn't wait to open those books and focus in on the material. I was finding out that I was really getting a free class on Brantt the Addict: with every page I turned I gained some insight into myself and why I did the things I did. I learned about the effects of drugs and booze on the brain, the way young people are especially vulnerable, the way addiction can be passed on from generation to generation, and how family can help break its grip. I learned how substances worm their way into our mind to make life's considerable challenges harder and its problems worse.

I loved every moment in class. For the first time I was actually interested in what was being taught. It helped that it was a subject dealing with my life, but it was still fun to do the homework, and so inspiring to be sitting at a desk with thirty other people studying. They were long days, but when it was time to close the books and head back to the hotel, I always felt I was further ahead than when I'd arrived that morning.

After six months I'd finished my courses. I passed them all, and so received my certificate. That was a big moment for me—and as I left the building with that certificate, I started to tear up again. I'd actually done something that was positive in every aspect. The tears came from my gratitude for the financial assistance.

Everything was coming together. I still didn't have a pot to piss in as far as the money went, but at that time it really didn't matter. Living in recovery was the most important thing. I knew that if I didn't stay sober, no matter what job I had or how much money I made, it would all disappear.

Back when I was at Astoria Pointe, I'd lie in bed and gaze at a lighthouse that blinked on and off in the darkness. I'd stare at that light throbbing out there in the fog and think to myself, I can't imagine my life ever becoming worth anything again.

Gratitude has a dangerous flip side. If you just take and take, eventually you start to feel worthless. It's human nature—you want to give back. Giving back is the only healthy response to generosity. If you don't, other people's generosity just creates another kind of debt. In other words, as great as Dan and the league had been, their help made me feel even worse in a lot of ways.

The thing that pulled me through was the promise I'd made to myself that somehow I'd help others. I didn't know how. Not exactly. But what I did know was that I'd gone further down the hole of substance abuse than anyone in the history of the league. I knew things that others didn't know. I'd made mistakes that others didn't need to make. Lying there in my bed in rehab, I swore I would use my hard-earned lessons to help others.

I felt that same need to give back when the league helped out with my tuition. Gratitude, definitely. But not just the everyday version of being thankful. I was also humbled, once again. I'd done a lot of work to pull my life together, but I hadn't even come close to doing it on my own. There is no way I could have made it that far without others. Many others, but especially the league, that brotherhood that had stood by me.

At that point I'd been sober for over a year. I hadn't solved all my problems by any means, but I felt different from the way I had for so long. Someone might think I should fix my own life before I tried to improve anyone else's. I mean, who the hell was I to be telling others how to live? But that overlooks the fact that helping others was exactly what I needed in order to help myself. I had taken enough. I needed to give.

It was time to make my proposal for the NHL and NHLPA. So I sat down at my computer and wrote for hours.

Dear Gary,

Thank you for taking the time to review this proposal. As I discussed previously with Doctor Lewis and Doctor Shaw, my goal is to enhance the substance abuse program available to current and former players. Having the personal experience of all four stages of the substance abuse program, and being the only player reinstated after Stage 4, I feel I am uniquely qualified to offer suggestions for the betterment of the program. I currently have 15 months of sobriety and recovery.

Objective
To establish a program where I am a full-time resource for all players who are encountering problems with substance abuse or lifestyle issues.

Goals
To be a first point of contact for any player who needs help addressing any addiction, substance abuse, or lifestyle issues. As a former player who dealt with addiction and lifestyle issues my entire career, one of the hardest things for me to do was to ask for help or share that I had a problem. My goal is to open a line of communication to me (a former player) who understands what a current player is going

through both professionally and personally. Another important goal is to remove the apprehension a player might have in contacting management, the league, family, teammates, or their agent.

Having an impartial person to call or meet with who has been through everything they are experiencing can help greatly in getting a player the help they might need. From a practical standpoint I believe this program can serve as a type of insurance policy for the hockey club. While every aspect of a player's life is heavily invested in by the organization, this is one area where I believe we can do more to help the players. Helping even one player as a person and consequently as a player will make this program a huge success.

After I finished the rest of the proposal I asked Rob if he could look it over and edit anything that needed editing. Then, when it was ready to go, I went down to Rob's office where I could FedEx it out. Altogether I sent eight of them: four to the NHL and four to the NHLPA.

As you can imagine, I was pretty nervous waiting for a response. After a couple weeks went by and I still hadn't heard anything, I decided to reach out. They told me they were glad I was doing well, but that I didn't have enough sober time under my belt. Looking at it from a doctor's point of view, they'd heard my "I'm doing good" story a hundred times already, so I understood.

I probably wouldn't have believed Brantt Myhres either.

17

I was really wanting to spend more time with Chloe—once every two weeks wasn't enough. So I called my friend Arnie in Edmonton to ask if I could stay with him when I came into the city. You might remember that Arnie was the guy I'd lived with before I went into treatment, back when we were getting fucked up. He had a drug problem still and was going downhill fast. But I thought that maybe if I stayed there he'd see how I was living and maybe it would rub off on him. So for the next little while I would travel into Edmonton for a day or two, see Chloe, then drive back to Red Deer.

When I called Shauna and told her it was time for Chloe to spend the night with me—that I didn't want to just see her for a couple hours, then leave—we agreed that she'd spend the night. That first night having her all to myself was so amazing. I set up a crib in my room and had it all arranged with stuffies and toys. We'd play all day, then I'd make dinner, give her a bath, and lay her down to sleep. And when she was sleeping I'd just rub her head and stare at her for hours. I couldn't believe that there was a mini Brantt.

It gave me a real sense of belonging in this world. I had such a love for Chloe that it's hard to explain. It was the first time in my life when I knew I would die for someone, no questions asked. And she also made the decision not to drink or do drugs that much easier. I now had a major responsibility in life. All the selfish acts had gone to the wayside. She was my number one priority. If I didn't stay sober I'd be no good to myself, let alone her.

After a few months of travelling back and forth, I asked Arnie if I could just stay there. Arnie still had his job where he'd go out of town for ten days, then come home for four. So the deal was that when he was gone I could stay in his room, and when he was home I'd sleep on the couch.

During that time I made up a proposal to the Western Hockey League, the league I'd played in for four years. I had a few meetings with them, but nothing was coming together as far as a job went. By now I was getting frustrated—no one was seeing I could be a positive influence on current players who had addiction issues. I still believed that, considering my past, it would be the perfect role for me: I would understand those players every step of the way. But I was getting a lot of nos.

Again, I had to just take a deep breath and keep moving forward. So while I stayed at Arnie's, I kept up with my routine: AA meetings and hitting the gym. It was keeping me sane. Plus, me and Chloe were building such a strong bond—every minute we were becoming closer.

Ever since I'd left rehab I'd gotten on my knees in the morning and at night before I went to bed to pray. I've never missed a day. And one night I remember getting on my knees before I went to sleep and taking a bit longer to pray this time.

> *Dear God, thank you for my sobriety and all the gifts you've blessed me with. I've been sober now for two and a half years, but I'm feeling lost, like I don't know what to do with my life. I believe there is something waiting for me out there, but waiting has been the hard part. I have no money left, and I know that you could never put a price on my sobriety the last two years, but if you could bless me with the strength to continue on no matter what my financial situation is I would really appreciate it. It's becoming frustrating, and I need to find some peace through all of this.*

I really meant what I'd said in that prayer; I couldn't see a future where I made a decent living, and it was weighing on me big-time. Thank god I had my AA meeting to go to and friends in the program to talk to. And I would always call my grandma when I was feeling down. She was always my rock when I needed it. She'd just say, Oh, dear, it's all going to work out. I'm so proud of you for staying sober. Don't let Grandma down—stay on the path.

My grandma's passing almost broke my heart.

I've always believed in angels—and when I talk about my grandma Jo, there was my angel. It's hard to explain, but when you have someone who's rescued you from harm and showered you with love, you become indebted to them. They have such a special place in your heart.

My grandma was a true Ukrainian, always cooking up the best dishes: perogies with bacon and onions, cabbage rolls in tomato sauce, baked ham with Caesar salad. My clothes were always washed and folded and I always had a few bucks in my pocket from Grams. She also had a side of her that was not to be crossed: you knew not to piss her off, or it would be grab-a-spoon time and watch out. Actually, I recall her only once ever grabbing the spoon, and looking back it was just a little love tap.

I really respected my grandma. She was such a hard worker, not only at the hardware store but when she got home as well—she was always preparing a big meal for family to come over. The one thing that sticks out with her was that she never ever lied to me. I could trust her no matter what. And when she met Chloe her eyes lit up with joy; she'd always have her on her lap, singing to her and brushing her hair. She made the best pickles, too—I'd have to stop Chloe from eating the whole jar, they were that good.

I knew my grandma was proud of the man I was becoming. I gave her my two-year coin of sobriety, and she later told me she kept it close to her bed. So yes, Grandma Jo was my rock. I pray to her every night, telling her how much I miss her.

I went home to Cold Lake for her funeral. My dad asked for a ride, and of course I agreed even though we still hadn't really talked since our blow-up.

During our trip home we started talking about my uncle Charlie, who was the Grand Chief of Treaty 7 Management Corporation. He was my uncle through marriage. And since I had Indigenous blood through my dad, who was a quarter Native, I had Métis status. I'd never spent much time on a reserve, so I didn't really understand the culture. But I started to think about how I could help some of the kids there who were dying from alcohol and drug abuse. I could make up a proposal for visiting schools on reserves and speaking to the kids on the pitfalls of abuse.

I'd grown up close to a reserve in Cold Lake, so I'd seen the issues these children faced. It was horrible. Kids at my junior high school would show up in dirty clothes and not have much food for lunch. In grade seven there was a guy in my class named Vinny who was living on a reserve. He would act out in class all the time, swearing at the teacher for no reason. Towards the end of the school year we came to class one morning to find out that Vinny had hanged himself—an awful thing to hear as grade seven kids.

I felt it would be the perfect job for me. I was close to being three years sober and had tons of experience with overcoming the odds. So after the funeral I went home and began to write the proposal. My father, who was good at writing, helped me with it. I told him that if I got hired I'd find a role for him—he hadn't worked in years, so it felt like the right thing to do, not to mention that he'd been a brilliant hockey mind back in the day. I was a little hesitant making that call since we had a history of not getting along, but I was in a different place in my life and it seemed like he was too.

On my uncle's suggestion I sent the proposal to a man named Ryan Robb, who was the CEO of Treaty 7. Then I waited by the computer the whole day. No response.

That night I was scheduled to go take care of Chloe, so that took my mind off how anxious I was. But once I got to Edmonton my truck needed gas and I had no cash left—and when I say no cash left, I mean I was at, like, zero. Arnie was away at the time but I knew he kept this jar of change in his room, so I went up, grabbed the jar, poured it out on the bed, and counted out sixty bucks. Then I texted Arnie and asked him if I could borrow it for gas so that I could go see Chloe. The message he sent back was, Of course buddy, it's all yours, no worries. Arnie might have been a drug addict, but he was a stand-up friend.

After I filled up the truck I headed out to see Chloe. It was a real snowy night out, and as I drove I was reflecting on everything current in my life. I then had one of those serene, peaceful moments . . . It's going to be fine, relax, go enjoy your daughter, you're sober and that's all that matters.

I woke up the next morning, made myself a cup of coffee, turned on my computer, and opened up my email. There was an email from Ryan Robb. My heart started pounding.

Hey Brantt, thank you for the proposal. Your vision sounds very intriguing. How about you come to Calgary to start on this vision? And how about you invoice us the six thousand you're requesting?

I jumped up and yelled out, *Six grand?!* Holy shit, I hadn't had that much money in my account for years.

Then I hit my knees and gave thanks for having my prayers answered. As they say, don't quit before the miracle happens, and I hadn't. In almost three years I'd never once strayed from the path—no matter how hard it got, or how down I was at times. And I wasn't going to give in this time. Now it was my time.

The first thing that came to my mind was that I could now buy Chloe a nice gift, and just how good it was going to feel not to worry about having enough gas money for my truck. I still had no damn clue what I was going to do, though. Nothing was set in stone—I was just winging it.

The next day I packed up and headed to Calgary with my dad. Treaty 7 put me up in a hotel while I was there, and actually paid me a per diem.

It felt like the good old days, back when I was playing. When I got to the office that first day, me and Ryan had a meeting. He suggested that I run with whatever I thought could work. You're your own boss now, he told me.

As I sat there I couldn't believe what I was hearing. My own boss now? I'm going to be a *boss*? This was just mind blowing! They even gave me an assistant right off the bat. Bev Latter was a lovely lady, full of energy and great at writing proposals. For the first week we just hit the boardroom and put down ideas on paper. Nothing was really sticking, but I knew I had to come up with something soon. We were going through ideas of how to run athletic programs on the reserve, since I knew that sport would be a huge component of the vision.

That's when I came across a school in Calgary called Edge Academy, a private boarding school with elite sports programs. When I drove there to check it out, I was just amazed by how big it was. They were changing the lives of all these students, combining academics with athletics, which is a recipe for success.

But by the way, enrolment cost tens of thousands of dollars. And hockey was tens of thousands on top of that.

So not everyone was going to find success that way. I certainly wouldn't have. The kids I knew growing up wouldn't have. The guys I knew in the show wouldn't have made it that way either. Sheldon Souray couldn't have taken that route. He was one of the only Indigenous players I knew who'd made it, but there was also Jordin Tootoo, Chris Simon, Sandy McCarthy, and a few more. And none of them had had the advantage of a private school education or a hockey academy, I can tell you that.

I started doing some research and found that there were thirty-three hockey academies in Alberta, but *none* were on reserve or catered to the cultural needs of Indigenous youth.

It hit me: why don't I try to build something like the Edge school but for Indigenous students? There were so many gifted kids out there, and all they needed was some direction, hope, and good role models.

I started working on a plan to create something similar to Notre Dame high school in Saskatchewan. The students would come from all over the province and live in Calgary during the term. We'd be starting with grades ten to twelve, and we'd have a women's team as well as a men's.

That's how the Greater Strides Hockey Academy was born. We were about to try and form the first charter school that catered to Indigenous students. Bev got to work on making a proposal to the government of Alberta, since we needed some cash to get us through.

After February 18 hit, I now had three years of sobriety. I remember sitting in my hotel room listening to music. It was the happiest I'd been in years. I couldn't stop singing and dancing around—for the first time since I'd played hockey, I felt like I finally had a purpose in life. Staying on the course with my sobriety was paying off. I'd known that one day it would, but when you're down and out it's hard to really believe it. Meanwhile, my little peanut Chloe was two years old, and she was the love of my life.

I'd been working in Calgary for a month now, and wanted to address my credit situation. I knew it would be ugly, but I had to start somewhere, right? So I went into CIBC and set up a meeting with this young guy. I was upfront with him from the start.

Hey man, I said, I've got terrible credit. I've been sober for three years now, but before that I was a mess. I'd love to get a Visa so that I can start to build my credit—can you look into that for me?

After that I went home and looked up my credit report. I had an R9, which is the worst—I owed $30,000 from old bills. I couldn't even qualify for a Walmart card! So I was sitting on the couch saying to myself, How the hell am I going to ever get out of this mess? Well Brantt, just like the last three years of your sobriety: one day at a time.

I received a call the next day from the guy at CIBC.

Hey Brantt, it's Cory. I pulled some strings for you and got you a $5000-limit Visa.

You're shitting me. A five grand limit? Wow, thank you so much, Cory! I'll never be late for a payment.

I hung up the phone and realized that this had been another God Shot. As long as I was working towards a better life, little gifts like that showed up out of nowhere. I also bought back my Gretzky stick and my Rolex watch that a stripper sold when we were doing coke—I went online and found the exact one I lost. I wanted to get back some of the material things I'd lost in my disease.

I was talking with Ryan Robb about some strategies moving forward with our school. We felt we needed to get our name out into the communities, so me and my partner Steve Parsons, my buddy and former teammate back in Providence, began planning a three-day hockey academy camp. I wanted to make it different from all the other hockey schools. I wanted to make it a bit over the top.

First off, I wanted there to be a cultural piece to it so that the students could better understand where they came from and how important it was to maintain their heritage. So I built in an hour when an Elder would come in to talk to the kids.

Then I wanted to add a nutrition piece, where we'd bring in healthy food and talk to the kids about the importance of eating well. I also wanted to include a piece where the kids would have some fun, so I added in swim time for an hour. And if we were to plan for eighty to a hundred kids, I wanted them to be safe, so I felt that having leaders for each group was important. I needed to find six or eight group leaders who were responsible.

Next was staff. You're only as good as the people you work with, so this was really vital. Steve mentioned that he had a friend named Travis Fleury; with Theo Fleury being his brother, he'd come from a hockey background. I met with him and thought he'd be perfect for the job: he would direct all on-ice activity.

I also wanted to have a woman on staff so that the other girls could relate. One day in walked this bright-eyed young woman who had an amazing résumé. Meagan Big Snake had been the first girl to leave her reserve and go to university in New York on a scholarship; she played on the women's hockey team while she went to school. After she left the interview, me and Steve looked at each other and were blown away. Well buddy, I said, looks like we found our girl. She was hired that night.

We then needed to find someone to run our off-ice conditioning. I got hooked up with a guy named Shane Spriggs who'd worked at Jarome Iginla's camp—he was perfect for the job. Then all the other staff fell into place.

Ryan came to me one day and said I should talk to this lady named Catherine from Enbridge Inc. Enbridge was, of course, a big player in the oil and gas sector. They were working on tons of reserves throughout Alberta, so they had a vested interest in sponsoring us, not to mention the cash. When we met to discuss our vision for the camp, Catherine loved it, and hired us to do our first one in Edmonton.

I was so excited. We were finally going to put Greater Strides on the map. It would be a free three-day hockey camp for a hundred reserve kids aged five to seventeen.

Our next challenge was to raise some money for our cause, so me and Steve decided to put on a charity golf tournament. And since we knew a lot of people, we had lots of work ahead of us. The first thing we did was put together a spreadsheet of all our contacts, then we started in. My good friend Sheldon Souray, a Métis, had played in the NHL for many years and had been an all-star a couple times. He agreed to fly in from Los Angeles to attend, as did Mike Green from the Washington Capitals— he had no Native in him, but was just a great guy from Calgary trying to support the cause. In total we had five NHL players agree to show up. It was looking good.

Around that time I decided to move in with Shauna. She lived in this tiny three-bedroom apartment. It was me, Chloe, Shauna, and Marcus, her six-year-old son. It worked out well, though, since I was home only two or three days a week, then at the hotel when I was in Calgary.

Our first camp was held in 2011. That camp, and the annual camps we held for the following five summers, turned out to be amazing. We were always pretty much full at that hundred mark. And we started getting interest from other companies as well, so that helped with funding. It was somewhat discouraging seeing the attendance from the parents, though—I mean, out of the hundred kids, there'd be maybe only ten to fifteen parents. It almost seemed like a place to drop their kids to be babysat for the day or weekend. But the parents who did attend were extremely grateful for the opportunity their kids had.

18

In July 2010 I was in L.A. visiting some friends when my cell phone rang. It was a friend from back home saying that Bob Probert had passed away from a heart attack. I was crushed. Probie was so young for that to happen. I remembered all the good times we had together and the amazing career he had.

But Probie wasn't just part of the hockey brotherhood, and he wasn't just a friend and workout partner. Losing someone like that will leave a hole in anyone's life. He was also a husband and a father. I sent his wife, Dani, a text message. I kept thinking about all those times sitting in Bob's kitchen, laughing together, shooting the breeze.

He was a good man. He would be missed—and the turnout at his funeral made it clear just how much. A who's who of hockey aristocracy was in attendance. Fans in Red Wings sweaters lined the route. Bob stood for so much that we all love about the game. He was the ultimate team player. He was as tough as they come.

That was what I idolized in Bob Probert before I met him. But then I realized what a toll it took on him. It cost him dearly to be the guy everyone revered. Not that he was faking it. He really did want to stand up for his teammates. God help you if you took liberties with Steve Yzerman. But Bob was a sweet guy. It was the sweetness that made him protective, not meanness.

I've been in a lot of hockey fights. And even I can't imagine what it was like to be the heavyweight champion for the better part of an era.

The pressure must have been crushing. The worst thing about losing a hockey fight isn't getting punched in the face—it's the pain of disappointing the people who believe in you. The GM who traded for you, the coach who sent you over the boards, the fans cheering for you, the teammates counting on you to make things right. The tough guy is the player who sees a situation that needs to be sorted out, and with his actions says, Don't worry, guys—I've got this.

If he loses, he's crushed.

And half the guys who do that lose.

And all of them wanted a shot at Bob Probert. So he had to put all that on the line—the faith that he was the best fighter of a generation—every time he stepped on the ice.

Like I said, crushing.

I knew that better than most, because he and I fought a lot of the same enforcers. We also fought a lot of the same demons.

I remembered the time I was over at his house in California, when he said that as soon as he was done playing, he was going to line up some vodka shots in front of the league doctors, give them the finger, and pound back the booze.

It was haunting to have seen not just the troubling fate that seemed to hang over a guy I truly cared about, but to have seen that there was something within this warm, caring, funny guy that had been drawn to that fate.

It wasn't much longer down the road when I got on the internet one day and the headline was Derek Boogaard dead from an overdose of drugs and booze. It was hard to read that, considering I could have or should have died many times from the same thing. I felt horrible for Derek and his family. The Boogeyman, as they called him, was six seven and weighed 280 pounds. What a name to have in the NHL—and you don't get that name by making saucer passes resulting in breakaways. But he probably hated it. I'd bet anything he hated the way people talked about him, the way coaches talked to him, the way he sat on the bench for whole periods in tight games. He probably made the decision to do whatever it took to make it to the NHL, then realized he was trapped.

I got out of the gym one day, jumped into my truck, and saw that my cell phone had missed calls: one from TSN, one from a reporter at Sportsnet, and one from CBC Sports. They asked me what I thought about the death of Wade Belak and Derek Boogaard.

What do you mean? Wade died too?

Yes, it looks like a suicide.

I was really taken aback. Bob, Derek, and now Wade: three guys like me. And now the media was trying to link their enforcer role with their deaths. I went on the radio in Edmonton the next day to talk about it.

My stance was that I felt that role was the hardest one in all of pro sports. It had taken such a toll on me since the age of sixteen, and the only way I'd known how to forget about it was to medicate. People have to remember that hockey is the only professional sport on the planet where you can fight bare-knuckled, and not only once, but three times before you get kicked out. There were countless nights when I couldn't sleep because I was so worried about hitting my head on the ice and dying.

I could see how this pressure could drive guys to drink or take drugs. Everyone was saying, Well, what if they weren't enforcers? What if they were goal scorers? Would the same thing have happened?

The answer to that is pretty simple: did three goal scorers just die? I'm not saying that skill guys don't have pressure, or that they don't drink. Trust me, they do. But I bet the skill guys would agree with me: the pressure of taking the entire team on your shoulders for forty seconds is something different. You'd have to actually be in that role to really understand what we go through on a daily basis.

Put it this way. If you've ever been to a hockey game and a fight has gone down, you know how the energy in the building changes. It's enough to drive twenty thousand fans into a frenzy. It's enough to lift a team of pro athletes. Well, that energy has to come from somewhere. Or someone. It takes a toll.

When I was five years old playing hockey on an outdoor rink, if some-one had come up to me and said, Hey, I've got a deal for you: the only way you're going to make the NHL one day is if you specialize in punch-ing people in the face. What do you think, kid? You up for it? That would have been the end of the conversation. I would never have played the game again.

It was shortly after that radio interview, in August 2011, when I got the news that Rick Rypien had also died. I just thought, Poor kid.

Then I got a call from TSN asking if I'd go on *Off the Record* to join a group discussion about enforcers and the role they had to play. I knew it would be based around their deaths as well. I'd always been a big fan of the show, so it was a tad nerve-racking, but really exciting at the same time. I flew to Toronto, and when I arrived at the TSN headquarters Michael Landsberg greeted me. He went over a few points pertaining to the show, and then said, Oh yeah, Brantt, I'll be doing a one-on-one with you at the start.

Holy shit. My heart started pounding and my palms were sweating.

But as in all things, I just said to myself, Time to go and get this done; just do your best. It was an amazing experience. I sort of blacked out during the questions 'cause this guy had been a legend to me growing up. Towards the end of the interview Michael suddenly asked me, Are you going to win the day? I knew what he meant. I was about to tear up, but I told myself to keep it together. Yeah, I said, I'm winning it so far. For me, every day that I don't drink or take a drug is a win for sure.

I woke up one morning after that to a message from HBO. They were doing a story on the three deaths and asked if I could be part of the inter-view. It now seemed like every time I turned around I was doing some type of interview on the topic. People were finally paying attention to just how hard that role was and the toll it took not only on the body but on the mind. I didn't want to be the guy taking a stand that the role of the fighter had made me do what I did, but it sure contributed to it no doubt.

I noticed that my memory wasn't what it used to be. It was getting frustrating—I mean, I'd forget the simplest things. And I knew that getting punched in the head over a thousand times over my life surely had to play a part. It would manifest itself in strange ways, like depression for one. I would isolate and not want to be around anyone. It would feel like a chore to interact with people.

On the other hand, my life was becoming sort of dreamlike. I'd been sober now for over three years and my bank account was growing. I went to work, went to AA meetings, went to the gym, and took care of my daughter. Those things seemed to keep my mind pretty clear. It may seem boring to some people, but I had to keep my life really simple. I'd had such an insane life before that having some serenity now felt so good.

I sent out another proposal to the NHL and the NHLPA. Now, with a new director in Donald Fehr, I was hoping for some traction. Donald got back to me—and other than the league's rejection of my first proposal it was the first time someone actually responded—and said he wanted to meet in Calgary. I really felt this was my chance to get an opportunity. So I drove to Calgary, met with Fehr at the Hilton hotel, and had a great discussion, or at least I thought so. He told me to stay on the path and keep in touch. So that's what I did, except that not much transpired.

Anyway, as I drove home to Edmonton I started to reflect on the last three and a half years. The sun was shining in my face, it was a beautiful day out, and I felt this overwhelming sense of gratitude mixed with joy rush over me. It was the same serene feeling I'd had when I'd first hit my knees and prayed to God for help back in 2008. First off, not once in the last three years had I ever felt even one urge to drink or do drugs, which was a blessing from God.

I had a great job. I'd cleaned up my credit. I'd put aside a sum of cash to one day put a deposit on a house. All my psoriasis had cleared. And me and my baby girl, Chloe, were building a love that no one could ever come between. She was my life, and I wasn't going to follow my parents in how they raised me.

If you were to tell me that all this stuff would happen when I checked into rehab for the fifth time—that I'd stay sober, that I'd never stop fighting, that I'd put my faith in the good of this universe—I would have said, Never in a million years, it's just not in the cards for me. I've sunk too far down, there's no way out of this mess I've created.

In April 2015 I was in Calgary for a meeting with the people who ran Treaty 7. I'd been hearing some rumblings that the money was drying up, and sure enough, they told me there would be no more funding for my hockey programs. I was really sad over the whole thing. I mean, I'd created something special, something to be proud of. We'd been able to help hundreds of kids and give them some hope. So I'd never envisioned the money coming to an end. I must say, though, that this was the first time in my life when I had no regrets. There'd been no lies followed by more lies—it had been an honest effort in making my life and others' lives better.

So I got in my car and started driving home. And just as before, I had this weird sort of feeling that everything was going to be okay. It was such a peaceful feeling—and I'm not sure why I felt that way because I really had no clue what I was going to do for work.

A few weeks later I said to Chloe, Hey, let's jump in the truck and head to Penticton for a week to just chill by the beach and get some sun. Uncle Lorenzo will be there with his girls, so you'll have someone to play with. We loaded up the truck and headed for B.C.

It was a real nice morning outside, very hot. I asked Lorenzo if he could watch Chloe while I went to the gym for an hour or so. I had a hard workout, then bought a protein shake and headed back to my truck. I had a BlackBerry back then and its red light was flashing, meaning I had a message.

It was an email from Dean Lombardi, the GM of the Los Angeles Kings. My heart was racing like crazy. When I opened it, all it said was Please call me.

I knew that within the last year three Kings players had been charged and arrested—Slava Voynov was charged with domestic abuse, Jarret Stoll was caught with ecstasy at a pool party in Las Vegas, and only a week or so before, Mike Richards was busted trying to cross the border with OxyContin. So I had a pretty good idea why Dean Lombardi was trying to get hold of me.

As I started driving back to the hotel, all these memories came flooding through me. The one that really stood out was from my first night at the Astoria Pointe treatment centre, the night I'd written in my journal that if I stayed sober, one day I would build a program to help players not go through the fucking nightmare I had to go through.

But I didn't want to get too excited. I mean, hey, Dean could have just wanted to talk and get some advice, right?

When I got back to the hotel I ran down to the beach. Lorenzo was there with all the kids, so I said, Bro, I have to call Dean Lombardi, can you watch Chloe for a bit? Then I went back to the room and called the number. His assistant picked up the phone, and when I asked for Dean I heard him say, Tell him I'll call him back in about thirty minutes. All I did for those thirty minutes was pace back and forth, non-stop, making sure I had full service on my cell phone every couple minutes or so.

Then the phone rings.

Hey Dean, long time no chat.

Hi Brantt. I'm sure you're aware of what's gone on here in L.A.?

I started going into a long-winded ramble about how I could help.

But Lombardi stopped me and said, Listen, there's no need to sell yourself. I was the one who called you, right?

I laughed. Yeah, you're right.

Can you come down to L.A. in the next couple of days to talk face to face?

Yes, of course I can.

Call my assistant back and she'll arrange your travel details.

As soon as the conversation ended, I fell to my knees and had tears coming down my face. I couldn't believe that after five years of sending proposals to the NHL and NHLPA, I finally had my chance.

19

No one's going to look back on my NHL career and want to talk about what I did on the ice. If my name comes up it'll be as the guy who set a record for substance-abuse suspensions. I get that. I'm not proud of it, but I get it.

There are a few guys like that. More than a few, probably. Think of Derek Sanderson. No one talks about his numbers. He figures in hockey lore not as the guy who teamed up with Bobby Orr as the sniper on the most exciting team in the game. He's remembered as the life of the party, and less cheerfully, as a guy who drank himself out of the game.

The tough guys often leave darker stories in their wake. Few people remember John Kordic's fights, but most hockey fans know that it took nine cops to subdue him the night a booze-, coke-, and steroid-fuelled rage ended in his death.

Sure, these are old-school guys who played back when there were tubs of iced beer in the dressing room and guys like Guy Lafleur still smoked cigarettes between periods. But if you think playing in today's NHL, with more money and more pressure, makes the temptations of booze and drugs easier to resist, you'd be wrong. For one thing, painkillers and sleeping pills are passed out like Halloween candy. Hockey players are always banged up, and therefore powerful drugs like OxyContin and Toradol are never hard to come by.

And that's just the legal stuff. Illegal drugs like coke and ecstasy are nearly as common. Back when Bob Probert was busted for coke, it was like everyone gasped in horror. But when images of Evgeny Kuznetsov doing coke showed up on social media, the response was more of a shrug. Not that anyone condones it. But no one is surprised anymore. It's everywhere. In fact, as guys lay off the booze to stay in shape, they often turn to drugs instead. Needless to say, that's not exactly a good-news story.

The point is not that my blunders are any less regrettable or embarrassing because other guys have also made mistakes. I still hold the record, after all. My point is that many of these tragedies are to some extent foreseeable. I can't tell you which guy is going to let his newfound fame and money convince him that he's invincible. But I can guarantee you that some young millionaire with no education is going let his partying get away from him. Or let his reliance on painkillers slip out of his control. Or find that the endless banquet of drugs and booze available to him helps take his mind off the pressure a little too much. It's going to happen.

And even if you know it's going to happen, you may not always be able to prevent it. But you can prevent it from becoming a promising young athlete's unintended legacy.

July 5, 2015

> In Edmonton airport, flying to LA to meet with the GM. Let's just
> say it's a very exciting day for me—even if nothing happens job
> wise, it will be a great experience.

As the plane descended into L.A. I was looking down at the ocean feeling like I just couldn't believe what was happening. It was like a dream. Once we'd landed I took a cab to the hotel, which was only a few blocks from the TSC, the Kings' practice rink.

> It's 11 pm and I'm sitting in my hotel room that the LA Kings
> got for me—I'll be here till Wednesday. My meeting is at 9 am

tomorrow with Dean Lombardi. I have no clue what to expect, but what I do know is that God is going to flow through me. I've worked the last 7 years for this meeting, and I must say that it feels like a fucking dream being here. I used to have dreams from time to time about Darryl and Dean, playing for the Sharks again, hockey dreams. Time to turn it over . . . Night. Amen.

I woke up early, had a shower, and put on some nice clothes. I was having some head issues—a tingly, almost spaced-out sort of feeling—and was hoping it wouldn't come back during the meeting. When I got to TSC I went upstairs to Dean's office. I was sitting on the couch in the reception area when he opened his door and said, Come on in. I went in and sat down.

So, he said, how are we going to do this?

Dean, it's all right here in these pages. I've had this in my head now for seven years.

He grabbed the pages and started reading. All was quiet.

Finally he said, This is some pretty good stuff.

Here's part of what I'd written.

Player Assistance Director: Los Angeles Kings Hockey Club

Objective: To act as a lifestyle director for all members of the Kings management staff under contract. I will be the main point of contact for any players in the Kings system for support regarding any substance abuse issues or issues pertaining to the pressures of a professional athlete.

Projections of the program: We need to build the trust of the players from the get-go. I have to put myself in their shoes, almost as if I were sitting in that dressing room with 23 other guys. How would I react to this person who has been hired by the team to perform this position?

I think the first step would be to speak with each player individually at camp rather than in a group setting. Speaking one on one will give them a place to open up and to feel there is no threat of the conversation leaving the room; you instantly build a relationship with the player, face to face. We can schedule it for 15 to 20 minutes each, no different from the players doing their fitness tests.

It is vital that I be a regular part of the day-to-day functions that occur. If I'm seen by other players as a part of the team, when they see me talking to someone (a player), the red flags won't go off—I will be seen as just one of the guys: this is very important. I do not want to be seen as a police officer.

This also pertains to the AHL club.

Stages
In order for these players to step up before it's an issue, there needs to be stages in place where they can come to me without my being obligated to contact management.

Stage 1
Player reaches out to me—he is having issues with alcohol, pain meds, or street drugs, or simply wants to talk about outside pressures. He casually wants to talk about the incident. I will meet with the player one on one. He will understand that our conversation is strictly confidential; it will not be heard by anyone else. I recommend that in Stage 1 there will be no name attached to the report—instead, just a number that I'll assign. That way management will have an understanding of an issue, but names will not be made public. The player will also be made aware of this.

Stage 2
The player has reoccurring issues that need attention. I will work with the player to determine what that will look like. The first step would be to see if the player is willing to attend recovery meetings

(AA) with me. The second step would be to connect the player with a local therapist; I have the resources in the recovery field to do that. My close friends in Los Angeles are very respected in the recovery world. I would then suggest to the player that in order to keep him honest in this process, I myself would oversee a random drug test throughout the year. I would suggest one test every two weeks. The player will not be made aware beforehand of this process.

Stage 3

If the player fails a drug test after Stages 1 and 2, we will then bring in Dean Lombardi and whomever else Dean feels should be there in the meeting. At that point we will all sit down and discuss the issues at hand. If the player or Dean feels like it is getting out of control, we will look at my staying with the player for a period of time, including rooming with him on the road. If I feel that the player is not progressing, we will then look at rehab. Now, rehab does not have to be a month-long process; I would recommend a two-week stay at least. What that does is give the player enough time to get involved in recovery as well as work on the issues regarding his drug or alcohol problem. It also instills in the player the idea that at this stage, this is very serious. This is all in house— we will not be contacting the NHL or NHLPA.

Stage 4

At some point in these stages, there needs to be consequences. I think that if the player hits Stage 4, consequences need to be implemented. Suspension and loss of pay are options. If there are no consequences, the player will look at it as, Oh well, if I get it, then I get it. There needs to be an understanding that if he does not follow what's been laid out, he will be held accountable for his actions.

The consequences will be put into a contract upon Stage 3, signed by both management and player.

At this point Dean put the pages down and yelled, Blakey, come on in here! Rob Blake was Dean's assistant GM.

Blakey, do you think the players will talk to Myze?

Ahh, I don't think so, Dean.

I looked at Rob. Well Rob, this program isn't meant for guys like you—when you played you were a Hall of Famer, an all-star player year after year, never struggled with booze or drugs. It's meant for the two or three guys who will need it—like the three players who were arrested last year.

Dean said, Good point, Brantt. So, how long should you be around for?

Dean, a key component of this program is that I'm ingrained in the team's day-to-day functions. If I only come in once a month and the players see me talking to someone, they're going to say, What's Myze doing talking to so-and-so? There must be a problem, right? So I suggest that out of every month I spend twenty days with the team, then go home for ten days.

There was no pushback from Dean. All that was left to talk about was money.

July 7, 2015 My Dream Job Came True

I first have to say that I am forever grateful to God for this opportunity. I just got hired by the LA Kings Hockey Club to be their Lifestyle Coach for the year. I'm at a loss for words at the moment. I have had this goal ever since my first night in rehab 7 years ago. It actually has come true. Never stop dreaming, it's sometimes all we have to keep us going. Again—this all happened so fast, within 3 days, so I'm trying to process it all. I'm so fucking proud and happy . . . Keep going, Brantt. The best is yet to come.

The next day I flew back to Edmonton on cloud nine. I knew I had a couple months to prepare a speech to the team, which almost made me sick with anxiety. The vision of standing in front of the team and coaches and delivering a speech would keep me up at night for the next two months.

It was around August, and the Kings had already made a trade for Milan Lucic at the draft. I was in Kelowna visiting some friends when my phone rang. It was Milan's agent, Gerry Johannson.

Brantt, I need to talk to you. Where are you?

I'm in Kelowna.

No way—this may work out then.

What?

Milan has been having some personal issues. He's having a real hard time with the suicide of his father and the fact of leaving Boston. Could you meet with him while you're there?

Sure, of course I will.

After we'd talked a bit more I hung up the phone and thought for a minute. I wasn't even on the Kings staff yet, so I wrestled with the question of how to handle confidentiality. But I finally figured that the right thing to do in this case was to be open with Dean. So I picked up the phone again.

Dean, I got a call from Gerry—he wants me to spend some time with Milan, get him on the right track, but mostly just have a guy to talk to, to have support.

Jesus fucking Christ, do I have to fucking worry here, Brantt? I just paid this guy six million fucking dollars!

Relax, Dean, I'm on it. It's all good. He'll be fine.

The next day I met Milan for the first time. We had lunch and talked about everything. I could see that he was feeling like the weight of the world was on his shoulders, but he's a strong guy, and felt he'd power through it.

So I told him, I'll see you at training camp in a few weeks, bud. Let's get together when I'm there and you're all settled.

Looch was such a great guy—I could see why so many teams were trying to trade for him and why the Kings got him. You could tell he was a team-first kind of player, that he loved his teammates and would do anything for them. It's funny, you see him on TV just crushing guys, then you meet him and think, What a kind soul, how the hell can he make that switch?

But the more I thought about it, I understood fully how he could. It felt good to actually have a guy on the team I could talk about fights with. Lucic was regarded as one of the toughest guys in the league. He'd paid his dues, and then some. (By the way, Lucic is the only guy I break confidentiality to mention by name, because he was one of the only players to mention mine in the press. Reading in a major publication that he thought I'd really helped him meant the world to me.)

When I got to L.A. in September, Dean wanted to meet with me about what I was going to do at training camp.

I said, Well, I'd like to start by addressing the whole team. But if anyone has any issues, they won't come forward in that atmosphere. So after that I'd like to have one-on-one meetings with each player at camp.

Okay, Dean said. I'm going to give a speech first, then I'll leave and you can take over.

That night in my hotel room was a complete blur. I was scared shitless about standing in front of the entire team, but of course it needed to be done. My head started to act up on me again—I was feeling out of it, and the tingling pressure was coming back. The only thing that helped was to put a hat on and lie down on the bed, taking deep breaths. The reason for the hat started a few years back when I had my first ever panic attack. I noticed that if I put my hand on my head, some of that pressure would go away. It was the same thing with the hat—if I put it a notch tighter, I'd feel better. It's hard to explain how scary it is to deal with brain issues. You know there has been some damage. There is no way around that if you've been punched in the head thousands of times, never mind the body checks and other rough stuff. But you don't know how much or exactly *what* has gone wrong. It's like you're walking on thin ice, worried that you can go through at any moment. And if that moment is when your life is finally back on track, the idea of having it all fall apart is terrifying.

When I got to TSC the next morning I had no office yet, so I was directed to a cubicle next to the lounge where all the players ate and hung out. I went over my speech time and time again in my head, right up until Dean came down and all the players and coaches gathered in the video room. There were about thirty people there for Dean's speech, which was based on what had happened to the three players who'd been arrested and how, as teammates, they needed to be more accountable to each other. Accountable: hockey players use that word a lot. They know how to step up on the ice (though whether they have the balls to actually do it is another question). But for most guys, dealing with a teammate's off-ice problems is difficult territory.

Dean went on for about half an hour. It was, by far, the best speech I've ever heard anyone give. His passion was over the top. The whole time, though, all I could think about was my own speech.

When Dean finished, the room was silent. Then he announced, That's all I have to say. Brantt, you're up. Then he left the room.

As I walked up to stand in front of everyone I could feel my heart racing and everything starting to get blurry. There in the first row were Darryl Sutter, Dustin Brown, Anže Kopitar, and Drew Doughty. Now I felt really fucked. Here was the core of a team that had just won the Stanley Cup and a coach I admired more than anyone in the game.

I started in, my voice sounding slow and my knees knocking together with nervousness. But I'd waited seven years for this opportunity, and it was finally here. All I could say to myself was that if I fainted I'd lose the job and it would be over. So keep it together, Brantt, come on, you can do this. Yeah, here were a bunch of big-league hockey players judging me. But it wasn't all that long ago that I was sitting where they were, probably being a smartass.

So I delivered my speech, giving them a rundown of my history and why I was there. Then it was over. And as they all got up and left, I felt the weight of the world leave my shoulders.

The next day was one-on-one meetings with each player. Now I was in my comfort zone. I had zero anxiety; these talks were right in my wheelhouse. I'd even built a program on my computer so that I could have a file on each guy.

The first player to come in was Jeff Carter. He sat down and then I asked him certain questions. Carts was a straight arrow, so there was no concern there. Actually, it was nice to just break the ice and have a personal talk. Carts was really close with Mike Richards, so that must have been tough for him.

That's pretty much how the next two days of interviews went. Some guys had a little more on their plate than others. But I'd already worked out a system in which I'd assign each player a colour, from green (meaning he was good to go), to yellow, to red. They all seemed suspicious of me, not giving me any more than I needed or asked for. I don't blame them.

After I'd done all the interviews, Dean said, Hey, we're going to take a car and head down to San Diego to meet with the Chargers staff. I understand they have a guy there in a similar role to yours—they call it Player Engagement. I'd like you to sit with him for the day.

It made sense to me that Dean was looking to the NFL, since he'd often said that the NHL was behind in their thinking when it came to supporting players on drugs and alcohol.

As we were driving there, though, my head started acting up again. And again I was trying to talk to myself, saying, Everything is fine, buddy, just hang in there, there's nothing to be worried about.

When we got to the stadium we met with the coach and GM as well as the Player Engagement guy. It was my first experience with the NFL, so I felt like a little kid, full of excitement. I had these moments during the day when I'd be sitting in the boardroom thinking, Okay Brantt, take a deep breath, I know you're sitting next to the GM and coach of an

NFL team and the GM of the Los Angeles Kings and I know you used to have dreams of playing again for Dean and Darryl but it's all good, buddy, no, this is no dream, it's as real as real gets . . .

They were all nice—no egos there, just class acts getting together to pick each other's brains. We had a good meeting. But the whole time I was feeling really off again—my head felt fucked, and I couldn't wait to head back. I never told anyone about this head issue I was having, but it was really scaring me. All I could think about was all the fights I'd been in and the damage that must have been done to my brain over it all. When we finally got back to L.A. and I went straight to the hotel to put my hat on and lie on the bed, taking those deep breaths.

The next day Dean called me up to his office and said, Well, we need to find you an office, young man, come with me. We went down and met with the head equipment trainer, Darren Granger.

Darren, Dean said, we need to find Myze an office, and it can't be anywhere near our offices upstairs.

So we looked around near the dressing room, but there was nothing. Then Darren said, I have an idea—let's go check out the jersey room next to the laundry room. When we opened its door all that was in there were practice jerseys hanging on a steel rod.

Dean said, Grange, can you add some carpet, paint the walls, and get a phone and desk put in here?

Yeah, no problem.

The next day guys were in there working away to turn the jersey room into a cool office.

Meanwhile, I had to get to know not only all the Kings players but also the entire AHL team and its prospects, not to mention all the staff— so we're talking about ninety people I had to make my way around and introduce myself to. It was a bit mind-blowing to say the least. Fortunately I already knew the head and the assistant coaches, Mike Stothers and Chris Hajt, from the Kings' minor team, the Ontario Reign. They were both awesome humans, and I really enjoyed driving the ninety minutes from L.A. to the city of Ontario to make my face more recognizable.

There's a difference in attitude between an NHL and an AHL player. In the AHL, each guy is so goddamn hungry to get that one shift in the NHL that his ego is minimal. By hockey standards they're making pretty much peanuts, but they're just so happy to be there. The big boys in the NHL are more guarded. There's more of a wall in front of them, and very few get behind that wall. I mean, when you're making millions of dollars a year, people are always asking for your autograph. It's tough to really let your guard down.

The PR guy from the Kings told me there'd be a press release about the hiring the next day, and to be ready for interviews. Sure enough, the *Los Angeles Times* called me that night in the hotel room and published a huge piece the next day on my new role. Once that happened, I had to do a conference call with about seven or eight different news media outlets, from TSN to NBC, to ESPN. The headline TSN's story was "From Lifetime Ban to Kings' Lifeline?"

It was feeling all sorts of surreal to have this type of attention. I mean, even when I'd played, this had never happened. So I knew that what I'd worked so hard towards for years had meaning in the hockey world.

One of my first meetings came about unexpectedly. Our team doctors were in the conference room when Dean came in and said, Hey, I want you in here for this. I was working out just then, so there I was in my workout clothes, still sweating, as I sat down and listened to what they were talking about.

The subject just then was Ambien. I had an idea of the league-wide problem with Ambien—team doctors were giving them out like candy. It bothered me, since I knew the dangers of sleeping pills if they were taken longer than a few days at a time.

So I asked our doctor, When the team goes on an East Coast road trip that's around a week long, and a player or coach comes to you and asks for some Ambien, how many do you prescribe?

He said, I give them thirty days' worth.

I was blown away by that. So I offered my thoughts.

When a player goes on the road, I began, these pills should only be used for the first couple of nights to get his sleep regulated. But what do you think is going to happen when the team gets back from that road trip and the player is now in his own bed in L.A., but he can't sleep within five minutes? He's going to say, Hey, there's twenty-three more Ambien in the bathroom, fuck this tossing around, I'm going to get up and take one. That way I'll know for sure I'll be asleep in under ten minutes. Now we're dealing with a dependency problem here. After taking those for longer than seven days, they really fuck with your head.

At this point our trainer, Chris Kingsley, spoke up and said, Myze, starting this year we'll be monitoring each and every pill that goes out to the players—they'll be getting them only if needed.

The next day I walked into Dean's office for a meeting.

So Brantt, he began, how the hell am I going to know if this program is working or not? You've got it set up so that I'm pretty much in the dark here unless it's Stage 3.

Dean, a great year is if you don't hear from me—not one phone call, text message, or knock on your office door. I know that sounds fucked up because you have to get reports weekly from all the staff, but it's true.

Well, you're right. I've hired you to do a job, and I'm going to let you do it. And if it gets to my desk, it's too late in my opinion.

The next morning I went to the rink and all the guys were sitting around this big table in the lounge area. That's where they'd always eat. After all, we had chefs who would cook all our meals, and it was incredible food. Anyway, I knew I had to place my ass right down in the middle of this table. Now, I'm no dummy; I knew this table was for players only. Not even the coaches sat there. But I knew I had to force myself—it was important that I had conversations with these guys, that I get to know them each day a little better. It was so strange hearing those guys call me Brantt when they'd walk by. It's always been Myze—I haven't been called by my first name since I was fourteen.

So I had to really push myself to interact with this group. And for the first few months they were really standoffish. But whenever I was around I'd just make sure to walk up to a guy and start asking him about his day.

I found out just how unknown I was to the team when Drew Doughty was sitting on the medical table getting some treatment one day, with about ten other guys in the room.

Hey Brantt, Drew said, so what kind of player were you? Did you score lots of goals or what?

I started to laugh. Nah Dewy, I was a fourth-line plug—I was paid to protect guys like you.

At that moment I was like, Shit, I feel like an outsider. Someone in a hockey dressing room not knowing what kind of player I was: that had never happened to me before.

Our captain that year was Dustin Brown. Brownie too seemed standoffish with me. If I walked by him and didn't say hi or good morning, he wasn't going to say anything. He reminded me of our captain in San Jose, Owen Nolan—they had similar personalities. I knew Brownie was a good guy somewhere deep down. I just needed to gain his trust; after all, it really was his team to lead.

Our other big gunner was Anže Kopitar. He'd been with the Kings his whole career and made the most money out of anyone. Kopie was from Slovenia, but he could have passed for a Canadian. He was this big cool human of a hockey player, real easy to talk to, and he led on the ice. It was clear to see that Brownie and Kopie didn't have any off-ice issues, so I was more or less just trying to create a conversation once in a while.

I already had a good idea of who to keep closer tabs on—it was pretty easy to figure that out just from hearing the stories the next day at the lounge table. Now, I could give a shit about them going out and having a good time. I encouraged it, actually: it's a big part of team bonding. I was never a guy to say, Now now boys, make sure you don't have much to drink and that you're home at a decent hour. Instead I was like, If you're going out, have a fucking blast—just make sure you don't cross that line of no return.

The line of no return is touching any drug that's illegal, driving after one drink, fighting with your girlfriend or wife where it escalates to laying a hand on them. I hadn't been brought in to act as a cop or watch guard; I was there for support if one of the players needed it. And if they didn't call or knock on my office door, my hands were tied, there was nothing I could do. I wasn't a miracle worker.

We had our first exhibition game in Phoenix. That afternoon I was at the hotel putting my suit on, looking in the mirror, feeling so proud of what I'd accomplished over the last eight years. It all still felt like a dream, but a great one no doubt. When we all got on the bus, Dean and Darryl sat at the front, Rob Blake and myself sitting across from each other. I just remember that it was a beautiful day out, and that as we were driving I'd look over at Dean and Darryl just to make sure it wasn't a dream. I kept saying to myself, Is this seriously fucking happening?

20

It was opening night, and our first home game. October 17, 2015. I believe we were playing Minnesota. My car radio was blasting as I pulled up to the Staples Center, which was just incredible; what a venue to play hockey at. I went down through security, headed to the press lounge— they always had a buffet laid out and games on the TV—grabbed a bite to eat, then headed up to the top where management sat in the boxes. I took a seat next to Jeff Solomon. What a great guy. I really liked Solly— he was Dean's right-hand man for anything to do with contracts, the collective bargaining agreement, or cap issues, a real brain to say the least.

I remember that night thinking, What should I do if we win? I was like, Fuck it, I'll stand in the hallway just outside the dressing room and high-five guys as they walk by. Then I started to get real nervous, thinking, What if they don't high-five me back? I'll look like an idiot!

But as I watched the game from the team suite, it was another "I can't believe what's happening to me" moment. I just tried to focus on the play. I know it sounds crazy, but I was so damn invested in this game—every time we had a scoring chance I'd tense up, and when we actually scored it felt like I was sitting on the bench, excited for my teammates. I wanted the boys to play well, and in part I mean that selfishly, because anyone who's around a team that's losing is no fun, and the atmosphere is dull and quiet. When you're winning, though, everyone is happy and smiling, in a good mood. So I was like, Come on boys, let's win this one so that I can go down to the dressing room after the game with a swagger on.

October 18 FIRST WIN AS A KING!

We had our first win last night against Minny—it sure felt great
to breathe again. We lost our first three games of the season so I
was feeling a bit like it was my fault. Of course I know that's not
the case, but I was like WTF—we should be winning every game.
I'm settling in with the club now. I would have to say my favourite
moment of this whole experience was last night when we won. I
stood outside the dressing room, and when the guys came off the
ice I was right there high-fiving all of them! It felt like a dream, it
really did. Thank you Lord for that moment! I will NEVER forget
it . . . Well, back to work! Amen.

After the game I sat in the players' lounge at the back of the dressing
room, chatting with a few of the guys. They were all just sitting around
checking stat sheets, talking about the game, eating some food that had
been catered in. It felt cool just to be a part of it all. I was the only
non-player in that room, but seeing all the boys in their towels walking around, laughing, discussing where they'd be going for a beer—it
brought back so many memories of when I'd played myself. Later I just
grabbed a Gatorade and drove back to the hotel.

Soon after that we headed off to Colorado for a two-game trip, and
when I got to the airport I realized we were taking a chartered plane.
I was like, Wow, I can't believe this! It had been maybe fourteen years
since I'd flown on a private plane. When I got to the top of the stairs
there was our travel guy with an envelope full of cash for meal money; he
showed me where I'd be sitting. As I sat down I said a little prayer, just
thanking God for this incredible opportunity. Then, after takeoff, the
next thing I know a girl is asking me what I'd like to eat—they even had
a menu with all this great food! Now and then I'd catch myself looking
over at Dean and Darryl, still in awe of what was really happening.

When we arrived at the hotel I went up to my room and took a video
of it, just talking about how awesome it was to be back again in the NHL.

Our time in Colorado was typical of how these trips would go for me: first off, we'd always stay in five-star hotels. In the morning I'd go with the players to the pre-game skate. We'd all pile on the team bus, where I'd usually sit with one of our assistant coaches, Davis Payne or John Stevens, and sometimes the video coach, Sammy Lee. At the rink I'd go into the dressing room to chat with the trainers, have a coffee, and wait for the team to hit the ice. After the skate we'd head back to the hotel for a pre-game meal with all the players, coaches, and video staff. And the meal laid out for us was incredible. Everything you could ever want was there—steak, all the veggies, pasta, all the sauces—nothing was left out. I guess that's why they call it the Never Hungry League.

I did from time to time question whether I was doing a good job or not—I mean, my role wasn't like a player's in any way: it was keep my antenna up, stay involved, and if there's any guys that need help, I'll be there. The role was similar to a SWAT team I guess: you have them on staff in case of an emergency and you may not use them for six months, but when you do, you're sure glad they're there. That's how I felt about my role.

When we were back in L.A. and I had a day off, I'd always go out to see my buddy Eli; he lived with his brother Yuri, and we were all very close. Eli was sober and in recovery, so I'd show up at their house around six and we'd head off to an AA meeting, then go get something to eat after. It was a blessing that they lived in the city—it really helped me out a lot, being under the stress of that job.

But when I say stress, I mean that it was self-inflicted. I was constantly worrying about my head issues, worrying if I was doing an okay job, worrying if I was liked by the players and the staff. When you've worked towards a job for seven years, had dreams about getting that job, it can bring a pretty heavy price tag with it.

When I'd get back to Edmonton, Shauna and I arranged it so that I'd take Chloe—or Peanut, as I always called her—for the ten straight days. It was awesome just being a dad, waking up with her each morning and making her lunch, then taking her to school. After that I'd head to the gym and get in a ninety minute workout. In the afternoon I'd pick her up from school at three thirty. During the winter it was sure nice knowing that I'd be heading back to L.A. in a week or so. It didn't matter where the team was on the road, I would just call Tiffany, their travel person, and she'd book me a flight to meet up with the team.

When one of our East Coast Hockey League (ECHL) players got charged with domestic abuse, Dean wanted me to go to Boston to meet with him. But about one a.m. the night before I was supposed to fly out, I got a call from management saying that one of our players in L.A. was in trouble. He was out-of-control drunk having a huge fight with his girlfriend, and wanted me to call him asap.

Now, this was one of our best players, and if his situation didn't get handled quickly, it was going to be on the front page on the L.A. Times. When he picked up the phone his voice was mangled, and it sounded to me like he was on more than just booze. I talked to him for half an hour trying to calm him and get the situation under control. I told him that he needed to go to bed and that we'd meet the next day at the rink. His neighbour was two seconds away from calling the cops, so thank god that didn't happen.

I had to message Dean around two a.m. saying there was a situation and I'd handled it, but I wouldn't be going to Boston since I needed to meet with the player to work things out.

When I got to the rink the next day, there was Dean, pacing the hallway.

Okay, he said, I don't need to know who it was, but on a scale of 1 to 10, how bad was it?

Well Dean, it should have been a 10, but it's down to a 7. Don't worry about it, it's under control.

Fuck me, he said, then walked away.

I have to say, I give Dean a ton of credit for letting me do my job. It must have been hard on him after what he'd gone through with Stoll, Richards, and Voynov, but he was true to his word and left me alone.

At the end of it all, we got it sorted out. The player was awesome in responding to after-care. I set him up with a good therapist, he always took my calls, and I never once had another issue with him.

I had a little routine I did for pretty much the entire three years I worked for the Kings. I'd get to the practice rink around seven a.m., check in with some guys, grab a coffee, and basically walk around and have conversations. The boys would start skating at ten a.m., so I'd watch practice till it was over. Then there'd be lunch made by one of the chefs. After that I'd go back to my office and write up any reports. At two o'clock I'd go work out with the coaches upstairs. That was quite the gym—the roof opened up, so when you worked out the sun would be shining on your face. Then I'd grab a steamer, shower, head back to the hotel, chill for an hour, put my suit on, and make the drive to Staples.

I became really close with the equipment trainers: Jojo, D-ball, and Grange. They were just awesome people and we all got along really well. I'd be sitting in my office, and when the door was open I'd be able to see who was in the trainers' room sitting down chatting. Anže Kopitar would always be in there with Jeff Carter, so I'd head over, sit down, and just strike up a conversation with the boys.

And with our AHL affiliate team in Ontario, California, just down the road, I'd go down to spend time with them, too. The same sort of thing applied there as well. It was nice to have the team so close.

I remember we had an East Coast road trip, starting in Florida. It would be a six-hour flight to Tampa—I had to Google that to find out, since I was really worried my head would act up again and I'd have a nervous breakdown right on the plane. If it was too long of a flight, I'd be fucked if I lost it. Since I'd gotten the job my head issues had become worse. It seemed to happen all the fucking time now, and it really scared me.

We got our asses kicked in Tampa, like 5–0. And when we got on the plane our travel guy said, Hey Brantt, you'll be sitting with Darryl on the way home.

I never usually sat with Darryl; usually it was with Solly or Blakey, or by myself. So I was like, Fuck! What am I going to say for six hours home? What if I freak out with these head issues I'm having? All these fears were coming at me at once. So as soon as I sat down I got my hat out of my bag and put it on. Darryl was probably wondering, What's this guy doing wearing a hat? And I'm sure everyone on that plane thought the same thing. If they only knew. I felt so much pressure and stress—I didn't want to fuck up, I wanted to do such a good job—that my head felt heavy all the time.

Anyway, the flight back went awesome. Me and Darryl just talked about old hockey stories for a few hours. And he told me a story I'd never heard before, one that I still laugh about today:

When Darryl was head coach for the Chicago Blackhawks, one of his players was a guy named Joe Murphy, who, as you may recall, has his own unique approach to dealing with other people. Chicago was in the playoffs—I believe they were playing against St. Louis, a real big game— when they took a penalty. And when Darryl told Joe to serve it, Joe gave him a look that said, You got to be fucking kidding me, I'm the goal scor-er on this team and you want me to go spend two minutes in the penalty box? Darryl's point of view was that when the penalty was over Joe might get a good scoring chance coming out of the box—he could get behind their defence without being seen. Joe's point of view was that Darryl was fucking him over. So the time counts down on the penalty and finally reaches zero, when Joe is supposed to leave the box and go help his team-mates. Instead his team is playing four against five and Joe's just sitting in the penalty box looking at Darryl and mouthing the words *Fuck you*.

Darryl was such a character. When I asked him where he kept his two Stanley Cup rings he said they were back at the farm on top of the fridge! As I got to talk more and more to him, it was mind-blowing just how smart this man was—not only was he one of the brightest minds in hockey, but he knew a lot about world issues as well.

After he went to sleep I was just counting the minutes till we land-ed, 'cause then if I needed a hospital it would be just around the corner.

I know it must sound crazy, but in the first year on the job that's where my head was at all the fucking time.

November 26, 2015

Well, we're on the plane going home from Tampa. I haven't been back in Tampa in 14 years—it's really changed to say the least. I've had a couple good days health wise. For some reason, I get just a little tight on flights. I mean, we travel so comfortably, and I'm with THE team, so I'm not worried about the flight per se—I guess it's just lingering stuff from before. I mean, I'm living out my dream job for fuck sakes, so I don't really know why I feel that way sometimes. I thank you Lord for blessing me with this job. I am really trying my best to live life these days, considering I was so fucked up a year ago. As I said, I'm sure the more I do this the easier it will become . . . Amen.

By this time I was getting calls from other teams asking me about my job.

Hey Brantt, we love what you guys are doing there in L.A. What would we have to do to get that role?

Well, first off, is there anyone in the org who's an ex-player who's sober and in recovery?

They'd all say, No, why?

Because, I'd tell them, that's the most important part of the job. First and foremost, players don't respond well to doctors or psychiatrists who've never been in their shoes. Second, you can't have someone trying to help another person if they're talking to them about addiction while drinking a glass of wine. Listen, if a person who has cancer wants to talk to someone, and if that someone has never had cancer and battled through it, well they can have sympathy for the person but they'll *never* have the same bond as you'd get from someone who's had cancer as well. Same goes for the person with a drug or alcohol problem.

So those conversations with other teams ended pretty quickly.

The problem is, there are very few, and do I mean very few, of these guys—former NHLers who got sober and went back to school—to choose from. That's probably why that role doesn't exist.

A lot of the players were complaining about Darryl Sutter being too hard on them. It was a common theme in the dressing room: they were not happy. I'd talk to Drew Doughty once in a while about certain things, and one day I knew he was on fire.

Drew, come into my office and tell me what's going on.

That mother fucker, I swear I'm gonna kill him. I can't stand it any longer—all this guy does is ride my ass the whole game!

I was like, Okay Dewy, let me go talk to Dean about this.

Knowing what kind of guy Dean was, the whole time I was walking up the stairs I sort of knew what the outcome was going to be.

Hey Dean, can I talk to you for a second?

Sure, come on in.

Dean, Dewy is really upset with the way Darryl is treating him. He says Darryl is riding him way too hard, and that he can't stand it any longer.

Boo fricken hoo. You tell Drew to take a hard look at his hand and the Stanley Cup rings that are on it. Give me a fucking break, "Darryl's being too hard"—get the hell out of my office!

Guess who won the Norris Trophy that year as the best defenceman in the NHL? Yup, number 8. Kind of shows you what kind of pressure it takes to make it to the very top.

In that first year, I spent time with Milan Lucic—we'd grab a bite to eat on the road and chat on the phone from time to time—mostly just trying to let him know that I was there for him if he needed it.

As for the team as a whole, that season went great. I believed we had first place locked up until the last game of the year when we lost to the Sharks. For me that first year was really just working on building relationships with twenty-four players and the staff, which was actually a ton of work. But the players were finally starting to let me into their little world, so the hard work seemed to be paying off.

I was wondering what was going to happen with my contract, which would be up on July 1, 2016, so I was relieved when Jeff Solomon called me and said, Hey, we'd like to re-up your deal. I said, Well, let me put something together. It was pretty much the same deal as the first year, but this time I wanted a two-year deal. There was no pushback whatsoever.

It was nice to have more than a one-year contract; although, in this game, who the hell knew what was going to happen?

When I went back for training camp, the first thing I noticed was that the guys were calling me Myze. Finally! Actually everyone was calling me by my nickname now, which was cool.

That year we went on a trip to Montreal that became my favourite memory of being on the road. The team flew out a few days earlier to go to this unreal resort called Mont Tremblant. I mean, this place looked like something out of a movie. It had this cabin vibe to it, but with a very wealthy feel. Our team dinners there were a riot, with all the guys drinking and having a blast. I was having a blast, too—when the boys were tying one on I'd leave them alone, usually sitting with Darryl, Matt Price, or Sammy. At one point I was told they had incredible spas about twenty minutes from the resort, so I jumped into an Uber and headed off. It was freezing that night—and when you're in your shorts outside in the snow jumping into the cold river and then running back into the hot tub, it's the best feeling ever.

One day sometime after that trip, Dean, who wanted me to be always refreshing my education, called me into his office and said he'd like me to take a substance abuse course that was credited for California. He'd pay for it out of his own pocket, he told me. It was another one of those moments where I felt like Dean was a father figure, that he really cared about me as a person. When I got my certificate I went straight to our trainer, Grange, and asked if he could help me hang it on the wall in my office. I was really proud of it.

In Year 2, the team was about average. I was still doing the deal— working with a couple guys in the big club and a couple in the AHL, visiting our draft picks in the summer. I was feeling more and more comfortable in the role, and now it seemed like I was just part of the mix, no big deal.

We didn't make the playoffs that year. The team was just not playing well, and the rumours started flying. On the day I was scheduled to have exit meetings with Dean and Darryl, I got to the rink in the morning and had a workout, then went to Big Wok, my favourite restaurant. I'd just gotten my meal when my buddy Yuri sent me a message from Twitter saying "The Kings fire GM Dean Lombardi and Head Coach Darryl Sutter." I instantly felt sick to my stomach.

And that feeling had nothing to do with me or the security of my job—it had to do with how bad I felt for them. Here were two guys who'd brought two Stanley Cups to that city in three years. Dean had built up that team over time to win, and they had. But while the players were rewarded with nice contracts and reputations as winners, Dean and Darryl were shown the door.

The next day I'll never forget. I got to the rink early, and as I walked by I saw Darryl cleaning out his office, putting his Stanley Cup pictures in a box.

Hey, Myze.

Yeah, Big D?

I walked into his office, not sure what to say.

Keep up the good work, Darryl told me. And if you ever need a reference, put me down.

That's the type of man Darryl Sutter is. Talk about loyal: here he is, just gotten fired and he's wanting to help me. The hard-ass style of leadership has been going out of style lately. But we need more hard-asses like Darryl Sutter.

In the end, Rob Blake took over from Dean as GM. And good for Blake. The guy's a winner. He played the game right. He has deep roots in the organization. He made sense.

He also had a different vision for the team. And if the team could part ways with big dogs like Dean and Darryl after they'd brought two Stanley Cups to the organization, Brantt Myhres could only be an after-thought. My time with the Kings was up.

After my last conversation with Blake, I drove away from the Staples Center thinking, Get over yourself. You had three amazing years, probably the best three years of your life, so consider that a gift and be grateful you even got to live your dream again.

And the thing is, what was so important about those three years wasn't the salary. It wasn't the chartered flights and five-star hotels and shooting the breeze with NHL stars. And while I loved my work and felt I'd made a difference in some players' lives, I'm not telling myself that I cured cancer or anything like that. I did a good job, but I wasn't looking for a medal.

What was most important to me was that I'd made it back. I never forgot that ten-year-old Brantt who dreamed of making it to the NHL and then let it slip through his fingers. I'd let something precious go, but then I'd sifted through the muck until I had it again. Making it to the NHL is something anyone should be proud of. I felt pretty good about doing it twice. It was harder the second time, I can tell you that.

And there was something else that made me stand up a little taller. I'd made a living protecting hockey players. I took care of things. Maybe it's easier to stick up for others than it is for yourself. Maybe I protected others because I knew what it was like to be left unprotected. I don't know. I guess a tough guy has a lot of different motivations.

I do know that, as grateful as I was for all the second chances, and for all the favours, and for all the times guys like Dan Cronin went the extra mile for me, I was never comfortable being the guy who others had to take care of. That's not who I really am. I'm sure no one wants to be that person.

But more than just being back in the NHL, it meant the world to me that I was back in the NHL to be there for other guys. I had the guys' backs. I had Dean's back too, and Darryl's. I could do that. I could be that person. I could give back. I could be part of that family again.

Much had been given to me, and much had been taken away. And there was more loss to come.

My dad died. I went to the hospital with terrible anxiety, knowing that he only had about a day to live. My father had declined dialysis; he told me he was going to go out his way, not the doctors', so they cut off all pain medication and all other means of keeping him alive. I told Chloe to stay home—I didn't want her to see her grandpa like that. When I walked into his hospital room he wasn't on medication anymore, just morphine to help with the pain. His legs were white and as skinny as toothpicks, his eyes were closed, and he was breathing lightly.

As I sat there in the chair alone in the room next to him, memories came flooding back. The bad ones to start. My father had a way with words, and they cut really fucking deep at times.

I've spoken of the night when, high on cocaine, I picked up the phone and called him, I was so lost and needing some fatherly love. What he said to me then was, I'm so embarrassed by you, you fucking loser, all you are is a washed-up NHLer druggie. That's why I hung up the phone and cried a while, and that's why I didn't talk to him for years afterwards.

Out of the five rehabs I went to, he came to see me only once, and his words were, Why are you here? You don't have a problem with this shit. Try and get the hell out.

I also remembered what he said to me one night sitting at the dinner table. He said, Brantt, you know what? I've never ever really loved you. Actually, I don't even like you.

I don't think anyone ever crushed me with words in the way he did that night.

As I sat in that hospital room, I reflected on the love I have for Chloe, my shining star, the gift from the heavens. And how my father did some things to me in my life that I would never repeat with my daughter. The pain I felt I would never wish upon her or anyone else. The thing is, in a funny way I learned a lot about being a father from my dad. When Brad was beating the shit out of me and my mom and I called him at six years old begging him to come rescue us, only to be disappointed that he never showed, it taught me something: when your kid needs you, you'd better show up.

My dad could be unkind. He could be an asshole. Did that mean I needed to be an asshole? There were lessons to be learned.

I looked at him lying there, and suddenly grabbed his frail hand. All the great memories of my father had now come rushing back.

He would stop and put two dollars' worth of gas in his tank just to get me to hockey practice, and then give me another dollar for a Slurpee afterwards. He'd make me my favourite hamburger soup during *Hockey Night in Canada*.

He would borrow money from friends to take me to hockey tournaments all over the country. I found that out from his friends later on. During the summer months in Edmonton when I was thirteen he'd take me to play shinny every night, making sure my skates were sharp and my stick was perfect. In the winter we'd listen to the Oilers game on the radio and talk about how one day I was going to make it to the NHL.

When I was sixteen and played for Portland in the WHL, he moved there to make sure I was on the right path. Then when I got traded to Lethbridge at seventeen, he moved there as well. He never missed a game that whole year. He was the smartest hockey man I knew, and he knew he needed to be there to guide me. Anything I needed, my father was there.

We used to fist-pump each other before every game, with him saying, Go get 'em, son. When I was playing my first year in Tampa I flew my father down for a game against the Montreal Canadiens. As I was walking down the tunnel to hit the ice, there was my dad against the rail, the biggest smile on his face. I walked up to him with a fist pump, saying, Dad, we did it.

He let me down, and I let him down too. There were lots of times I fucked him over—lying, not showing up when I was supposed to, falling short of strong character to say the least. I was not the best son to have. He had every right to judge me harshly. I certainly did.

My dad's father died when he was only twenty-one, so he never really had a role model, and he grew up poor. That explains a lot of the reasons why my dad lived the way he did. He had me when he was twenty-two, just a kid himself. My Lord all I have to do is think about having Chloe at twenty-two. He did a way better job with me than I probably would have done with Chloe at that age.

Did my father fall short of expectations at times? Sure he did, but we all do, folks. The biggest thing is looking at your part in life, good or bad, and trying to correct it. Now that he's left this earth, I can't ever talk hockey with him anymore, or have that hamburger soup he used to make me. Life is really short. So remember the good in people, and don't hold grudges; they'll only hurt you in the long run. Tell someone you're upset with that you love them and forgive them for hurting you. It will free your soul.

Dad, thank you for giving me what you had. I will keep all our memories close. I love you, and I will miss you.

EPILOGUE

I wasn't feeling great that summer. So I decided to rent this awesome condo on the beach in Kelowna, B.C., for a week, just to get away, ride my Harley, hit the gym. Arnie, my old drinking and drugging buddy, was living in B.C., so I gave him a call. Turned out he wanted to move back to Edmonton and start working again. I was so fucking lonely that I said, Hey bud, why don't you just move into my house while you get a job and get back on your feet? I won't charge you a penny. Better yet, come see me in Kelowna.

But when Arnie arrived I was feeling really off. Things were eating at me, I was feeling like saying, Fuck all of this, I just want to escape, I want my head to shut the fuck up for a night. We went to play a round of golf, and the whole time I was thinking about maybe just going hard for the night. Then I'd get right back on the sober train the next day.

By the way, I hadn't been to AA in a while. I figured I was in the clear. I didn't really need AA anymore. I wasn't like the other people in the program anyway.

We got back to the condo and were sitting out by the pool.

Hey Arnie, why don't we get dressed up and head out to this bar down the street?

Sure man, let's go!

So we get to the bar and the waitress shows up. What would you guys like to drink?

Arnie: I'll have a double vodka with soda.

Sir, what would you like?

Brantt: Umm, I'll just have a Diet Coke.

But the whole time my fucking head was just racing to order a cocktail.

And as Arnie sipped his drink, my mind kept reeling. I looked at his vodka.

Hey Arnie, why don't you pass that glass over?

Myze, are you sure?

Yeah man, I'll be okay.

I grabbed the glass and put it up to my mouth, the vodka slightly touching my lips. But all I could think about was Chloe saying, Daddy, no, please don't do it! It shocked me into putting the glass down and sliding it back to Arnie. All I said was, Not tonight, bud.

But my mind still wouldn't shut the fuck off. Then this thought came into my head: Well, why don't you just buy some cocaine and watch Arnie do it? It would be pretty cool to see cocaine again and watch someone else snort a line.

Hey Arnie, do you have that guy's number to get some coke?

Yup, I sure do!

Cool, buddy. I'll buy it—let's hit the bank machine.

I got out eight hundred bucks just in case we needed more at the end of the night. The old emotions were rushing through my veins, as if I was already raging. The excitement was dizzying.

We went back to the bar where the guy was waiting in his car. Arnie got out of the truck, went over to buy the bag of coke, and when he returned he said, Let's go back to the condo and I'll do a couple big blasts before we head out on the town.

But when we arrived I said, Arnie, give me that bag. I want to crush up that rock and make a few lines for you.

No problem, buddy.

I crushed the rock into powder, sliced off three huge lines of cocaine, and rolled up the bill. My heart was racing a thousand miles per second. I kept thinking, I'm doing this, fuck it, let's go. I gave Arnie the bill, he bent his head down and snorted a line, waited ten seconds, then did another one. Then he gave me the plate.

As I was staring at that last line my head said to me, Okay, Brantt, you don't have to snort it, just dip your finger in and open your mouth and rub your gums with it—no big deal. So I put my finger in the cocaine, but as I'm bringing it up to my mouth these flashes came over me—five rehabs, being broke, working my ass off to stay sober on a daily basis, Chloe wailing No Daddy, achieving my goal of making it back to the NHL. The last flash was, IT'S ALL GOING TO BE GONE IF YOU DO THIS.

It was overwhelming. I turned on the tap water, made sure it was hot, then put my finger under the tap and washed off all the coke. I looked at Arnie and said, I need to go to bed dude, I'm just really tired. See you in the morning.

I went straight up to my room and hit my knees, thanking God for giving me clarity, giving me the strength to say *no*. Then I fell into a deep, peaceful sleep.

I woke up at eight a.m. and heard the music still going downstairs. I was like, No fucking way, he's still up! Good god, this is what happens if you stop going to AA? I went downstairs and there was Arnie sitting on the couch looking just weathered. I felt sick to my stomach—I knew that would have been me if I'd given in.

Dude, holy fuck you're still up?

Yeah, Myze, haven't slept yet.

I had to get out of there, so I said, I'm going to the gym and then to grab some lunch. And I'll be going to an AA meeting tonight if you want to come. You probably need it.

But when I got back Arnie was still in the same spot doing blow. So I jumped on my Harley and went for a long ride to clear my head. I kept thinking, How the hell can I have this guy live with me when we get back to Edmonton? My place has no bad memories of anything—no drugs, no booze—and I just can't live with that in my house. But how the hell can I tell him no?

Arnie had packed up all his belongings, his car was full—he'd been counting on moving in, and had nowhere else to go. It was eating at me big-time.

I drove my Harley to the AA meeting and told all the people there what had happened and the insanity I was in. It was good just to get it off my chest.

It was about nine thirty that night when I got back to the condo. Arnie was still sitting there, doing coke and drinking vodka. I was like, Holy fuck man, this is gross, he's been going for a day and a half and can't stop!

I walked up to my room, shut the door, got on my knees, and prayed again.

When I woke up in the morning Arnie was in his room. I opened the door and there he was, just lying in bed looking at the ceiling, his eyes wide open. I shut the door and headed out the door to the pool.

Then I called my good buddy Cort, a friend from L.A. who had years of sobriety. I just needed to talk to someone. And when I told him about what had been happening the last couple days, he said, Myze, you need to tell him to leave, NOW. Get him the fuck out of there asap. I don't care how you say it, just do it now. He's no good for you—and if you don't do it you're going to relapse, I promise you that.

Soon after that call Arnie came out to the pool and sat down next to me. I said, Listen man, we go back a long ways, but the last couple days were fucked up. I was so close to throwing it all away. I hate to tell you this, but you can't live with me. You're going to have to find a different place to live.

But Myze, I have nowhere to go!

Sorry, Arnie, but I have to make this decision. My head has not been in a good place for some time now, and the last two days have just shown me how much work I need to put back into my program.

Arnie got up. He was pissed. But he walked back into the house and started packing.

That wasn't easy for me. It still weighs on me. Remember, when I had nowhere else to go Arnie had let me stay at his place. He'd given me the change in his jar so that I could fill up my gas tank. Yes, he drank, but he'd always been good to me, and we were really tight.

I actually really miss him. I've never laughed so hard with a friend in my life, and I fucked him over. I don't feel good about it. I've tried to call him five times, I've sent him messages, but he won't return my calls. I'd told him to pack up his belongings and move in with me, then I left him stranded with nowhere to live. And all because he went along with my idea of grabbing some blow. That's on me, not him.

That was the last time I hung around with Arnie, and the last time I came close to booze or drugs. I went to an AA meeting every day I was there till I went home. I knew I needed to get refocused or I was going to relapse, and to relapse for me would be pretty much suicide. My life depended on it. I wasn't going to give up on staying sober and doing the next right thing. I'd worked too hard for too many years to give in to that same old voice and tear down my world.

I do wonder what I was thinking that day. I know now that what freed me was humility. I don't know if that's the therapy talking, or faith in God. But I do know that even when I was so consumed by self-loathing that I couldn't face myself in the mirror without a drink, I was still thinking I was special. That's not the same as confidence. That's not the same as believing in yourself. It's more like the opposite of those things. It's more like selfishness—the idea that whatever you're going through right now is the most important thing in the world. So maybe that day I was just feeling cocky.

I'm not proud of that. And the fact that I wanted to be cocky about being humble shows that I still have a lot to learn.

But I'm lucky to have had many lessons in humility. The seemingly endless series of second chances reminds me every day that I wouldn't be here now without other people. That so many people have helped me, even in ways they never intended, is humbling. There is no way I can claim to have done anything on my own.

To be perfectly honest, there've been times when I've been hanging on by a thread. But God has a way in my life of inserting reasons to stay sober, even if I fucking *hate* doing it. Even if what I actually want is to get fucked up. When I got let go from the Kings my head started talking loud again, and they were not good thoughts. More than once, I've been tempted to my very core to throw away all I've worked for. It's not that I just want a drink, or a nice fat line, or whatever, and that I'm willing to put my life at risk. It's that what I want, deep down, is to ruin my life. Getting wrecked is just a way to do that.

Ruining your life is not incidental. It is the whole point. It's what gets you to the edge of the abyss. You're not kicking and screaming, believe me. You're usually in a rush to get there, and maybe beyond. It's a fight to not set foot on that path. A constant fight. An exhausting fight. Exhausting to fight it, and exhausting to be reminded that it's never going to stop.

If it were just about me, I would have thrown in the towel. But there are the people who've saved me that I have to think about, and the people I would betray, like my daughter. And there are the people I might save. In the end, it's not about me. It's much bigger than me, and any other thought is just selfish.

But that's just another way of talking about love, isn't it? Love is a daily reminder that I am far from being the most important person in my universe. As long as I have love to give, and to keep me humble, I think I'll be safe from my own demons.

Not that I'm in the clear. I don't think anyone ever is. There's something out there capable of tripping just about anyone up. All you can do is live your life the right way—and doing things the right way is really just a shortcut to making good decisions. We can all convince ourselves that a bad decision is a good one, and playing by the rules you set out for yourself is a good way of avoiding the kind of tricks I played for years. It took me a long time to develop the humility to even *want* to live life right.

The thing is, you can change. But the life you used to live doesn't just disappear, because the people in it live on. I think every day about the people whose lives mine touched. And when your life is a train wreck, touching others isn't likely to be something they remember fondly. It hurts me that I hurt others, who deserved much better.

I haven't seen Brooke in twenty years. She moved to Calgary and is married now, with two young girls. She won't accept any requests on social media. I don't blame her. All these years later, the way things worked out is still unfair to her. I get to remember that afternoon when we held hands in the back seat of my buddy's car as the Alberta landscape flew by. I get to remember the sweet intensity of teenage love. She's stuck with the memory of years spent hoping a guy with such a sense of entitlement that he cheated on her without a second thought might get his shit together. I'm not surprised it's not a memory she wants to cherish.

Megan is living back in Sacramento. She has two kids, and that's all I really know of her. I've tried a few times to call her and apologize, but she won't return my calls or even acknowledge I'm alive. I don't even know that an apology from me would be worth anything to her. I'd get something out of it, but would she? It may be that there's nothing I can give to her that would be of any value.

That love could end in such a black hole is a warning I take seriously. Love is something we're all lucky to stumble upon. I deserve the cold shoulder from Brooke and Megan, but I wish them love, happiness, and health. If it hadn't been for those two, I would never have known what it is to be in love. I will always be grateful.

My sister Cher's story is the one that really haunts me. We haven't talked in years. She went in to get back surgery five years ago and came out with a painkiller addiction. I know all too well how it must have happened.

The fentanyl must have made her whole life feel better, not just her back. If your prescription is the highlight of your day, you're in danger. Now it's been that way every day for years. She's not the same person I knew before the surgery, and I miss her.

If I could have it my way, I'd speak to her every day. But the pain meds have made her turn into a recluse, so it's hard. One day we were fighting on the phone. I was telling her I'd pay for her treatment; all she had to do was get on the plane. That had been done for me, and I wanted to do it for her. She shouted at me, Brantt, I can't go, I'm not as strong as you are. And of course I told her I didn't get sober because I was strong. Maybe I had put in some painful work, but it wasn't strength that got me back on track. I don't get to take credit. I was *lucky*.

I was lucky to have way more than my fair share of last chances. I had friends, teammates, coaches, and general managers step in when everything was about to go terribly wrong. Cher didn't have that. And she didn't have guys like Dan Cronin on the other end of the phone when all hope seemed lost. He moved mountains for me, when you'd think most people would have been ready to give up. And he made sure I did it right. Rehab veterans call a short stint a "spin dry." Sober up a bit, and leave. Dan knew a spin dry wasn't going to work. He kept me in until he knew I'd finally come around.

I think each and every day about what my life would have been like without Dan. He saved me. No question. And Dave Lewis from the league, and Brian Shaw from the NHLPA—they drove me crazy by trying to keep me away from the booze and drugs I loved so much. I hated them sometimes. But they *saved* me. I owe the league, and those guys, everything. My sobriety is not a testament to how strong I am, it's a testament to how generous, and caring, those guys are, even when I gave them every reason to turn their backs on me.

That's what I tried to tell Cher. And when it comes to strength, Cher, you have no idea just how strong you are—you got pregnant at fourteen, which meant you were living on your own at fifteen. You survived the physical and mental abuse while living with our mother and her dead-beat boyfriends. You had no role models in your life to guide you or show you the way. You are a survivor, so don't tell me you're not that strong, Cher. I know you are. But words alone can't turn someone around. I know that as well as anyone.

My heart is missing my sister. I hope she's doing okay.

My brother Devon is five years younger than me—and today he's the only one from my family I talk to. I felt really sorry for Devon having Brad as his dad. He didn't start out life holding great cards, and I wasn't everything a guy could hope for in a big brother. When I'd come home I'd take him out and get him wasted. I gave him his first line of coke when he was fifteen. I could have done more for him, but that's what I thought a big brother should do. But he's made a good life for himself. He works for Husky in the oil and gas field. I'm not used to men saying they love me, but he does.

I didn't hear that a lot growing up, or as a younger man. I didn't know how to say it either. I respect Devon for saying what I couldn't for so long, and I'm grateful that he's there to say it.

It's funny, the way we think love is something you can deserve. Or not deserve. You blame others when you don't get the love you think you're entitled to. And hate yourself when you think you don't meet the standards that would allow others to properly love you. But you don't love someone because they pass some kind of test. And people don't love you because you're especially good. I thought that way for a long time, and I was wrong.

Now, when I think of those who've given shape to my life, whether good or bad, and those whose lives I've had some part in shaping, good or bad, I know better than to think it falls to me to judge. Who am I to judge others? And who am I even to judge myself? All I can do is take responsibility. That, and be open. To love, and to accept love when it's offered.

———

I've never liked being alone.

I felt isolated enough even when I was with other people. Being completely by myself was always close to unbearable.

But that was how I spent my birthday in 2020. The coronavirus had everyone holed up. So there was no way around it. Everyone I loved was somewhere else. Chloe was with her mom. No one would be coming by.

I thought I'd head down to the mailbox to see if anyone had sent me a birthday card. As I was sifting through the mail I saw an envelope from my mother. Instantly I felt bad. Her birthday is only a week before mine and I hadn't sent her anything. I haven't sent her anything in years. The truth is, we haven't talked much in years.

When I opened the card, sixty dollars fell out. It read, *Happy Birthday son, I love and miss you.*

Of course she sent me a card. It's her job, right? But you can't buy forgiveness for sixty bucks.

My mother still lives at the top of that hill in Brady Heights in Grand Centre. I haven't seen her in three years, and even then it was just for five minutes. She's only sixty-three, but looks ninety. She is not in good health. Looking back now, I understand that my mother dealt with serious mental health issues. She stopped working in my grandparents' store before she was forty and has never worked since. She's given up.

I guess that, at the end of the day, thank god she had enough sense to put me and Cher in the car and head to Grandma's. More than one person has said, Your mother did the best she could back then with what she knew or had. But there are some things in life you may not be able to shake off. For years now I've been striving for that moment when I'm able to pick up the phone and say, Mom, I love you and I forgive you, because I've made some really bad decisions too.

Now the card was eating me up inside. There I was, all alone in my house. Whenever I feel torn I put on some music, open my journal, and start writing away my feelings—and this time I decided to listen to one of my favourite bands, Fleetwood Mac. When I heard the first few bars of "Songbird," a memory crashed into my mind. I was a little kid living with my mom in the trailer park. I was sitting on her lap. She had her arms around me. Fleetwood Mac was playing.

It was one of the only memories I had of my mom wrapping her arms around me. I'm sure there were many more, but that's the one I remember. Mom. With her arms around me on the couch.

Suddenly, anger wasn't the right emotion.

Maybe, if it were all about me, it would be okay to be angry at what felt like the shortcomings of others. But how could it be just about me? When there was this other person to consider, this person hugging me and humming along to "Songbird"? Something about that song brought to life for me the young woman who held me.

She was only eighteen when she had me. I started to think about life in Swan Hills, in a trailer with us kids. I started to think about my mom getting the shit beaten out of her in front of me and Cher. Going from one horrible relationship with Brad to the next one. And so on. The mental abuse my mom went through, the crushing weight of hopelessness, the frustration of seeing the future narrowing down to a repetition of familiar mistakes, the cyclical trauma of being hurt by those she loves. The burden of what she lived through was impossible to imagine, even for me, even for a guy who'd lost everything. She was just a kid herself when she had me. What kind of parent would I have been at eighteen?

I picked up the phone. I called her.

I said, Hey Mom, it's Brantt. How are you doing? I know it's been years since we talked.

Just like that, something changed. We didn't fix every problem or right every wrong. But we both felt better, and we both wanted to talk about the things that brought us closer together. Tough times bring people closer together too.

I told her I'd written a book. I told her that it recounts some things about my childhood that will be hard for her to read. I wanted to give her the heads-up.

Oh, son, it's okay, you write down whatever you feel you need to put on paper. I can take it, she said. I just want you to know something. Believe me, I've paid for what I did. I lost you as a son, and if I could take it back I would in a second. But I can't, and I'm sorry.

There's no need to say sorry, Mom. I don't think I'll ever forget some of those memories, but forty years have passed. I'm far from perfect, and there's so many things I wish I could take back as well.

We talked for an hour. I'm glad I made the call.

ACKNOWLEDGMENTS

I wanted to thank Dan Cronin, Dave Lewis, Brian Shaw, and Dave Lewis from the NHL and NHLPA. Thanks to my coach Darryl Sutter, who cared more about Brantt the human than Brantt the hockey player. Thanks to my tribe of sober friends in Los Angeles. To my editor Nick Garrison: thank you for your professionalism, and vision to take this journey together. And thanks to my grade 6 teacher, who told me to stop practicing my autograph, because I'd never make the NHL.

INDEX